THE LETTERS OF ROBERT LOUIS STEVENSON

TO HIS FAMILY AND FRIENDS

SELECTED AND EDITED, WITH NOTES AND INTRODUCTION, BY

SIDNEY COLVIN

VOLUME II

NEW YORK
CHARLES SCRIBNER'S SONS
1901

CONTENTS

VIII

LIFE AT BOURNEMOUTH (*Continued*)

IX

THE UNITED STATES AGAIN

WINTER IN THE ADIRONDACKS

CONTENTS

X

PACIFIC VOYAGES

XI

LIFE IN SAMOA

XII

LIFE IN SAMOA (*Continued*)

CONTENTS

LIST OF ILLUSTRATIONS

VIII

LIFE AT BOURNEMOUTH

Continued

(JANUARY, 1886–JULY, 1887)

VIII

LIFE AT BOURNEMOUTH

Continued

(JANUARY, 1886–JULY, 1887)

THE following section gives the pith of the writer's correspondence from the date of the publication of *Jekyll and Hyde* in January, 1886, down to that of his father's death in May, 1887. The period was one of trying ill-health and of meagre production, but at the same time of fast-growing literary reputation and popularity. *Jekyll and Hyde,* after threatening for the first week or two to fall flat, in no long time caught the attention of all classes of readers, was quoted from a hundred pulpits, and made the writer's name familiar to multitudes both in England and America whom it had never reached before. A success scarcely inferior, though of another kind, was made a few months afterwards by *Kidnapped,* which Stevenson finished in the spring, and which was published in the early summer. After completing this task in March, he was able to do little work during the remainder of the year, except in preparing materials for the *Life of Fleeming Jenkin,* and in writing occasional verses which helped to make up the collection published in the following year under the title *Underwoods*.

For some weeks of April he was much taken up with a scheme which had nothing to do with literature, and which the few friends to whom he confided it regarded as wildly Quixotic and unwise. In these years he had, as we have seen, taken deeply to heart both what he thought the guilty remissness of Government action in the matter of the Soudan garrisons and of Gordon, and the tameness of acquiescence with which the national conscience appeared to take the results. He had been not less disturbed at the failure, hitherto, of successive administrations to assert the reign of law in Ireland. He was no blind partisan of the English cause in that country, and had even written of the hereditary hatred of Irish for English as a sentiment justified by the facts of history. But he held strongly that private warfare, the use of dynamite and the knife, with the whole system of agrarian vengeances and the persecution of the weak, were means which no end could justify; and that redress of grievances, whatever form it might ultimately take, must be preceded by the re-establishment of law. In *More New Arabian Nights*, published the year before, he had endeavoured "to make dynamite ridiculous if he could not make it horrible," and to the old elements of fantastic invention, and humorously solemn realism in the unreal, had added the new element of a witty and scornful criminal psychology. A case that now appealed to him with especial force was that of the cruel persecution kept up against the widow and daughters of the murdered man Curtin. He determined that if no one else would take up the duty of resisting such persecution without regard to consequences, he would take it up himself, in the hope of more effectually rousing the public conscience to the evils of the time. His plan was to go with his family, occupy and live upon the derelict farm, and let happen what would. This, as the letters referring to the matter plainly show, was no irresponsible dream or whim, but a purpose conceived in absolute and sober earnest. His wife and household were prepared to follow, though under protest, had he persisted; as it seemed for some weeks that he certainly would, until at last the arguments of his friends persuaded him to give up his purpose. The one consideration, I believe, which in the end prevailed with him was that of his father's declining health. But to the last, I think, he was never well satisfied that in giving way he had not been a coward, preferring fireside ease and comfort to the calls of a public duty. In the early autumn of the same year, 1886, he took a longer and more successful excursion from home than usual, staying without breakdown for two or three weeks at the Monument, as he always called my house at the British Museum, and seeing something of kindred spirits among his elders, such as Mr. Robert Browning, Mr. J. R. Lowell, the painters Burne-Jones and W. B. Richmond, and others who had hitherto delighted in his work and now learned to delight no less in his society.

Thence he went with Mr. Henley for a short trip to Paris, chiefly in order to see the sculptor Rodin and his old friends Mr. and Mrs. W. H. Low. From this trip he returned none the worse, but during all the later autumn and winter at Bournemouth was again hampered in his work by renewed and prolonged attacks of illness. A further cause of trouble was the distressing failure of his father's health and spirits, attended by symptoms which plainly indicated the beginning of the end. After spending a part of the winter at Bournemouth and a part at Torquay, both parents returned to Edinburgh in April, 1887; and within a few weeks after their arrival Stevenson was summoned north to his father's death-bed.

To Mrs. de Mattos

1886
ÆT. 36

With this cousin the writer had always been on terms of close affection, and he now dedicated to her *The Strange Case of Dr. Jekyll and Mr. Hyde.* In the dedication as published onlv the second verse stands.

[Skerryvore, Bournemouth], *January 1st, 1886.*

DEAREST KATHARINE,—Here, on a very little book and accompanied with lame verses, I have put your name. Our kindness is now getting well on in years; it must be nearly of age; and it gets more valuable to me with every time I see you. It is not possible to express any sentiment, and it is not necessary to try, at least between us. You know very well that I love you dearly, and that I always will. I only wish the verses were better, but at least you like the story; and it is sent to you by the one that loves you—Jekyll, and not Hyde.

R. L. S.

Ave!

Bells upon the city are ringing in the night;
High above the gardens are the houses full of light;
On the heathy Pentlands is the curlew flying free;
And the broom is blowing bonnie in the north countrie.

We cannae break the bonds that God decreed to bind,
Still we'll be the children of the heather and the wind;
Far away from home, O, it 's still for you and me
That the broom is blowing bonnie in the north countrie!

R. L. S.

To Alison Cunningham

[Skerryvore, Bournemouth], *Jan. 1st, 1886.*

My dear Kinnicum,—I am a very bad dog, but not for the first time. Your book, which is very interesting, came duly; and I immediately got a very bad cold indeed, and have been fit for nothing whatever. I am a bit better now, and aye on the mend; so I write to tell you, I thought of you on New Year's Day; though, I own, it would have been more decent if I had thought in time for you to get my letter then. Well, what can't be cured must be endured, Mr. Lawrie; and you must be content with what I give. If I wrote all the letters I ought to write, and at the proper time, I should be very good and very happy; but I doubt if I should do anything else.

I suppose you will be in town for the New Year; and I hope your health is pretty good. What you want

1886 ÆT. 36 is diet; but it is as much use to tell you that as it is to tell my father. And I quite admit a diet is a beastly thing. I doubt, however. if it be as bad as not being allowed to speak, which I have tried fully, and do not like. When, at the same time, I was not allowed to read, it passed a joke. But these are troubles of the past, and on this day, at least, it is proper to suppose they won't return. But we are not put here to enjoy ourselves: it was not God's purpose; and I am prepared to argue, it is not our sincere wish. As for our deserts, the less said of them the better, for somebody might hear, and nobody cares to be laughed at. A good man is a very noble thing to see, but not to himself; what he seems to God is, fortunately, not our business; that is the domain of faith; and whether on the first of January or the thirty-first of December, faith is a good word to end on.

My dear Cummy, many happy returns to you and my best love.—The worst correspondent in the world,

ROBERT LOUIS STEVENSON.

TO MR. AND MRS. THOMAS STEVENSON

[SKERRYVORE, BOURNEMOUTH], *January 1st, 1886.*

MY DEAR PEOPLE,—Many happy returns of the day to you all; I am fairly well and in good spirits; and much and hopefully occupied with dear Jenkin's life. The inquiry in every detail, every letter that I read, makes me think of him more nobly. I cannot imagine how I got his friendship; I did not deserve it. I believe the notice will be interesting and useful.

My father's last letter, owing to the use of a quill pen

and the neglect of blotting-paper, was hopelessly illegible. Every one tried, and every one failed to decipher an important word on which the interest of one whole clause (and the letter consisted of two) depended. 1886 ÆT. 36

I find I can make little more of this; but I'll spare the blots.—Dear people, ever your loving son, R. L. S.

I will try again, being a giant refreshed by the house being empty. The presence of people is the great obstacle to letter-writing. I deny that letters should contain news (I mean mine; those of other people should). But mine should contain appropriate sentiments and humorous nonsense, or nonsense without the humour. When the house is empty, the mind is seized with a desire—no, that is too strong—a willingness to pour forth unmitigated rot, which constitutes (in me) the true spirit of correspondence. When I have no remarks to offer (and nobody to offer them to), my pen flies, and you see the remarkable consequence of a page literally covered with words and genuinely devoid of sense. I can always do that, if quite alone, and I like doing it; but I have yet to learn that it is beloved by correspondents. The deuce of it is, that there is no end possible but the end of the paper; and as there is very little left of that—if I cannot stop writing—suppose you give up reading. It would all come to the same thing; and I think we should all be happier. . . .

To W. H. Low

In the following letter R. L. S. accepts the dedication of Mr. Low's illustrated edition of Keats's *Lamia*, and sends him in return the newly

1886 published *Jekyll and Hyde,* and a set of verses afterwards printed in the
ÆT. 36 *Century Magazine* and *Underwoods*, and engraved by Mr. St. Gaudens on his medallion portrait of the author. The terms of the *Lamia* dedication are as follows: "In testimony of loyal friendship and of a common faith in doubtful tales from Faery-Land, I dedicate to Robert Louis Stevenson my work in this book." The Latin legend inscribed above the design runs: "Neque est ullum certius amicitiæ vinculum quam consensus et societas consiliorum et voluntatum."

[SKERRYVORE, BOURNEMOUTH], *Jan. 2nd, 1886.*

MY DEAR LOW,—*Lamia* has come, and I do not know how to thank you, not only for the beautiful art of the designs, but for the handsome and apt words of the dedication. My favourite is "Bathes unseen," which is a masterpiece; and the next, "Into the green recessed woods," is perhaps more remarkable, though it does not take my fancy so imperiously. The night scene at Corinth pleases me also. The second part offers fewer opportunities. I own I should like to see both *Isabella* and the *Eve* thus illustrated; and then there 's *Hyperion*—O, yes, and *Endymion!* I should like to see the lot: beautiful pictures dance before me by hundreds: I believe *Endymion* would suit you best. It also is in faery-land; and I see a hundred opportunities, cloudy and flowery glories, things as delicate as the cobweb in the bush; actions, not in themselves of any mighty purport, but made for the pencil: the feast of Pan, Peona's isle, the "slabbed margin of a well," the chase of the butterfly, the nymph, Glaucus, Cybele, Sleep on his couch, a farrago of unconnected beauties. But I divagate; and all this sits in the bosom of the publisher.

What is more important, I accept the terms of the

dedication with a frank heart, and the terms of your 1886
Latin legend fairly. The sight of your pictures has ÆT. 36
once more awakened me to my right mind; something may come of it; yet one more bold push to get free of this prisonyard of the abominably ugly, where I take my daily exercise with my contemporaries. I do not know, I have a feeling in my bones, a sentiment which may take on the forms of imagination, or may not. If it does, I shall owe it to you; and the thing will thus descend from Keats even if on the wrong side of the blanket. If it can be done in prose — that is the puzzle — I divagate again. Thank you again: you can draw and yet you do not love the ugly: what are you doing in this age? Flee, while it is yet time; they will have your four limbs pinned upon a stable door to scare witches. The ugly, my unhappy friend, is *de rigueur:* it is the only wear! What a chance you threw away with the serpent! Why had Apollonius no pimples? Heavens, my dear Low, you do not know your business. . . .

I send you herewith a Gothic gnome for your Greek nymph; but the gnome is interesting, I think, and he came out of a deep mine, where he guards the fountain of tears. It is not always the time to rejoice.—Yours ever,

R. L. S.

The gnome's name is *Jekyll & Hyde;* I believe you will find he is likewise quite willing to answer to the name of Low or Stevenson.

Same day.— I have copied out on the other sheet some bad verses, which somehow your picture sug-

1886 ÆT. 36 gested; as a kind of image of things that I pursue and cannot reach, and that you seem — no, not to have reached — but to have come a thought nearer to than I. This is the life we have chosen: well, the choice was mad, but I should make it again.

What occurs to me is this: perhaps they might be printed in (say) the *Century* for the sake of my name; and if that were possible, they might advertise your book. It might be headed as sent in acknowledgment of your *Lamia.* Or perhaps it might be introduced by the phrases I have marked above. I dare say they would stick it in: I want no payment, being well paid by *Lamia.* If they are not, keep them to yourself.

To Will H. Low

Damned bad lines in return for a beautiful book.

Youth now flees on feathered foot.
Faint and fainter sounds the flute;
Rarer songs of Gods.
And still,
Somewhere on the sunny hill,
Or along the winding stream,
Through the willows, flits a dream;
Flits, but shows a smiling face,
Flees, but with so quaint a grace,
None can choose to stay at home,
All must follow — all must roam.

This is unborn beauty: she
Now in air floats high and free,

Takes the sun, and breaks the blue;—
Late, with stooping pinion flew
Raking hedgerow trees, and wet
Her wing in silver streams, and set
Shining foot on temple roof.
Now again she flies aloof,
Coasting mountain clouds, and kissed
By the evening's amethyst.

In wet wood and miry lane
Still we pound and pant in vain;
Still with earthy foot we chase
Waning pinion, fainting face;
Still, with grey hair, we stumble on
Till—behold!—the vision gone!

Where has fleeting beauty led?
To the doorway of the dead!
qy. omit? [Life is gone, but life was gay:
We have come the primrose way!][1]

R. L. S.

To Edmund Gosse

Skerryvore, Bournemouth, *Jan. 2nd, 1886.*

My dear Gosse,—Thank you for your letter, so interesting to my vanity. There is a review in the *St. James's*, which, as it seems to hold somewhat of your opinions, and is besides written with a pen and not a poker, we think may possibly be yours. The *Prince*[2]

[1] In *Underwoods* the lines thus queried stand with the change:
"Life is over; life was gay."

[2] *Prince Otto.*

1886 ÆT. 36 has done fairly well in spite of the reviews, which have been bad: he was, as you doubtless saw, well slated in the *Saturday;* one paper received it as a child's story; another (picture my agony) described it as a "Gilbert comedy." It was amusing to see the race between me and Justin M'Carthy: the Milesian has won by a length.

That is the hard part of literature. You aim high, and you take longer over your work, and it will not be so successful as if you had aimed low and rushed it. What the public likes is work (of any kind) a little loosely executed; so long as it is a little wordy, a little slack, a little dim and knotless, the dear public likes it; it should (if possible) be a little dull into the bargain. I know that good work sometimes hits; but, with my hand on my heart, I think it is by an accident. And I know also that good work must succeed at last; but that is not the doing of the public; they are only shamed into silence or affectation. I do not write for the public; I do write for money, a nobler deity; and most of all for myself, not perhaps any more noble, but both more intelligent and nearer home.

Let us tell each other sad stories of the bestiality of the beast whom we feed. What he likes is the newspaper; and to me the press is the mouth of a sewer, where lying is professed as from an university chair, and everything prurient, and ignoble, and essentially dull, finds its abode and pulpit. I do not like mankind; but men, and not all of these — and fewer women. As for respecting the race, and, above all, that fatuous rabble of burgesses called "the public," God save me from such irreligion! — that way lies disgrace and dishonour.

There must be something wrong in me, or I would not be popular. 1886 ÆT. 36

This is perhaps a trifle stronger than my sedate and permanent opinion. Not much, I think. As for the art that we practise, I have never been able to see why its professors should be respected. They chose the primrose path; when they found it was not all primroses, but some of it brambly, and much of it uphill, they began to think and to speak of themselves as holy martyrs. But a man is never martyred in any honest sense in the pursuit of his pleasure; and *delirium tremens* has more of the honour of the cross. We were full of the pride of life, and chose, like prostitutes, to live by a pleasure. We should be paid if we give the pleasure we pretend to give; but why should we be honoured?

I hope some day you and Mrs. Gosse will come for a Sunday; but we must wait till I am able to see people. I am very full of Jenkin's life; it is painful, yet very pleasant, to dig into the past of a dead friend, and find him, at every spadeful, shine brighter. I own, as I read, I wonder more and more why he should have taken me to be a friend. He had many and obvious faults upon the face of him; the heart was pure gold. I feel it little pain to have lost him, for it is a loss in which I cannot believe; I take it, against reason, for an absence; if not to-day, then to-morrow, I still fancy I shall see him in the door; and then, now when I know him better, how glad a meeting! Yes, if I could believe in the immortality business, the world would indeed be too good to be true; but we were put here to do what service we can, for honour and not for hire: the sods

1886 ÆT. 36 cover us, and the worm that never dies, the conscience, sleeps well at last; these are the wages, besides what we receive so lavishly day by day; and they are enough for a man who knows his own frailty and sees all things in the proportion of reality. The soul of piety was killed long ago by that idea of reward. Nor is happiness, whether eternal or temporal, the reward that mankind seeks. Happinesses are but his wayside campings; his soul is in the journey; he was born for the struggle, and only tastes his life in effort and on the condition that he is opposed. How, then, is such a creature, so fiery, so pugnacious, so made up of discontent and aspiration, and such noble and uneasy passions—how can he be rewarded but by rest? I would not say it aloud; for man's cherished belief is that he loves that happiness which he continually spurns and passes by; and this belief in some ulterior happiness exactly fits him. He does not require to stop and taste it; he can be about the rugged and bitter business where his heart lies; and yet he can tell himself this fairy tale of an eternal tea-party, and enjoy the notion that he is both himself and something else; and that his friends will yet meet him, all ironed out and emasculate, and still be lovable,—as if love did not live in the faults of the beloved only, and draw its breath in an unbroken round of forgiveness! But the truth is, we must fight until we die; and when we die there can be no quiet for mankind but complete resumption into—what?—God, let us say—when all these desperate tricks will lie spellbound at last.

Here came my dinner and cut this sermon short—*excusez*. R. L. S.

SKERRYVORE.

To James Payn

The late Mrs. Buckle, a daughter of Mr. James Payn married to the editor of the *Times*, had laughingly remonstrated, through her father, on recognising some features of her own house in Queen Square, Bloomsbury, in the description of that tenanted by the fair Cuban in the section of Stevenson's *Dynamiter* which tells the story of the Brown Box.

Skerryvore, Bournemouth, *Jan. 2nd, 1886.*

Dear James Payn,—Your very kind letter came very welcome; and still more welcome the news that you see ——'s tale. I will now tell you (and it was very good and very wise of me not to tell it before) that he is one of the most unlucky men I know, having put all his money into a pharmacy at Hyères, when the cholera (certainly not his fault) swept away his customers in a body. Thus you can imagine the pleasure I have to announce to him a spark of hope, for he sits to-day in his pharmacy, doing nothing and taking nothing, and watching his debts inexorably mount up.

To pass to other matters: your hand, you are perhaps aware, is not one of those that can be read running; and the name of your daughter remains for me undecipherable. I call her, then, your daughter—and a very good name too—and I beg to explain how it came about that I took her house. The hospital was a point in my tale; but there is a house on each side. Now the true house is the one before the hospital: is that No. 11? If not, what do you complain of? If it is, how can I help what is true? Everything in *The Dynamiter* is not true; but the story of the Brown Box is, in almost every particular; I lay my hand on my heart and swear

1886 ÆT. 36 to it. It took place in that house in 1884; and if your daughter was in that house at the time, all I can say is she must have kept very bad society.

But I see you coming. Perhaps your daughter's house has not a balcony at the back? I cannot answer for that; I only know that side of Queen Square from the pavement and the back windows of Brunswick Row. Thence I saw plenty of balconies (terraces rather); and if there is none to the particular house in question, it must have been so arranged to spite me.

I now come to the conclusion of this matter. I address three questions to your daughter:—

1st. Has her house the proper terrace?
2nd. Is it on the proper side of the hospital?
3rd. Was she there in the summer of 1884?

You see, I begin to fear that Mrs. Desborough may have deceived me on some trifling points, for she is not a lady of peddling exactitude. If this should prove to be so, I will give your daughter a proper certificate, and her house property will return to its original value.

Can man say more?—Yours very truly,

ROBERT LOUIS STEVENSON.

I saw the other day that the Eternal had plagiarised from *Lost Sir Massingberd:* good again, sir! I wish he would plagiarise the death of Zero.

To W. H. Low

The late Sir Percy and Lady Shelley had in these days attached themselves warmly to R. L. S., and saw in his ways and character a living image of those of the poet, Sir Percy's father, as they imagined him.

SKERRYVORE, BOURNEMOUTH,
Jan. Somethingorother-th, 1886.

MY DEAR LOW,—I send you two photographs: they are both done by Sir Percy Shelley, the poet's son, which may interest. The sitting down one is, I think, the best; but if they choose that, see that the little reflected light on the nose does not give me a turn-up; that would be tragic. Don't forget "Baronet" to Sir Percy's name.

We all think a heap of your book; and I am well pleased with my dedication.—Yours ever,

R. L. STEVENSON.

P. S.—*Apropos* of the odd controversy about Shelley's nose: I have before me four photographs of myself, done by Shelley's son: my nose is hooked, not like the eagle, indeed, but like the accipitrine family in man: well, out of these four, only one marks the bend, one makes it straight, and one suggests a turn-up. This throws a flood of light on calumnious man—and the scandal-mongering sun. For personally I cling to my curve. To continue the Shelley controversy: I have a look of him, all his sisters had noses like mine; Sir Percy has a marked hook; all the family had high cheek-bones like mine; what doubt, then, but that this turn-up (of which Jeaffreson accuses the poet, along with much other *fatras*) is the result of some accident similar to what has happened in my photographs by his son?

R. L. S.

TO THOMAS STEVENSON

[SKERRYVORE, BOURNEMOUTH, *January 25, 1886.*]

MY DEAR FATHER,—Many thanks for a letter quite like yourself. I quite agree with you, and had already planned

1886 ÆT. 36 a scene of religion in *Balfour;* the Society for the Propagation of Christian Knowledge furnishes me with a catechist whom I shall try to make the man. I have another catechist, the blind, pistol-carrying highway robber, whom I have transferred from the Long Island to Mull. I find it a most picturesque period, and wonder Scott let it escape. The *Covenant* is lost on one of the Tarrans, and David is cast on Earraid, where (being from inland) he is nearly starved before he finds out the island is tidal; then he crosses Mull to Toronsay, meeting the blind catechist by the way; then crosses Morven from Kinlochaline to Kingairloch, where he stays the night with the good catechist; that is where I am; next day he is to be put ashore in Appin, and be present at Colin Campbell's death. To-day I rest, being a little run down. Strange how liable we are to brain fag in this scooty family! But as far as I have got, all but the last chapter, I think David is on his feet, and (to my mind) a far better story and far sounder at heart than *Treasure Island.*

I have no earthly news, living entirely in my story, and only coming out of it to play patience. The Shelleys are gone; the Taylors kinder than can be imagined. The other day, Lady Taylor drove over and called on me; she is a delightful old lady, and great fun. I mentioned a story about the Duchess of Wellington which I had heard Sir Henry tell; and though he was very tired, he looked it up and copied it out for me in his own hand.—Your most affectionate son,

ROBERT LOUIS STEVENSON.

To C. W. Stoddard

Skerryvore, Bournemouth, *Feb. 13th, 1886.*

MY DEAR STODDARD,—I am a dreadful character; but, you see, I have at last taken pen in hand; how long I may hold it, God knows. This is already my sixth letter to-day, and I have many more waiting; and my wrist gives me a jog on the subject of scrivener's cramp, which is not encouraging.

I gather you were a little down in the jaw when you wrote your last. I am as usual pretty cheerful, but not very strong. I stay in the house all winter, which is base; but, as you continue to see, the pen goes from time to time, though neither fast enough nor constantly enough to please me.

My wife is at Bath with my father and mother, and the interval of widowery explains my writing. Another person writing for you when you have done work is a great enemy to correspondence. To-day I feel out of health, and sha'n't work; and hence this so much overdue reply.

I was re-reading some of your *South Sea Idyls* the other day: some of the chapters are very good indeed; some pages as good as they can be.

How does your class get along? If you like to touch on *Otto*, any day in a by-hour, you may tell them—as the author's last dying confession—that it is a strange example of the difficulty of being ideal in an age of realism; that the unpleasant giddy-mindedness, which spoils the book and often gives it a wanton air of unreality and juggling with air-bells, comes from unsteadiness of key; from the too great realism of some chapters and passages—some of which I have now spotted, others

1886 I dare say I shall never spot — which disprepares the
ÆT. 36 imagination for the cast of the remainder.

Any story can be made *true* in its own key; any story can be made *false* by the choice of a wrong key of detail or style: Otto is made to reel like a drunken — I was going to say man, but let us substitute cipher — by the variations of the key. Have you observed that the famous problem of realism and idealism is one purely of detail? Have you seen my "Note on Realism" in Cassell's *Magazine of Art;* and "Elements of Style" in the *Contemporary;* and "Romance" and "Humble Apology" in *Longmans'?* They are all in your line of business; let me know what you have not seen and I'll send 'em.

I am glad I brought the old house up to you. It was a pleasant old spot, and I remember you there, though still more dearly in your own strange den upon a hill in San Francisco; and one of the most San Francisco-y parts of San Francisco.

Good-bye, my dear fellow, and believe me your friend, ROBERT LOUIS STEVENSON.

TO J. A. SYMONDS

SKERRYVORE, BOURNEMOUTH [*Spring, 1886*].

MY DEAR SYMONDS,—If we have lost touch, it is (I think) only in a material sense; a question of letters, not hearts. You will find a warm welcome at Skerryvore from both the lightkeepers; and, indeed, we never tell ourselves one of our financial fairy tales, but a run to Davos is a prime feature. I am not changeable in friendship; and I think I can promise you you have a pair of trusty well-wishers and friends in Bournemouth:

whether they write or not is but a small thing; the flag may not be waved, but it is there. 1886 ÆT. 36

Jekyll is a dreadful thing, I own; but the only thing I feel dreadful about is that damned old business of the war in the members. This time it came out; I hope it will stay in, in future.

Raskolnikoff[1] is easily the greatest book I have read in ten years; I am glad you took to it. Many find it dull: Henry James could not finish it: all I can say is, it nearly finished me. It was like having an illness. James did not care for it because the character of Raskolnikoff was not objective; and at that I divined a great gulf between us, and, on further reflection, the existence of a certain impotence in many minds of to-day, which prevents them from living *in* a book or a character, and keeps them standing afar off, spectators of a puppet show. To such I suppose the book may seem empty in the centre; to the others it is a room, a house of life, into which they themselves enter, and are tortured and purified. The Juge d'Instruction I thought a wonderful, weird, touching, ingenious creation: the drunken father, and Sonia, and the student friend, and the uncircumscribed, protoplasmic humanity of Raskolnikoff, all upon a level that filled me with wonder: the execution also, superb in places. Another has been translated — *Humiliés et Offensés*. It is even more incoherent than *Le Crime et le Châtiment*, but breathes much of the same lovely goodness, and has passages of power. Dostoieffsky is a devil of a swell, to be sure. Have you heard that he became a stout, imperialist conservative? It is interesting to know. To some-

[1] The name of the hero in Dostoieffsky's *Le Crime et le Châtiment.*

1886 ÆT. 36 thing of that side, the balance leans with me also in view of the incoherency and incapacity of all. The old boyish idea of the march on Paradise being now out of season, and all plans and ideas that I hear debated being built on a superb indifference to the first principles of human character, a helpless desire to acquiesce in anything of which I know the worst assails me. Fundamental errors in human nature of two sorts stand on the skyline of all this modern world of aspirations. First, that it is happiness that men want; and second, that happiness consists of anything but an internal harmony. Men do not want, and I do not think they would accept, happiness; what they live for is rivalry, effort, success — the elements our friends wish to eliminate. And, on the other hand, happiness is a question of morality — or of immorality, there is no difference — and conviction. Gordon was happy in Khartoum, in his worst hours of danger and fatigue; Marat was happy, I suppose, in his ugliest frenzy; Marcus Aurelius was happy in the detested camp; Pepys was pretty happy, and I am pretty happy on the whole, because we both somewhat crowingly accepted a *via media*, both liked to attend to our affairs, and both had some success in managing the same. It is quite an open question whether Pepys and I ought to be happy; on the other hand, there is no doubt that Marat had better be unhappy. He was right (if he said it) that he was *la misère humaine*, cureless misery — unless perhaps by the gallows. Death is a great and gentle solvent; it has never had justice done it, no, not by Whitman. As for those crockery chimney-piece ornaments, the bourgeois (*quorum pars*), and their cowardly dislike of dying and killing, it is merely one symptom of a thousand how utterly they have got out of touch of life. Their dislike of capital punishment and their treatment of their domestic servants are for me the two flaunting emblems of their hollowness. 1886 ÆT. 36

God knows where I am driving to. But here comes my lunch.

Which interruption, happily for you, seems to have stayed the issue. I have now nothing to say, that had formerly such a pressure of twaddle. Pray don't fail to come this summer. It will be a great disappointment, now it has been spoken of, if you do.—Yours ever,

ROBERT LOUIS STEVENSON.

To W. H. Low

The following letter relates to a suggestion which Mr. Gilder, as editor of the *Century Magazine*, had already made in the Hyères time nearly three years previously, and had now lately revived, that Stevenson and his friend Mr. W. H. Low should make a joint excursion down the Rhone, the result to be a book written by R. L. S. and illustrated by Mr. Low. Considerations of health caused the plan to be promptly abandoned for the second time.

[SKERRYVORE, BOURNEMOUTH, *March, 1886.*]

MY DEAR LOW,—This is the most enchanting picture. Now understand my state: I am really an invalid, but of a mysterious order. I might be a *malade imaginaire*, but for one too tangible symptom, my tendency to bleed from the lungs. If we could go, (*1st*) We must have money enough to travel with *leisure and comfort*—especially the first. (*2nd*) You must be prepared for a comrade who would go to bed some part of every day

1886 ÆT. 36 and often stay silent. (*3rd*) You would have to play the part of a thoughtful courier, sparing me fatigue, looking out that my bed was warmed, etc. (*4th*) If you are very nervous, you must recollect a bad hæmorrhage is always on the cards, with its concomitants of anxiety and horror for those who are beside me.

Do you blench? If so, let us say no more about it.

If you are still unafraid, and the money were forthcoming, I believe the trip might do me good, and I feel sure that, working together, we might produce a fine book. The Rhone is the river of Angels. I adore it: have adored it since I was twelve, and first saw it from the train.

Lastly, it would depend on how I keep from now on. I have stood the winter hitherto with some credit, but the dreadful weather still continues, and I cannot holloa till I am through the wood.

Subject to these numerous and gloomy provisos, I embrace the prospect with glorious feelings.

I write this from bed, snow pouring without, and no circumstance of pleasure except your letter. That, however, counts for much. I am glad you liked the doggerel: I have already had a liberal cheque, over which I licked my fingers with a sound conscience. I had not meant to make money by these stumbling feet, but if it comes, it is only too welcome in my handsome but impecunious house.

Let me know soon what is to be expected—as far as it does not hang by that inconstant quantity, my want of health. Remember me to Madam with the best thanks and wishes; and believe me your friend,

Robert Louis Stevenson.

To Mrs. Fleeming Jenkin

[Skerryvore, Bournemouth, *April, 1886.*]

MY DEAR MRS. JENKIN,—I try to tell myself it is good nature, but I know it is vanity that makes me write.

I have drafted the first part of Chapter VI., Fleeming and his friends, his influence on me, his views on religion and literature, his part at the Savile; it should boil down to about ten pages, and I really do think it admirably good. It has so much evoked Fleeming for myself that I found my conscience stirred just as it used to be after a serious talk with him: surely that means it is good? I had to write and tell you, being alone.

I have excellent news of Fanny, who is much better for the change. My father is still very yellow, and very old, and very weak, but yesterday he seemed happier, and smiled, and followed what was said; even laughed, I think. When he came away, he said to me, "Take care of yourself, my dearie," which had a strange sound of childish days, and will not leave my mind.

You must get Litolf's *Gavottes Célèbres:* I have made another trover there: a musette of Lully's. The second part of it I have not yet got the hang of; but the first—only a few bars! The gavotte is beautiful and pretty hard, I think, and very much of the period; and at the end of it, this musette enters with the most really thrilling effect of simple beauty. O—it 's first-rate. I am quite mad over it. If you find other books containing Lully, Rameau, Martini, please let me know; also you might tell me, you who know Bach, where the easiest

1886 is to be found. I write all morning, come down, and
ÆT. 36 never leave the piano till about five; write letters, dine, get down again about eight, and never leave the piano till I go to bed. This is a fine life.—Yours most sincerely,

R. L. S.

If you get the musette (Lully's), please tell me if I am right, and it was probably written for strings. Anyway, it is as neat as—as neat as Bach—on the piano; or seems so to my ignorance.

I play much of the Rigadoon; but it 's strange, it don't come off *quite* so well with me!

There is the first part of the musette copied (from memory, so I hope there 's nothing wrong). Is it not angelic? But it ought, of course, to have the gavotte before. The gavotte is in G, and ends on the keynote thus (if I remember):—

staccato, I think. Then you sail into the musette.

N. B.—Where I have put an "A," is that a dominant

eleventh, or what? or just a seventh on the D? and if the latter, is that allowed? It sounds very funny. Never mind all my questions; if I begin about music (which is my leading ignorance and curiosity), I have always to babble questions: all my friends know me now, and take no notice whatever. The whole piece is marked allegro; but surely could easily be played too fast? The dignity must not be lost; the periwig feeling. 1886 ÆT. 36

To Thomas Stevenson

Want of health preventing the author at this time from carrying the adventures of David Balfour, as narrated in *Kidnapped*, through to their issue as originally designed, it was resolved to wind them up for the present with the discomfiture of the wicked uncle, leaving open the possibility of a sequel, which was supplied six years later in *Catriona*.

[Skerryvore, Bournemouth, *March, 1886.*]

My dear Father,—The David problem has to-day been decided. I am to leave the door open for a sequel if the public take to it, and this will save me from butchering a lot of good material to no purpose. Your letter from Carlisle was pretty like yourself, sir, as I was pleased to see; the hand of Jekyll, not the hand of Hyde. I am for action quite unfit, and even a letter is beyond me; so pray take these scraps at a vast deal more than their intrinsic worth. I am in great spirits about David, Colvin agreeing with Henley, Fanny, and myself in thinking it far the most human of my labours hitherto. As to whether the long-eared British public may take to it, all think it more than doubtful; I wish they would, for I could do a second volume with ease

1886 ÆT. 36 and pleasure, and Colvin thinks it sin and folly to throw away David and Alan Breck upon so small a field as this one.—Ever your affectionate son, R. L. S.

To Mrs. Fleeming Jenkin

The following sets forth the *pros* and *cons* which were balancing each other in his mind in regard to his scheme of going to make a stand in his own person against agrarian outrage in Ireland.

[Skerryvore, Bournemouth],
April 15 or 16 (the hour not being known), 1886.

MY DEAR MRS. JENKIN,—It is I know not what hour of the night; but I cannot sleep, have lit the gas, and here goes.

First, all your packet arrived: I have dipped into the Schumann already with great pleasure. Surely, in what concerns us there is a sweet little chirrup; the *Good Words* arrived in the morning just when I needed it, and the famous notes that I had lost were recovered also in the nick of time.

And now I am going to bother you with my affairs: premising, first, that this is *private;* second, that whatever I do the *Life* shall be done first, and I am getting on with it well; and third, that I do not quite know why I consult you, but something tells me you will hear with fairness.

Here is my problem. The Curtin women are still miserable prisoners; no one dare buy their farm of them, all the manhood of England and the world stands aghast before a threat of murder. (1) Now, my work can be done anywhere; hence I can take up without loss a backgoing Irish farm, and live on, though not (as I had originally written) in it: First Reason. (2) If I should be killed, there are a good many who would feel it: writers are so much in the public eye, that a writer being murdered would attract attention, throw a bull's-eye light upon this cowardly business: Second Reason. (3) I am not unknown in the States, from which the funds come that pay for these brutalities: to some faint extent, my death (if I should be killed) would tell there: Third Reason. (4) *Nobody else is taking up this obvious and crying duty:* Fourth Reason. (5) I have a crazy health and may die at any moment, my life is of no purchase in an insurance office, it is the less account to husband it, and the business of husbanding a life is dreary and demoralising: Fifth Reason.

I state these in no order, but as they occur to me. And I shall do the like with the objections.

First Objection: It will do no good; you have seen Gordon die, and nobody minded; nobody will mind if you die. This is plainly of the devil. Second Objection: You will not even be murdered, the climate will miserably kill you, you will strangle out in a rotten damp heat, in congestion, etc. Well, what then? It changes nothing: the purpose is to brave crime; let me brave it, for such time and to such an extent as God allows. Third Objection: The Curtin women are probably highly uninteresting females. I have n't a doubt of it. But the Government cannot, men will not, protect them. If I am the only one to see this public duty, it is to the public and the Right I should perform it—not to Mesdames Curtin. Fourth Objection: I am

1886 married. "I have married a wife!" I seem to have
ÆT. 36 heard it before. It smells ancient! what was the context? Fifth Objection: My wife has had a mean life (1), loves me (2), could not bear to lose me (3). (1) I admit: I am sorry. (2) But what does she love me for? and (3) she must lose me soon or late. And after all, because we run this risk, it does not follow we should fail. Sixth Objection: My wife would n't like it. No, she would n't. Who would? But the Curtins don't like it. And all those who are to suffer if this goes on, won't like it. And if there is a great wrong, somebody must suffer. Seventh Objection: I won't like it. No, I will not; I have thought it through, and I will not. But what of that? And both she and I may like it more than we suppose. We shall lose friends, all comforts, all society: so has everybody who has ever done anything; but we shall have some excitement, and that 's a fine thing; and we shall be trying to do the right, and that 's not to be despised. Eighth Objection: I am an author with my work before me. See Second Reason. Ninth Objection: But am I not taken with the hope of excitement? I was at first. I am not much now. I see what a dreary, friendless, miserable, God-forgotten business it will be. And anyway, is not excitement the proper reward of doing anything both right and a little dangerous? Tenth Objection: But am I not taken with a notion of glory? I dare say I am. Yet I see quite clearly how all points to nothing coming, to a quite inglorious death by disease and from the lack of attendance; or even if I should be knocked on the head, as these poor Irish promise, how little any one will care. It will be a smile at a thousand breakfast-

tables. I am nearly forty now; I have not many illusions. And if I had? I do not love this health-tending, housekeeping life of mine. I have a taste for danger, which is human, like the fear of it. Here is a fair cause; a just cause; no knight ever set lance in rest for a juster. Yet it needs not the strength I have not, only the passive courage that I hope I could muster, and the watchfulness that I am sure I could learn. 1886 ÆT. 36

Here is a long midnight dissertation; with myself; with you. Please let me hear. But I charge you this: if you see in this idea of mine the finger of duty, do not dissuade me. I am nearing forty, I begin to love my ease and my home and my habits, I never knew how much till this arose; do not falsely counsel me to put my head under the bed-clothes. And I will say this to you: my wife, who hates the idea, does not refuse. "It is nonsense," says she, "but if you go, I will go." Poor girl, and her home and her garden that she was so proud of! I feel her garden most of all, because it is a pleasure (I suppose) that I do not feel myself to share.

1. Here is a great wrong.
2. " a growing wrong.
3. " a wrong founded on crime.
4. " crime that the Government cannot prevent.
5. " crime that it occurs to no man to defy.
6. But it has occurred to me.
7. Being a known person, some will notice my defiance.
8. Being a writer, I can *make* people notice it.
9. And, I think, *make* people imitate me.

1886
ÆT. 36

10. Which would destroy in time this whole scaffolding of oppression.
11. And if I fail, however ignominiously, that is not my concern. It is, with an odd mixture of reverence and humorous remembrances of Dickens, be it said — it is A-nother's.

And here, at I cannot think what hour of the morning, I shall dry up, and remain,—Yours, really in want of a little help, R. L. S.

Sleepless at midnight's dewy hour.
" " witching "
" " maudlin "
etc.

Next morning.— Eleventh Objection: I have a father and mother. And who has not? Macduff's was a rare case; if we must wait for a Macduff. Besides, my father will not perhaps be long here. Twelfth Objection: The cause of England in Ireland is not worth supporting. *A qui le dites vous?* And I am not supporting that. Home Rule, if you like. Cause of decency, the idea that populations should not be taught to gain public ends by private crime, the idea that for all men to bow before a threat of crime is to loosen and degrade beyond redemption the whole fabric of man's decency.

To Mrs. Fleeming Jenkin

The first paragraph of the following refers to the *Life of Fleeming Jenkin;* the second, to a remark of his correspondent that a task such as he had proposed to himself in Ireland should be undertaken by a society rather than an individual.

[SKERRYVORE, BOURNEMOUTH, *April, 1886.*] 1886 ÆT. 36

MY DEAR MRS. JENKIN,—The Book—It is all drafted: I hope soon to send you for comments Chapters III., IV., and V. Chapter VII. is roughly but satisfactorily drafted: a very little work should put that to rights. But Chapter VI. is no joke; it is a *mare magnum:* I swim and drown and come up again; and it is all broken ends and mystification: moreover, I perceive I am in want of more matter. I must have, first of all, a little letter from Mr. Ewing about the phonograph work: *If* you think he would understand it is quite a matter of chance whether I use a word or a fact out of it. If you think he would not: I will go without. Also, could I have a look at Ewing's *précis?* And lastly, I perceive I must interview you again about a few points; they are very few, and might come to little; and I propose to go on getting things as well together as I can in the meanwhile, and rather have a final time when all is ready and only to be criticised. I do still think it will be good. I wonder if Trélat would let me cut? But no, I think I would n't after all; 't is so quaint and pretty and clever and simple and French, and gives such a good sight of Fleeming: the plum of the book, I think.

You misunderstood me in one point: I always hoped to found such a society; that was the outside of my dream, and would mean entire success. *But*—I cannot play Peter the Hermit. In these days of the Fleet Street journalist, I cannot send out better men than myself, with wives or mothers just as good as mine, and sisters (I may at least say) better, to a danger and a long-drawn dreariness that I do not share. My wife

1886 ÆT. 36 says it 's cowardice; what brave men are the leader-writers! Call it cowardice; it is mine. Mind you, I may end by trying to do it by the pen only: I shall not love myself if I do; and is it ever a good thing to do a thing for which you despise yourself?—even in the doing? And if the thing you do is to call upon others to do the thing you neglect? I have never dared to say what I feel about men's lives, because my own was in the wrong: shall I dare to send them to death? The physician must heal himself; he must honestly *try* the path he recommends: if he does not even try, should he not be silent?

I thank you very heartily for your letter, and for the seriousness you brought to it. You know, I think when a serious thing is your own, you keep a saner man by laughing at it and yourself as you go. So I do not write possibly with all the really somewhat sickened gravity I feel. And indeed, what with the book, and this business to which I referred, and Ireland, I am scarcely in an enviable state. Well, I ought to be glad, after ten years of the worst training on earth—valetudinarianism—that I can still be troubled by a duty. You shall hear more in time; so far, I am at least decided: I will go and see Balfour when I get to London.

We have all had a great pleasure: a Mrs. Rawlinson came and brought with her a nineteen-year-old daughter, simple, human, as beautiful as—herself; I never admired a girl before, you know it was my weakness: we are all three dead in love with her. How nice to be able to do so much good to harassed people by—yourself!—Ever yours, R. L. S.

To Miss Rawlinson

Here follows a compliment in verse to the young lady last mentioned, whose Christian name was May.

[Skerryvore, Bournemouth, *April, 1886.*]

Of the many flowers you brought me,
  Only some were meant to stay,
And the flower I thought the sweetest
  Was the flower that went away.

Of the many flowers you brought me,
  All were fair and fresh and gay,
But the flower I thought the sweetest
  Was the blossom of the May.

Robert Louis Stevenson.

To Miss Monroe

The next is in answer to criticisms on *Prince Otto* received from a lady correspondent in Chicago.

Skerryvore, Bournemouth, *May 25th, 1886.*

Dear Miss Monroe,—(I hope I have this rightly) I must lose no time in thanking you for a letter singularly pleasant to receive. It may interest you to know that I read to the signature without suspecting my correspondent was a woman; though in one point (a reference to the Countess) I might have found a hint of the truth. You are not pleased with Otto; since I judge you do not like weakness; and no more do I. And yet I have more than tolerance for Otto, whose faults

1886 ÆT. 36 are the faults of weakness, but never of ignoble weakness, and who seeks before all to be both kind and just. Seeks, not succeeds. But what is man? So much of cynicism to recognise that nobody does right is the best equipment for those who do not wish to be cynics in good earnest. Think better of Otto, if my plea can influence you; and this I mean for your own sake—not his, poor fellow, as he will never learn your opinion; but for yours, because, as men go in this world (and women too), you will not go far wrong if you light upon so fine a fellow; and to light upon one and not perceive his merits is a calamity. In the flesh, of course, I mean; in the book the fault, of course, is with my stumbling pen. Seraphina made a mistake about her Otto; it begins to swim before me dimly that you may have some traits of Seraphina?

With true ingratitude you see me pitch upon your exception; but it is easier to defend oneself gracefully than to acknowledge praise. I am truly glad that you should like my books; for I think I see from what you write that you are a reader worth convincing. Your name, if I have properly deciphered it, suggests that you may be also something of my countrywoman; for it is hard to see where Monroe came from, if not from Scotland. I seem to have here a double claim on your good nature: being myself pure Scotch and having appreciated your letter, make up two undeniable merits which, perhaps, if it should be quite without trouble, you might reward with your photograph.—Yours truly, ROBERT LOUIS STEVENSON.

To Miss Monroe

[Skerryvore, Bournemouth, *June, 1886.*]

My dear Miss Monroe,—I am ill in bed and stupid, incoherently stupid; yet I have to answer your letter, and if the answer is incomprehensible you must forgive me. You say my letter caused you pleasure; I am sure, as it fell out, not near so much as yours has brought to me. The interest taken in an author is fragile: his next book, or your next year of culture, might see the interest frosted or outgrown; and himself, in spite of all, you might probably find the most distasteful person upon earth. My case is different. I have bad health, am often condemned to silence for days together—was so once for six weeks, so that my voice was awful to hear when I first used it, like the whisper of a shadow—have outlived all my chief pleasures, which were active and adventurous, and ran in the open air: and being a person who prefers life to art, and who knows it is a far finer thing to be in love, or to risk a danger, than to paint the finest picture or write the noblest book, I begin to regard what remains to me of my life as very shadowy. From a variety of reasons, I am ashamed to confess I was much in this humour when your letter came. I had a good many troubles; was regretting a high average of sins; had been recently reminded that I had outlived some friends, and wondering if I had not outlived some friendships; and had just, while boasting of better health, been struck down again by my haunting enemy, an enemy who was exciting at first, but has now, by the iteration of his strokes, become merely annoying and inex-

1886 ÆT. 36 pressibly irksome. Can you fancy that to a person drawing towards the elderly this sort of conjunction of circumstances brings a rather aching sense of the past and the future? Well, it was just then that your letter and your photograph were brought to me in bed; and there came to me at once the most agreeable sense of triumph. My books were still young; my words had their good health and could go about the world and make themselves welcome; and even (in a shadowy and distant sense) make something in the nature of friends for the sheer hulk that stays at home and bites his pen over the manuscripts. It amused me very much to remember that I had been in Chicago, not so many years ago, in my proper person; where I had failed to awaken much remark, except from the ticket collector; and to think how much more gallant and persuasive were the fellows that I now send instead of me, and how these are welcome in that quarter to the sitter of Herr Platz, while their author was not very welcome even in the villainous restaurant where he tried to eat a meal and rather failed.

And this leads me directly to a confession. The photograph which shall accompany this is not chosen as the most like, but the best-looking. Put yourself in my place, and you will call this pardonable. Even as it is, even putting forth a flattered presentment, I am a little pained; and very glad it is a photograph and not myself that has to go; for in this case, if it please you, you can tell yourself it is my image—and if it displease you, you can lay the blame on the photographer; but in that, there were no help, and the poor author might belie his labours.

Kidnapped should soon appear; I am afraid you may not like it, as it is very unlike *Prince Otto* in every way; but I am myself a great admirer of the two chief characters, Alan and David. *Virginibus Puerisque* has never been issued in the States. I do not think it is a book that has much charm for publishers in any land; but I am to bring out a new edition in England shortly, a copy of which I must try to remember to send you. I say try to remember, because I have some superficial acquaintance with myself: and I have determined, after a galling discipline, to promise nothing more until the day of my death: at least, in this way, I shall no more break my word, and I must now try being churlish instead of being false.

I do not believe you to be the least like Seraphina. Your photograph has no trace of her, which somewhat relieves me, as I am a good deal afraid of Seraphinas — they do not always go into the woods and see the sunrise, and some are so well mailed that even that experience would leave them unaffected and unsoftened. The "hair and eyes of several complexions" was a trait taken from myself; and I do not bind myself to the opinions of Sir John. In this case, perhaps — but no, if the peculiarity is shared by two such pleasant persons as you and I (as you and me — the grammatical nut is hard), it must be a very good thing indeed, and Sir John must be an ass.

The *Book Reader* notice was a strange jumble of fact and fancy. I wish you could have seen my father's old assistant and present partner when he heard my father described as an "inspector of lighthouses," for we are all very proud of the family achievements, and

1886 ÆT. 36 the name of my house here in Bournemouth is stolen from one of the sea-towns of the Hebrides which are our pyramids and monuments. I was never at Cambridge, again; but neglected a considerable succession of classes at Edinburgh. But to correct that friendly blunderer were to write an autobiography.—And so now, with many thanks, believe me yours sincerely,

ROBERT LOUIS STEVENSON.

To R. A. M. STEVENSON

During these months, as already indicated, Stevenson was very much taken up, in by-hours, with trying to learn something of the theory and practice of music, and spent much of his time "pickling," as he called it, in an elementary manner on the piano. He even tried his hand in an experimental way at composition, and had sent one of his attempts for criticism to his cousin, Mr. R. A. M. Stevenson, who was better versed in the art.

SKERRYVORE, BOURNEMOUTH, *July, 1886.*

SIR,—Your foolish letter was unduly received. There may be hidden fifths, and if there are, it shows how dam spontaneous the thing was. I could tinker and tic-tac-toe on a piece of paper, but scorned the act with a Threnody, which was poured forth like blood and water on the groaning organ. If your heart (which was what I addressed) remained unmoved, let us refer to the affair no more: crystallised emotion, the statement and the reconciliation of the sorrows of the race and the individual, is obviously no more to you than supping sawdust. Well, well. If ever I write another Threnody! My next op. will probably be a Passepied and fugue in G (or D).

The mind is in my case shrunk to the size and sp. gr. of an aged Spanish filbert. O, I am so jolly silly. I now pickle with some freedom (1) the refrain of Martini's *Moutons ;* (2) *Sul margine d'un rio,* arranged for the infant school by the Aged Statesman; (3) the first phrase of Bach's musette (Sweet Englishwoman, No. 3),[1] the rest of the musette being one prolonged cropper, which I take daily for the benefit of my health. All my other works (of which there are many) are either arranged (by R. L. Stevenson) for the manly and melodious forefinger, or else prolonged and melancholy croppers. . . . I find one can get a notion of music very nicely. I have been pickling deeply in the Magic Flute; and have arranged *La dove prende,* almost to the end, for two melodious forefingers. I am next going to score the really nobler *Colomba o tortorella* for the same instruments.

This day is published
The works of Ludwig van Beethoven
arranged
and wiederdurchgearbeiteted
for two melodious forefingers
by,
Sir,—Your obedient servant,
PIMPERLY STIPPLE.

That 's a good idea? There 's a person called Lenz who actually does it—beware his den; I lost eighteen-pennies on him, and found the bleeding corpses of pieces of music divorced from their keys, despoiled of their graces, and even changed in time; I do not wish

1 *Suite anglaise.*

1886 ÆT. 36 to regard music (nor to be regarded) through that bony Lenz. You say you are "a spumfed idiot"; but how about Lenz? And how about me, sir, me?

I yesterday sent Lloyd by parcel post, at great expense, an empty matchbox and empty cigarette-paper book, a bell from a cat's collar, an iron kitchen spoon, and a piece of coal more than half the superficies of this sheet of paper. They are now (appropriately enough) speeding towards the Silly Isles; I hope he will find them useful. By that, and my telegram with prepaid answer to yourself, you may judge of my spiritual state. The finances have much brightened; and if *Kidnapped* keeps on as it has begun, I may be solvent. —Yours, THRENODIÆ AVCTOR

(The authour of ane Threnodie).

Op. 2: Scherzo (in G Major) expressive of the Sense of favours to come.

To R. A. M. STEVENSON

SKERRYVORE [BOURNEMOUTH, *July, 1886*].

DEAR BOB,—Herewith another shy; more melancholy than before, but I think not so abjectly idiotic. The musical terms seem to be as good as in Beethoven, and that, after all, is the great affair. Bar the dam bareness of the bass, it looks like a piece of real music from a distance. I am proud to say it was not made one hand at a time; the bass was of synchronous birth with the treble; they are of the same age, sir, and may God have mercy on their souls!—Yours, THE MAESTRO.

To Mr. and Mrs. Thomas Stevenson

Mr. and Mrs. Thomas Stevenson had been thinking of trying a winter at Bournemouth for the sake of being near their son, a plan which was eventually carried out. The health of the former was now fast and painfully breaking. Mr. J. W. Alexander, the well-known American artist, had been down at Skerryvore with an introduction from Mr. Gosse, and had made a drawing of Stevenson's head.

[Skerryvore, Bournemouth], *July 7th, 1886.*

My dear People,—It is probably my fault, and not yours, that I did not understand. I think it would be well worth trying the winter in Bournemouth; but I would only take the house by the month—this after mature discussion. My leakage still pursues its course; if I were only well, I have a notion to go north and get in (if I could) at the inn at Kirkmichael, which has always smiled upon me much. If I did well there, we might then meet and do what should most smile at the time.

Meanwhile, of course, I must not move, and am in a rancid box here, feeling the heat a great deal, and pretty tired of things. Alexander did a good thing of me at last; it looks like a mixture of an Aztec idol, a lion, an Indian Rajah, and a woman; and certainly represents a mighty comic figure. F. and Lloyd both think it is the best thing that has been done of me up to now.

You should hear Lloyd on the penny whistle, and me on the piano! Dear powers, what a concerto! I now live entirely for the piano, he for the whistle; the neigh-

1886 ÆT. 36 bours, in a radius of a furlong and a half, are packing up in quest of brighter climes.—Ever yours,

R. L. S.

P. S.—Please say if you can afford to let us have money for this trip, and if so, how much. I can see the year through without help, I believe, and supposing my health to keep up; but can scarce make this change on my own metal. R. L. S.

To Charles Baxter

[Skerryvore, Bournemouth, *July, 1886.*]

Dear Charles,—Doubtless, if all goes well, towards the 1st of August we shall be begging at your door. Thanks for a sight of the papers, which I return (you see) at once, fearing further responsibility.

Glad you like Dauvit; but eh, man, yon 's terrible strange conduc' o' thon man Rankeillor. Ca' him a legal adviser! It would make a bonny law-shuit, the Shaws case; and yon paper they signed, I 'm thinking, wouldnae be muckle thought o' by Puggy Deas.—Yours ever, R. L. S.

To Thomas Stevenson

"Coolin," mentioned below, had been a favourite Skye terrier of Heriot Row days.

[Skerryvore, Bournemouth], *July 28, 1886.*

My dear Father,—We have decided not to come to Scotland, but just to do as Dobell wished, and take an outing. I believe this is wiser in all ways; but I own it is a disappointment. I am weary of England; like Alan,

"I weary for the heather," if not for the deer. Lloyd has gone to Scilly with Katharine and C., where and with whom he should have a good time. David seems really to be going to succeed, which is a pleasant prospect on all sides. I am, I believe, floated financially; a book that sells will be a pleasant novelty. I enclose another review; mighty complimentary, and calculated to sell the book too. 1886 ÆT. 36

Coolin's tombstone has been got out, honest man! and it is to be polished, for it has got scratched, and have a touch of gilding in the letters, and be sunk in the front of the house. Worthy man, he, too, will maybe weary for the heather, and the bents of Gullane, where (as I dare say you remember) he gaed clean gyte, and jumped on to his crown from a gig, in hot and hopeless chase of many thousand rabbits. I can still hear the little cries of the honest fellow as he disappeared; and my mother will correct me, but I believe it was two days before he turned up again at North Berwick: to judge by his belly, he had caught not one out of these thousands, but he had had some exercise.

I keep well.—Ever your affectionate son,

R. L. S.

To Mrs. Thomas Stevenson

Having given up going to Scotland for a summer change, Stevenson had started on the "outing" which he mentions in the last letter. It took the shape of a ten days' visit to my house at the British Museum, followed by another made in the company of Mr. Henley to Paris, chiefly for the sake of seeing the W. H. Low's and the sculptor Rodin.

British Museum [*August 10th, 1886*].

MY DEAR MOTHER,—We are having a capital holiday, and I am much better, and enjoying myself to the nines.

1886 ÆT. 36 Richmond is painting my portrait. To-day I lunch with him, and meet Burne-Jones; to-night Browning dines with us. That sounds rather lofty work, does it not? His path was paved with celebrities. To-morrow we leave for Paris, and next week, I suppose, or the week after, come home. Address here, as we may not reach Paris. I am really very well.—Ever your affectionate son,

R. L. S.

To T. Watts-Dunton

Skerryvore, Bournemouth [*September, 1886*].

DEAR MR. WATTS,—The sight of the last *Athenæum* reminds me of you, and of my debt, now too long due. I wish to thank you for your notice of *Kidnapped;* and that not because it was kind, though for that also I valued it, but in the same sense as I have thanked you before now for a hundred articles on a hundred different writers. A critic like you is one who fights the good fight, contending with stupidity, and I would fain hope not all in vain; in my own case, for instance, surely not in vain.

What you say of the two parts in *Kidnapped* was felt by no one more painfully than by myself. I began it partly as a lark, partly as a pot-boiler; and suddenly it moved, David and Alan stepped out from the canvas, and I found I was in another world. But there was the cursed beginning, and a cursed end must be appended; and our old friend Byles the butcher was plainly audible tapping at the back door. So it had to go into the world, one part (as it does seem to me) alive, one part merely galvanised: no work, only an essay. For a man of tentative method, and weak health, and a scarcity of private means, and not too much of that frugality which is the artist's proper virtue, the days of sinecures and patrons look very golden: the days of professional literature very hard. Yet I do not so far deceive myself as to think I should change my character by changing my epoch; the sum of virtue in our books is in a relation of equality to the sum of virtues in ourselves; and my *Kidnapped* was doomed, while still in the womb and while I was yet in the cradle, to be the thing it is.

And now to the more genial business of defence. You attack my fight on board the *Covenant:* I think it literal. David and Alan had every advantage on their side—position, arms, training, a good conscience; a handful of merchant sailors, not well led in the first attack, not led at all in the second, could only by an accident have taken the round-house by attack; and since the defenders had firearms and food, it is even doubtful if they could have been starved out. The only doubtful point with me is whether the seamen would have ever ventured on the second onslaught; I half believed they would not; still the illusion of numbers and the authority of Hoseason would perhaps stretch far enough to justify the extremity.—I am, dear Mr. Watts, your very sincere admirer,

ROBERT LOUIS STEVENSON.

TO FREDERICK LOCKER-LAMPSON

Mr. Locker-Lampson, better known as Frederick Locker, the friend of Tennyson and most accomplished writer of *vers de société* in his

1886 time, had asked Stevenson, through their common friend Mr. Andrew
ÆT. 36 Lang, for a set of verses, and he had sent the following—hitherto only printed, I believe, at the head of a very scarce volume:—"Rowfant Rhymes, by Frederick Locker, with an introduction by Austin Dobson. Cleveland, The Rowfant Club, 1895. 127 copies only printed."

SKERRYVORE, *September 4, 1886.*

Not roses to the rose, I trow,
The thistle sends, nor to the bee
Do wasps bring honey. Wherefore now
Should Locker ask a verse from me?

Martial, perchance,—but he is dead,
And Herrick now must rhyme no more;
Still burning with the muse, they tread
(And arm in arm) the shadowy shore.

They, if they lived, with dainty hand,
To music as of mountain brooks,
Might bring you worthy words to stand
Unshamed, dear Locker, in your books.

But tho' these fathers of your race
Be gone before, yourself a sire,
To-day you see before your face
Your stalwart youngsters touch the lyre.

On these—on Lang, or Dobson—call,
Long leaders of the songful feast.
They lend a verse your laughing fall—
A verse they owe you at the least.

To Frederick Locker-Lampson

To Mr. Locker's acknowledgment of these verses Stevenson replied as follows, asking his correspondent's interest on behalf of a friend who had been kind to him at Hyères, in procuring a nomination for her son to the Blue-Coat School.

[Skerryvore], Bournemouth, *September, 1886.*

Dear Locker,—You take my verses too kindly, but you will admit, for such a bluebottle of a versifier to enter the house of Gertrude, where her necklace hangs, was not a little brave. Your kind invitation, I fear, must remain unaccepted; and yet—if I am very well—perhaps next spring—(for I mean to be very well)—my wife might. . . . But all that is in the clouds with my better health. And now look here: you are a rich man and know many people, therefore perhaps some of the Governors of Christ's Hospital. If you do, I know a most deserving case, in which I would (if I could) do anything. To approach you, in this way, is not decent; and you may therefore judge by my doing it, how near this matter lies to my heart. I enclose you a list of the Governors, which I beg you to return, whether or not you shall be able to do anything to help me.

The boy's name is ——; he and his mother are very poor. It may interest you in her cause if I tell you this: that when I was dangerously ill at Hyères, this brave lady, who had then a sick husband of her own (since dead) and a house to keep and a family of four to cook for, all with her own hands, for they could afford no servant, yet took watch-about with my wife,

1886 and contributed not only to my comfort, but to my re-
ÆT. 36 covery in a degree that I am not able to limit. You can conceive how much I suffer from my impotence to help her, and indeed I have already shown myself a thankless friend. Let not my cry go up before you in vain!—Yours in hope, ROBERT LOUIS STEVENSON.

TO FREDERICK LOCKER-LAMPSON

Mr. Locker, apparently misunderstanding the application, had replied with a cheque.

SKERRYVORE, BOURNEMOUTH, *September, 1886.*

MY DEAR LOCKER,—That I should call myself a man of letters, and land myself in such unfathomable ambiguities! No, my dear Locker, I did not want a cheque; and in my ignorance of business, which is greater even than my ignorance of literature, I have taken the liberty of drawing a pen through the document and returning it; should this be against the laws of God or man, forgive me. All that I meant by my excessively disgusting reference to your material weli-being was the vague notion that a man who is well off was sure to know a Governor of Christ's Hospital; though how I quite arrived at this conclusion I do not see. A man with a cold in the head does not necessarily know a ratcatcher; and the connection is equally close—as it now appears to my awakened and somewhat humbled spirit. For all that, let me thank you in the warmest manner for your friendly readiness to contribute. You say you have hopes of becoming a miser: I wish I had; but indeed I believe you deceive yourself, and are as far from it as ever. I wish I had any excuse to keep your cheque, for it is much more elegant to receive than to return; but I have my way of making it up to you, and I do sincerely beg you to write to the two Governors. This extraordinary outpouring of correspondence would (if you knew my habits) convince you of my great eagerness in this matter. I would promise gratitude; but I have made a promise to myself to make no more promises to anybody else, having broken such a host already, and come near breaking my heart in consequence; and as for gratitude, I am by nature a thankless dog, and was spoiled from a child up. But if you can help this lady in the matter of the Hospital, you will have helped the worthy. Let me continue to hope that I shall make out my visit in the spring, and believe me, yours very truly, ROBERT LOUIS STEVENSON.

It may amuse you to know that a very long while ago, I broke my heart to try to imitate your verses, and failed hopelessly. I saw some of the evidences the other day among my papers, and blushed to the heels.

R. L. S.

I give up finding out your name in the meantime, and keep to that by which you will be known — Frederick Locker.

TO FREDERICK LOCKER-LAMPSON

[SKERRYVORE, BOURNEMOUTH],
24th September, 1886.

MY DEAR LOCKER,—You are simply an angel of light, and your two letters have gone to the post; I trust they will reach the hearts of the recipients—at least, that

1886 ÆT. 36 could not be more handsomely expressed. About the cheque: well now, I am going to keep it; but I assure you Mrs. —— has never asked me for money, and I would not dare to offer any till she did. For all that I shall stick to the cheque now, and act to that amount as your almoner. In this way I reward myself for the ambiguity of my epistolary style.

I suppose, if you please, you may say your verses are thin (would you so describe an arrow, by the way, and one that struck the gold? It scarce strikes me as exhaustively descriptive), and, thin or not, they are (and I have found them) inimitably elegant. I thank you again very sincerely for the generous trouble you have taken in this matter which was so near my heart, and you may be very certain it will be the fault of my health and not my inclination, if I do not see you before very long; for all that has passed has made me in more than the official sense sincerely yours,

ROBERT LOUIS STEVENSON.

To Sidney Colvin

The following refers first, if I remember right, to some steps that were being taken to obtain recognition in the form of a knighthood for the elder Stevenson's public services; next, to the writer's own work at the time in hand; and lastly to my volume on Keats then in preparation for Mr. Morley's series.

SKERRYVORE, *Dec. 14, 1886.*

MY DEAR COLVIN,—This is first-rate of you, the Lord love you for it! I am truly much obliged. He—my father—is very changeable; at times, he seems only a slow quiet edition of himself; again, he will be very heavy and blank; but never so violent as last spring; and therefore, to my mind, better on the whole. 1887 ÆT. 37

I am splendid. I have been writing much verse—quite the bard, in fact; and also a dam tale to order, which will be what it will be: I don't love it, but some of it is passable in its mouldy way, *The Misadventures of John Nicholson*. All my bardly exercises are in Scotch; I have struck my somewhat ponderous guitar in that tongue to no small extent: with what success, I know not, but I think it 's better than my English verse; more marrow and fatness, and more ruggedness.

How goes *Keats?* Pray remark, if he (Keats) hung back from Shelley, it was not to be wondered at, *when so many of his friends were Shelley's pensioners.* I forget if you have made this point; it has been borne in upon me reading Dowden and the *Shelley Papers;* and it will do no harm if you have made it. I finished a poem to-day, and writ 3000 words of a story, *tant bien que mal;* and have a right to be sleepy, and (what is far nobler and rarer) am so.—My dear Colvin, ever yours,

THE REAL MACKAY.

TO FREDERICK LOCKER-LAMPSON

Stevenson suffered more even than usual after the turn of the year and during the spring of 1887, and for several months his correspondence almost entirely fails. This is in reply to an invitation to Rowfant for Easter.

SKERRYVORE, BOURNEMOUTH, *February 5th, 1887.*

MY DEAR LOCKER,—Here I am in my bed as usual, and it is indeed a long while since I went out to dinner.

1887 ÆT. 37 You do not know what a crazy fellow this is. My winter has not so far been luckily passed, and all hope of paying visits at Easter has vanished for twelve calendar months. But because I am a beastly and indurated invalid, I am not dead to human feelings; and I neither have forgotten you nor will forget you. Some day the wind may round to the right quarter and we may meet; till then I am still truly yours,

ROBERT LOUIS STEVENSON.

To Henry James

[SKERRYVORE, BOURNEMOUTH, *February, 1887.*]

MY DEAR JAMES,—My health has played me it in once more in the absurdest fashion, and the creature who now addresses you is but a stringy and white-faced *bouilli* out of the pot of fever, with the devil to pay in every corner of his economy. I suppose (to judge by your letter) I need not send you these sheets, which came during my collapse by the rush. I am on the start with three volumes, that one of tales,[1] a second one of essays,[2] and one of—ahem—verse.[3] This is a great order, is it not? After that I shall have empty lockers. All new work stands still; I was getting on well with Jenkin when this blessed malady unhorsed me, and sent me back to the dung-collecting trade of the republisher. I shall reissue *Virg. Puer.* as Vol. I. of *Essays*, and the new vol. as Vol. II. of ditto; to be sold, however, separately. This is but a dry maundering; however, I am quite unfit—"I am for action quite unfit Either of exercise or wit." My father is in a variable

[1] *The Merry Men.* [2] *Memories and Portraits.* [3] *Underwoods.*

state; many sorrows and perplexities environ the house of Stevenson; my mother shoots north at this hour on business of a distinctly rancid character; my father (under my wife's tutorage) proceeds to-morrow to Salisbury; I remain here in my bed and whistle; in no quarter of heaven is anything encouraging apparent, except that the good Colvin comes to the hotel here on a visit. This dreary view of life is somewhat blackened by the fact that my head aches, which I always regard as a liberty on the part of the powers that be. This is also my first letter since my recovery. God speed your laudatory pen!

My wife joins in all warm messages.—Yours,

R. L. S.

To W. H. Low

Mr. Low and his wife, who were at this time leaving Paris for good, had been meditating a visit to the Stevensons at Bournemouth on their way home to the United States.

[*April, 1887.*]

MY DEAR LOW,—The fares to London may be found in any continental Bradshaw or sich; from London to Bournemouth impoverished parties who can stoop to the third class get their ticket for the matter of 10*s*., or, as my wife loves to phrase it, "a half a pound." You will also be involved in a 3*s*. fare to get to Skerryvore; but this, I dare say, friends could help you in on your arrival; so that you may reserve your energies for the two tickets—costing the matter of a pound—and the usual gratuities to porters. This does not seem to me much: considering the intellectual pleasures that await

1887 you here, I call it dirt cheap. I *believe* the third class
ÆT. 37 from Paris to London (*viâ* Dover) is *about* forty francs, but I cannot swear. Suppose it to be fifty.

	frcs.
50 × 2 = 100	100
The expense of spirit or spontaneous lapse of coin on the journey, at 5 frcs. a head, 5 × 2 = 10	10
Victuals on ditto, at 5 frcs. a head, 5 × 2 = 10	10
Gratuity to stewardess, in case of severe prostration, at *3* francs	*3*
One night in London, on a modest footing, say 20	20
Two tickets to Bournemouth at 12.50, 12.50 × 2 = 25	25
Porters and general devilment, say 5 . .	5
Cabs in London, say 2 shillings, and in Bournemouth, *3* shillings = 5 shillings, 6 frcs. 25	6.25
frcs. .	179.25

Or, the same in pounds, £7 *3s. 6½d.*
Or, the same in dollars, $35.45,

if there be any arithmetical virtue in me. I have left out dinner in London in case you want to blow out, which would come extry, and with the aid of *vangs fangs* might easily double the whole amount—above all if you have a few friends to meet you.

In making this valuable project, or budget, I discovered for the first time a reason (frequently overlooked) for the singular costliness of travelling with your wife.

Anybody would count the tickets double; but how few would have remembered — or indeed has any one ever remembered? — to count the spontaneous lapse of coin double also? Yet there are two of you, each must do his daily leakage, and it must be done out of your travelling fund. You will tell me, perhaps, that you carry the coin yourself: my dear sir, do you think you can fool your Maker? Your wife has to lose her quota; and by God she will — if you kept the coin in a belt. One thing I have omitted: you will lose a certain amount on the exchange, but this even I cannot foresee, as it is one of the few things that vary with the way a man has.— I am, dear sir, yours financially,

SAMUEL BUDGETT.

TO ALISON CUNNINGHAM

SKERRYVORE, *April 16th, 1887.*

MY DEAREST CUMMY,— As usual, I have been a dreary bad fellow and not written for ages; but you must just try to forgive me, to believe (what is the truth) that the number of my letters is no measure of the number of times I think of you, and to remember how much writing I have to do. The weather is bright, but still cold; and my father, I 'm afraid, feels it sharply. He has had — still has, rather — a most obstinate jaundice, which has reduced him cruelly in strength, and really upset him altogether. I hope, or think, he is perhaps a little better; but he suffers much, cannot sleep at night, and gives John and my mother a severe life of it to wait upon him. My wife is, I think, a little

1887 better, but no great shakes. I keep mightily respect-
ÆT. 37 able myself.

Coolin's tombstone is now built into the front wall of Skerryvore, and poor Bogie's (with a Latin inscription also) is set just above it. Poor, unhappy wee man, he died, as you must have heard, in fight, which was what he would have chosen; for military glory was more in his line than the domestic virtues. I believe this is about all my news, except that, as I write, there is a blackbird singing in our garden trees, as it were at Swanston. I would like fine to go up the burnside a bit, and sit by the pool and be young again — or no, be what I am still, only there instead of here, for just a little. Did you see that I had written about John Todd? In this month's *Longman* it was; if you have not seen it, I will try and send it you. Some day climb as high as Halkerside for me (I am never likely to do it for myself), and sprinkle some of the well-water on the turf. I am afraid it is a pagan rite, but quite harmless, and *ye can sain it wi' a bit prayer.* Tell the Peewies that I mind their forebears well. My heart is sometimes heavy, and sometimes glad to mind it all. But for what we have received, the Lord make us truly thankful. Don't forget to sprinkle the water, and do it in my name; I feel a childish eagerness in this.

Remember me most kindly to James, and with all sorts of love to yourself, believe me, your laddie,

ROBERT LOUIS STEVENSON.

P. S.— I suppose Mrs. Todd ought to see the paper about her man; judge of that, and if you think she would not dislike it, buy her one from me, and let me know. The article is called "Pastoral," in *Longman's Magazine* for April. I will send you the money; I would to-day, but it 's the Sabbie day, and I cannae. 1887 ÆT. 37

R. L. S.

Remembrances from all here.

To Sidney Colvin

Within a fortnight after the date of the above Stevenson went himself, and for the last time, to Scotland; not, indeed, to visit his old haunts among the Pentlands, but to be present, too late for recognition, at the death of his father (May 8, 1887). Business detained him for some weeks, and the following was written just before his return to Bournemouth.

[Edinburgh, *June, 1887.*]

My dear S. C.,—At last I can write a word to you. Your little note in the *P. M. G.* was charming. I have written four pages in the *Contemporary*, which Bunting found room for: they are not very good, but I shall do more for his memory in time.

About the death, I have long hesitated, I was long before I could tell my mind; and now I know it, and can but say that I am glad. If we could have had my father, that would have been a different thing. But to keep that changeling—suffering changeling—any longer, could better none and nothing. Now he rests; it is more significant, it is more like himself. He will begin to return to us in the course of time, as he was and as we loved him.

My favourite words in literature, my favourite scene—"O let him pass," Kent and Lear—was played for me here in the first moment of my return. I believe

1887 Shakespeare saw it with his own father. I had no
ÆT. 37 words; but it was shocking to see. He died on his feet, you know; was on his feet the last day, knowing nobody — still he would be up. This was his constant wish; also that he might smoke a pipe on his last day. The funeral would have pleased him; it was the largest private funeral in man's memory here.

We have no plans, and it is possible we may go home without going through town. I do not know; I have no views yet whatever; nor can have any at this stage of my cold and my business.— Ever yours, R. L. S.

IX

THE UNITED STATES AGAIN:

WINTER IN THE ADIRONDACKS

(August, 1887–October, 1888)

IX

THE UNITED STATES AGAIN:

WINTER IN THE ADIRONDACKS

(August, 1887–October, 1888)

DURING the two years and nine months of Stevenson's residence at Bournemouth, preceding the date of his father's death, he had made no apparent progress towards recovery. Every period of respite had been quickly followed by a relapse, and all his work, brilliant and varied as it was, had been done under conditions which would have reduced almost any other man to inactivity. The close and frequently recurring struggles against the danger of death from hæmorrhage and exhaustion, which he had been used, when they first occurred, to find exciting, grew in the long run merely irksome; and even his persistent high courage and gaiety, sustained as they were by the devoted affection of his wife and many friends, began occasionally, for the first time, to fail him. Accordingly, when in May, 1887, the death of his father severed the strongest of the ties which bound him to the old country, he was very ready to listen to the advice of his physicians, who were unanimous in thinking his case not hopeless, but urged him to try some complete change of climate, surroundings, and mode of life. His wife's connections pointing to the West, he thought of the mountain health-resorts of Colorado, and of their growing reputation for the cure of lung patients. Having let his house at Bournemouth, he accordingly took passage on board the ss. *Ludgate Hill*, sailing for New York from London on August 21st, 1887, with his whole party, consisting of his wife, his widowed mother, whom they had persuaded to join them, his young stepson, and a trusted servant, Valentine Roch.

It was the moment when his reputation had first reached its height in the United States, owing to the popularity first of *Treasure Island* and then of *Kidnapped*, and more especially to the immense impression made by *The Strange Case of Dr. Jekyll and Mr. Hyde*. He experienced consequently for the first time the pleasures, such as they were, of celebrity, and also its inconveniences; found the most hospitable of refuges in the house of his kind friends, Mr. and Mrs. Charles Fairchild, at Newport; and quickly made many other friends, including Mr. C. Scribner and Mr. E. L. Burlingame, the owner and the editor of *Scribner's Magazine*, from whom he immediately received and accepted very advantageous offers of work. Having been dissuaded from braving for the present the fatigue of the long journey to Colorado and the extreme rigour of its winter climate, he determined to try instead a season at Saranac Lake in the Adirondack Mountains, New York State, which had lately been coming into reputation as a place of cure. There, under the care of the well-known resident physician, Dr. Trudeau, he spent nearly seven months, from the end of September, 1887, to the end of April, 1888, with results on the whole favourable to his own health, though not to that of his wife, who was never well at these high altitudes. His work during the winter consisted of the twelve papers published in the course of 1888 in *Scribner's Magazine,* including perhaps the most striking of all his essays, *A Chapter on Dreams, Pulvis et Umbra, Beggars, The Lantern Bearers, Random Memories,* etc.; as well as the greater part of *The Master of Ballantrae* and *The Wrong Box*—the last originally conceived and drafted by Mr. Lloyd Osbourne.

The following letters are selected from those which tell of his preparations to leave his Bournemouth home in the summer of 1887, of his voyage to New York and reception there at this date, and of his winter's life and work at Saranac.

To W. E. Henley

During the two months following his father's death Stevenson had suffered much both from his old complaints and from depression of mind. His only work had been in preparing for press the verse collection *Underwoods,* the *Life of Fleeming Jenkin,* and the volume of essays called *Memories and Portraits.* 1887 ÆT. 37

[Skerryvore, Bournemouth], *August, 1887.*

Dear Lad,—I write to inform you that Mr. Stevenson's well-known work, *Virginibus Puerisque,* is about to be reprinted. At the same time a second volume called *Memories and Portraits* will issue from the roar-

1887 ing loom. Its interest will be largely autobiographical,
ÆT. 37 Mr. S. having sketched there the lineaments of many departed friends, and dwelt fondly, and with a m'istened eye, upon bygone pleasures. The two will be issued under the common title of *Familiar Essays;* but the volumes will be vended separately to those who are mean enough not to hawk at both.

The blood is at last stopped: only yesterday. I began to think I should not get away. However, I hope — I hope — remark the word — no boasting — I hope I may luff up a bit now. Dobell, whom I saw, gave as usual a good account of my lungs, and expressed himself, like his neighbours, hopefully about the trip. He says, my uncle says, Scott says, Brown says — they all say — You ought not to be in such a state of health; you should recover. Well, then, I mean to. My spirits are rising again after three months of black depression: I almost begin to feel as if I should care to live: I would, by God! And so I believe I shall.—Yours,

BULLETIN M'GURDER.

How has the Deacon gone?

To W. H. Low

[SKERRYVORE, BOURNEMOUTH], *August 6th, 1887.*

MY DEAR LOW,— We — my mother, my wife, my stepson, my maidservant, and myself, five souls — leave, if all is well, Aug. 20th, per Wilson line ss. *Ludgate Hill.* Shall probably evade N. Y. at first, cutting straight to a watering-place: Newport, I believe, its name. Afterwards we shall steal incognito into *la bonne ville,* and see no one but you and the Scribners, if it may be so managed. You must understand I have been very seedy indeed, quite a dead body; and unless the voyage does miracles, I shall have to draw it dam fine. Alas, "The Canoe Speaks" is now out of date; it will figure in my volume of verses now imminent. However, I may find some inspiration some day.—Till very soon, yours ever,

R. L. S.

To Miss Adelaide Boodle

The lady to whom the following (and much correspondence yet to come) is addressed had been an attached friend of the Skerryvore household. She had given R. L. S. a paper-cutter by way of farewell token at his starting.

Bournemouth, *August 19th, 1887.*

MY DEAR MISS BOODLE,—I promise you the paper-knife shall go to sea with me; and if it were in my disposal, I should promise it should return with me too. All that you say, I thank you for very much; I thank you for all the pleasantness that you have brought about our house; and I hope the day may come when I shall see you again in poor old Skerryvore, now left to the natives of Canada, or to worse barbarians, if such exist. I am afraid my attempt to jest is rather *à contre-cœur*. Good-bye — *au revoir* — and do not forget your friend,

Robert Louis Stevenson.

To Messrs. Chatto and Windus

The titles and proofs mentioned in the text are presumably those of *Underwoods* and *Memories and Portraits*.

Bournemouth [*August, 1887*].

DEAR SIRS,—I here enclose the two titles. Had you not better send me the bargains to sign? I shall be

1887 ÆT. 37 here till Saturday; and shall have an address in London (which I shall send you) till Monday, when I shall sail. Even if the proofs do not reach you till Monday morning, you could send a clerk from Fenchurch Street Station at 10.23 A. M. for Galleons Station, and he would find me embarking on board the *Ludgate Hill*, Island Berth, Royal Albert Dock. Pray keep this in case it should be necessary to catch this last chance. I am most anxious to have the proofs with me on the voyage.—Yours very truly, ROBERT LOUIS STEVENSON.

TO SIDNEY COLVIN

A succession of Stevenson's friends had visited and spent part of the day or evening with him at Armfield's hotel on Sunday, August 20th, each bringing some farewell gift or another (as related by Mr. Gosse in his volume *Critical Kitcats*, p. 297). Among these, Mr. Henry James's gift had been a case of champagne for consumption during the journey. On the morning of the 21st I accompanied him to the docks, saw him and his party embarked on board the steamer *Ludgate Hill*, a vessel sailing from the port of London and carrying animals and freight as well as passengers. They had chosen to go by this route for the sake alike of economy and amusement, rather than by one of the sumptuous liners sailing from Liverpool or Southampton. Leaving the ship's side as she weighed anchor, and waving farewell to the party from the boat which landed me, I little knew what was the truth, that I was looking on the face of my friend for the last time. The letters next following were written during or immediately after his passage across the Atlantic. "The Commodore" is of course R. L. S.

H. M. S. "VULGARIUM," OFF HAVRE DE GRACE,
this 22nd day of August [*1887*].

SIR,—The weather has been hitherto inimitable. The berths are excellent, the pasture swallowable, the champagne of H. James (to recur to my favourite adjective) inimitable. As for the Commodore, he slept awhile in the evening, tossed off a cup of Henry James with his plain meal, walked the deck till eight, among sands and floating lights and buoys and wrecked brigantines, came down (to his regret) a minute too soon to see Margate lit up, turned in about nine, slept, with some interruptions, but on the whole sweetly, until six, and has already walked a mile or so of deck, among a fleet of other steamers waiting for the tide, within view of Havre, and pleasantly entertained by passing fishing-boats, hovering sea-gulls, and Vulgarians pairing on deck with endearments of primitive simplicity. There, sir, can be viewed the sham quarrel, the sham desire for information, and every device of these two poor ancient sexes (who might, you might think, have learned in the course of the ages something new) down to the exchange of head-gear.

I am, sir, yours,
Bold Bob Boltsprit.

B. B. B. (*alias* the Commodore) will now turn to his proofs. Havre de Grace is a city of some show. It is for-ti-fied; and, so far as I can see, is a place of some trade. It is situ-ated in France, a country of Europe. You always complain there are no facts in my letters.

R. L. S.

1887
ÆT. 37

To Sidney Colvin

Newport, R. I., U. S. A. [*September, 1887*].

MY DEAR COLVIN,—So long it went excellent well, and I had a time I am glad to have had; really enjoying my life. There is nothing like being at sea, after all. And O, why have I allowed myself to rot so long on land? But on the Banks I caught a cold, and I have not yet got over it. My reception here was idiotic to the last degree. . . . It is very silly, and not pleasant, except where humour enters; and I confess the poor interviewer lads pleased me. They are too good for their trade; avoided anything I asked them to avoid, and were no more vulgar in their reports than they could help. I liked the lads.

O, it was lovely on our stable-ship, chock full of stallions. She rolled heartily, rolled some of the fittings out of our state-room, and I think a more dangerous cruise (except that it was summer) it would be hard to imagine. But we enjoyed it to the masthead, all but Fanny; and even she perhaps a little. When we got in, we had run out of beer, stout, cocoa, soda-water, water, fresh meat, and (almost) of biscuit. But it was a thousandfold pleasanter than a great big Birmingham liner like a new hotel; and we liked the officers, and made friends with the quartermasters, and I (at least) made a friend of a baboon (for we carried a cargo of apes), whose embraces have pretty near cost me a coat. The passengers improved, and were a very good specimen lot, with no drunkard, no gambling that I saw, and less grumbling and backbiting than one would have asked of poor human nature. Apes, stallions, cows, matches, hay, and poor men-folk, all, or almost all, came successfully to land.—Yours ever, R. L. S. 1887 ÆT. 37

To Henry James

[Newport, U. S. A., *September, 1887.*]

MY DEAR JAMES,—Here we are at Newport in the house of the good Fairchilds; and a sad burthen we have laid upon their shoulders. I have been in bed practically ever since I came. I caught a cold on the Banks after having had the finest time conceivable, and enjoyed myself more than I could have hoped on board our strange floating menagerie: stallions and monkeys and matches made our cargo; and the vast continent of these incongruities rolled the while like a haystack; and the stallions stood hypnotised by the motion, looking through the ports at our dinner-table, and winked when the crockery was broken; and the little monkeys stared at each other in their cages, and were thrown overboard like little bluish babies; and the big monkey, Jacko, scoured about the ship and rested willingly in my arms, to the ruin of my clothing; and the man of the stallions made a bower of the black tarpaulin, and sat therein at the feet of a raddled divinity, like a picture on a box of chocolates; and the other passengers, when they were not sick, looked on and laughed. Take all this picture, and make it roll till the bell shall sound unexpected notes and the fittings shall break loose in our state room, and you have the voyage of the

1887 ÆT. 37 *Ludgate Hill.* She arrived in the port of New York, without beer, porter, soda-water, curaçoa, fresh meat, or fresh water; and yet we lived, and we regret her.

My wife is a good deal run down, and I am no great shakes.

America is, as I remarked, a fine place to eat in, and a great place for kindness; but, Lord, what a silly thing is popularity! I envy the cool obscurity of Skerryvore. If it even paid, said Meanness! and was abashed at himself.—Yours most sincerely, R. L. S.

TO SIDNEY COLVIN

[NEW YORK: *end of September, 1887.*]

MY DEAR S. C.,—Your delightful letter has just come, and finds me in a New York hotel, waiting the arrival of a sculptor (St. Gaudens) who is making a medallion of yours truly and who is (to boot) one of the handsomest and nicest fellows I have seen. I caught a cold on the Banks; fog is not for me; nearly died of interviewers and visitors, during twenty-four hours in New York; cut for Newport with Lloyd and Valentine, a journey like fairy-land for the most engaging beauties, one little rocky and pine-shaded cove after another, each with a house and a boat at anchor, so that I left my heart in each and marvelled why American authors had been so unjust to their country; caught another cold on the train; arrived at Newport to go to bed and to grow worse, and to stay in bed until I left again; the Fairchilds proving during this time kindness itself; Mr. Fairchild simply one of the most engaging men in the world, and one of the children, Blair, *æt.* ten, a great joy and amusement in his solemn adoring attitude to the author of *Treasure Island*. 1887 ÆT. 37

Here I was interrupted by the arrival of my sculptor. I have begged him to make a medallion of himself and give me a copy. I will not take up the sentence in which I was wandering so long, but begin fresh. I was ten or twelve days at Newport; then came back convalescent to New York. Fanny and Lloyd are off to the Adirondacks to see if that will suit; and the rest of us leave Monday (this is Saturday) to follow them up. I hope we may manage to stay there all winter. I have a splendid appetite and have on the whole recovered well after a mighty sharp attack. I am now on a salary of £500 a year for twelve articles in *Scribner's Magazine* on what I like; it is more than £500, but I cannot calculate more precisely. You have no idea how much is made of me here; I was offered £2000 for a weekly article—eh heh! how is that? but I refused that lucrative job. The success of *Underwoods* is gratifying. You see, the verses are sane; that is their strong point, and it seems it is strong enough to carry them.

A thousand thanks for your grand letter.—Ever yours,

R. L. S.

To W. E. Henley

The verses herein alluded to were addressed to Dr. Gordon Hake in return for some received from him. They are those beginning "In the beloved hour that ushers day," and printed as No. xix. in *Songs of Travel*.

New York [*September, 1887*].

MY DEAR LAD,—Herewith verses for Dr. Hake, which please communicate. I did my best with the inter-

1887 ÆT. 37 viewers; I don't know if Lloyd sent you the result; my heart was too sick: you can do nothing with them; and yet they literally sweated with anxiety to please, and took me down in long hand.

I have been quite ill, but go better. I am being not busted, but medallioned, by St. Gaudens, who is a first-rate, plain, high-minded artist and honest fellow; you would like him down to the ground. I believe sculptors are fine fellows when they are not demons. O, I am now a salaried person, £600 a year,[1] to write twelve articles in *Scribner's Magazine;* it remains to be seen if it really pays, huge as the sum is, but the slavery may overweigh me. I hope you will like my answer to Hake, and specially that he will.

Love to all.— Yours affectionately, R. L. S.

(*le salarié*).

To R. A. M. Stevenson

Saranac Lake, Adirondacks,
New York, U. S. A. [*October, 1887*].

MY DEAR BOB,—The cold [of Colorado] was too rigorous for me; I could not risk the long railway voyage, and the season was too late to risk the Eastern, Cape Hatteras side of the steamer one; so here we stuck and stick. We have a wooden house on a hill-top, overlooking a river, and a village about a quarter of a mile away, and very wooded hills; the whole scene is very Highland, bar want of heather and the wooden houses.

I have got one good thing of my sea voyage: it is proved the sea agrees heartily with me, and my mother

[1] The sum was really £700.

likes it; so if I get any better, or no worse, my mother will likely hire a yacht for a month or so in summer. Good Lord! What fun! Wealth is only useful for two things: a yacht and a string quartette. For these two I will sell my soul. Except for these I hold that £700 a year is as much as anybody can possibly want; and I have had more, so I know, for the extry coins were for no use, excepting for illness, which damns everything. 1887 ÆT. 37

I was so happy on board that ship, I could not have believed it possible. We had the beastliest weather, and many discomforts; but the mere fact of its being a tramp-ship gave us many comforts; we could cut about with the men and officers, stay in the wheel-house, discuss all manner of things, and really be a little at sea. And truly there is nothing else. I had literally forgotten what happiness was, and the full mind—full of external and physical things, not full of cares and labours and rot about a fellow's behaviour. My heart literally sang; I truly care for nothing so much as for that. We took so north a course, that we saw Newfoundland; no one in the ship had ever seen it before.

It was beyond belief to me how she rolled; in seemingly smooth water, the bell striking, the fittings bounding out of our state-room. It is worth having lived these last years, partly because I have written some better books, which is always pleasant, but chiefly to have had the joy of this voyage. I have been made a lot of here, and it is sometimes pleasant, sometimes the reverse; but I could give it all up, and agree that —— was the author of my works, for a good seventy-ton schooner and the coins to keep her on.

1887 ÆT. 37 And to think there are parties with yachts who would make the exchange! I know a little about fame now; it is no good compared to a yacht; and anyway there is more fame in a yacht, more genuine fame; to cross the Atlantic and come to anchor in Newport (say) with the Union Jack, and go ashore for your letters and hang about the pier, among the holiday yachtsmen—that 's fame, that 's glory, and nobody can take it away; they can't say your book is bad; you *have* crossed the Atlantic. I should do it south by the West Indies, to avoid the damned Banks; and probably come home by steamer, and leave the skipper to bring the yacht home.

Well, if all goes well, we shall maybe sail out of Southampton water some of these days and take a run to Havre, and try the Baltic, or somewhere.

Love to you all.—Ever your afft.,

ROBERT LOUIS STEVENSON.

TO EDMUND GOSSE

The following refers to a review by Mr. Gosse of Stevenson's volume of verse called *Underwoods*. The book had been published a few weeks previously, and is dedicated, as readers will remember, to a number of physicians who had attended him at sundry times and places.

SARANAC LAKE, *Oct. 8th, 1887.*

MY DEAR GOSSE,—I have just read your article twice, with cheers of approving laughter. I do not believe you ever wrote anything so funny: Tyndall's "shell," the passage on the Davos press and its invaluable issues, and that on V. Hugo and Swinburne, are exquisite; so,

I say it more ruefully, is the touch about the doctors. For the rest, I am very glad you like my verses so well; and the qualities you ascribe to them seem to me well found and well named. I own to that kind of candour you attribute to me: when I am frankly interested, I suppose I fancy the public will be so too; and when I am moved, I am sure of it. It has been my luck hitherto to meet with no staggering disillusion. "Before" and "After" may be two; and yet I believe the habit is now too thoroughly ingrained to be altered. About the doctors, you were right, that dedication has been the subject of some pleasantries that made me grind, and of your happily touched reproof which made me blush. And to miscarry in a dedication is an abominable form of book-wreck; I am a good captain, I would rather lose the tent and save my dedication.

I am at Saranac Lake in the Adirondacks, I suppose for the winter: it seems a first-rate place; we have a house in the eye of many winds, with a view of a piece of running water — Highland, all but the dear hue of peat — and of many hills — Highland also, but for the lack of heather. Soon the snow will close on us; we are here some twenty miles — twenty-seven, they say, but this I profoundly disbelieve — in the woods; communication by letter is slow and (let me be consistent) aleatory; by telegram is as near as may be impossible.

I had some experience of American appreciation; I liked a little of it, but there is too much; a little of that would go a long way to spoil a man; and I like myself better in the woods. I am so damned candid and ingenuous (for a cynic), and so much of a "cweatu' of im-

1887 pulse—aw" (if you remember that admirable Leech),
ÆT. 37 that I begin to shirk any more taffy; I think I begin to like it too well. But let us trust the Gods; they have a rod in pickle; reverently I doff my trousers, and with screwed eyes await the *amari aliquid* of the great God Busby.

I thank you for the article in all ways, and remain yours affectionately, R. L. S.

To W. H. Low

[SARANAC LAKE, *October, 1887.*]

SIR,—I have to trouble you with the following *paroles bien senties.* We are here at a first-rate place. "Baker's" is the name of our house, but we don't address there; we prefer the tender care of the Post-Office, as more aristocratic (it is no use to telegraph even to the care of the Post-Office, who does not give a single damn[1]). Baker's has a prophet's chamber, which the hypercritical might describe as a garret with a hole in the floor: in that garret, sir, I have to trouble you and your wife to come and slumber. Not now, however: with manly hospitality, I choke off any sudden impulse. Because, first, my wife and my mother are gone (a note for the latter, strongly suspected to be in the hand of your talented wife, now sits silent on the mantel shelf), one to Niagara and t' other to Indianapolis. Because, second, we are not yet installed. And because, third, I won't have you till I have a buffalo robe and leggings,

1 "But he was more than usual calm;
He did not give a single damn."—*Marjorie Fleming.*

THE COTTAGE AT SARANAC LAKE OCCUPIED BY ROBERT LOUIS STEVENSON.

lest you should want to paint me as a plain man, which I am not, but a rank Saranacker and wild man of the woods.—Yours, ROBERT LOUIS STEVENSON. 1887 ÆT. 37

TO WILLIAM ARCHER

The Wondrous Tale referred to in the following is Stevenson's *Black Arrow*, which had been through Mr. Archer's hands in proof.

SARANAC LAKE, *October, 1887*.

DEAR ARCHER,—Many thanks for the Wondrous Tale. It is scarcely a work of genius, as I believe you felt. Thanks also for your pencillings; though I defend "shrew," or at least many of the shrews.

We are here (I suppose) for the winter in the Adirondacks, a hill and forest country on the Canadian border of New York State, very unsettled and primitive and cold, and healthful, or we are the more bitterly deceived. I believe it will do well for me; but must not boast.

My wife is away to Indiana to see her family; my mother, Lloyd, and I remain here in the cold, which has been exceeding sharp, and the hill air, which is inimitably fine. We all eat bravely, and sleep well, and make great fires, and get along like one o'clock.

I am now a salaried party; I am a *bourgeois* now; I am to write a weekly paper for *Scribner's*, at a scale of payment which makes my teeth ache for shame and diffidence. The editor is, I believe, to apply to you; for we were talking over likely men, and when I instanced you, he said he had had his eye upon you from the first. It is worth while, perhaps, to get in tow with the Scribners; they are such thorough gentlefolk

1887 ÆT. 37 in all ways that it is always a pleasure to deal with them. I am like to be a millionaire if this goes on, and be publicly hanged at the social revolution: well, I would prefer that to dying in my bed; and it would be a godsend to my biographer, if ever I have one. What are you about? I hope you are all well and in good case and spirits, as I am now, after a most nefast experience of despondency before I left; but indeed I was quite run down. Remember me to Mrs. Archer, and give my respects to Tom.—Yours very truly,

ROBERT LOUIS STEVENSON.

TO HENRY JAMES

The "dear Alexander" mentioned below is Mr. J. W. Alexander, the well-known American artist, who had been a welcome visitor to Stevenson at Bournemouth, and had drawn his portrait there. The humorous romance proceeding from Mr. Osbourne's typewriter was the first draft of *The Wrong Box;* or, as it was originally called, *The Finsbury Tontine*, or *A Game of Bluff.* The article by Mr. Henry James referred to in the last paragraph is one on R. L. S. which had appeared in the *Century Magazine* for October, and was reprinted in *Partial Portraits.*

[SARANAC LAKE, *October, 1887.*] I know not the day;
but the month it
is the drear Octo-
ber by the ghoul-
haunted woodland
of Weir.

MY DEAR HENRY JAMES,—This is to say, *First,* the voyage was a huge success. We all enjoyed it (bar my wife) to the ground: sixteen days at sea with a cargo of hay, matches, stallions, and monkeys, and in a ship with no style on, and plenty of sailors to talk to, and the endless pleasures of the sea — the romance of it, the sport of the scratch dinner and the smashing crockery, the pleasure — an endless pleasure — of balancing to the swell: well, it 's over. 1887 ÆT. 37

Second, I had a fine time, rather a troubled one, at Newport and New York; saw much of and liked hugely the Fairchilds, St. Gaudens the sculptor, Gilder of the *Century* — just saw the dear Alexander — saw a lot of my old and admirable friend Will Low, whom I wish you knew and appreciated — was medallioned by St. Gaudens, and at last escaped to

Third, Saranac Lake, where we now are, and which I believe we mean to like and pass the winter at. Our house — emphatically "Baker's" — is on a hill, and has a sight of a stream turning a corner in the valley — bless the face of running water! — and sees some hills too, and the paganly prosaic roofs of Saranac itself; the Lake it does not see, nor do I regret that; I like water (fresh water I mean) either running swiftly among stones, or else largely qualified with whisky. As I write, the sun (which has been long a stranger) shines in at my shoulder; from the next room, the bell of Lloyd's typewriter makes an agreeable music as it patters off (at a rate which astonishes this experienced novelist) the early chapters of a humorous romance; from still further off — the walls of Baker's are neither ancient nor massive — rumours of Valentine about the kitchen stove come to my ears; of my mother and Fanny I hear nothing, for the excellent reason that they have gone sparking off, one to Niagara, one to Indian-

1887 ÆT. 37 apolis. People complain that I never give news in my letters. I have wiped out that reproach.

But now, *Fourth*, I have seen the article; and it may be from natural partiality, I think it the best you have written. O—I remember the Gautier, which was an excellent performance; and the Balzac, which was good; and the Daudet, over which I licked my chops; but the R. L. S. is better yet. It is so humorous, and it hits my little frailties with so neat (and so friendly) a touch; and Alan is the occasion for so much happy talk, and the quarrel is so generously praised. I read it twice, though it was only some hours in my possession; and Low, who got it for me from the *Century*, sat up to finish it ere he returned it; and, sir, we were all delighted. Here is the paper out, nor will anything, not even friendship, not even gratitude for the article, induce me to begin a second sheet; so here with the kindest remembrances and the warmest good wishes, I remain, yours affectionately, R. L. S.

To Charles Baxter

[Saranac Lake], *18th November, 1887.*

MY DEAR CHARLES,—No likely I 'm going to waste a sheet of paper. . . . I am offered £1600 ($8000) for the American serial rights on my next story! As you say, times are changed since the Lothian Road. Well, the Lothian Road was grand fun too; I could take an afternoon of it with great delight. But I 'm awfu' grand noo, and long may it last!

Remember me to any of the faithful—if there are

any left. I wish I could have a crack with you.— 1887 ÆT. 37
—Yours ever affectionately, R. L. S.

I find I have forgotten more than I remembered of business. . . . Please let us know (if you know) for how much Skerryvore is let; you will here detect the female mind; I let it for what I could get; nor shall the possession of this knowledge (which I am happy to have forgot) increase the amount by so much as the shadow of a sixpenny piece; but my females are agog.
—Yours ever, R. L. S.

To Charles Scribner

Shortly after the date of the present correspondence Stevenson, to his great advantage, put all his publishing arrangements (as he had already put his private business) into the hands of his friend, Mr. Baxter. Meantime he was managing them himself; and an occasional lapse of memory or attention betrayed him once or twice into misunderstandings, and once at least into conflicting agreements with two different publishers, both his friends. He was the first to denounce the error when he became aware of it, and suffered sharply from the sense of his own unintentional fault. The next two letters, and some allusions in those which follow, relate to this affair.

[Saranac Lake, *November 20 or 21, 1887.*]

My dear Mr. Scribner,— Heaven help me, I am under a curse just now. I have played fast and loose with what I said to you; and that, I beg you to believe, in the purest innocence of mind. I told you you should have the power over all my work in this country; and about a fortnight ago, when M'Clure was here, I calmly signed a bargain for the serial publication of a story. You will scarce believe that I did this in mere oblivion; but I

1887 ÆT. 37 did; and all that I can say is that I will do so no more, and ask you to forgive me. Please write to me soon as to this.

Will you oblige me by paying in for three articles, as already sent, to my account with John Paton & Co., 52 William Street. This will be most convenient for us.

The fourth article is nearly done; and I am the more deceived, or it is *A Buster*.

Now as to the first thing in this letter, I do wish to hear from you soon; and I am prepared to hear any reproach, or (what is harder to hear) any forgiveness; for I have deserved the worst.—Yours sincerely,

ROBERT LOUIS STEVENSON.

TO E. L. BURLINGAME

[SARANAC LAKE, *November, 1887*.]

DEAR MR. BURLINGAME,—I enclose corrected proof of *Beggars*, which seems good. I mean to make a second sermon, which, if it is about the same length as *Pulvis et Umbra*, might go in along with it as two sermons, in which case I should call the first "The Whole Creation," and the second "Any Good." We shall see; but you might say how you like the notion.

One word: if you have heard from Mr. Scribner of my unhappy oversight in the matter of a story, you will make me ashamed to write to you, and yet I wish to beg you to help me into quieter waters. The oversight committed—and I do think it was not so bad as Mr. Scribner seems to think it—and discovered, I was in a miserable position. I need not tell you that my first impulse was to offer to share or to surrender the price agreed upon when it should fall due; and it is almost to my credit that I arranged to refrain. It is one of these positions from which there is no escape; I cannot undo what I have done. And I wish to beg you—should Mr. Scribner speak to you in the matter—to try to get him to see this neglect of mine for no worse than it is: unpardonable enough, because a breach of an agreement; but still pardonable, because a piece of sheer carelessness and want of memory, done, God knows, without design and since most sincerely regretted. I have no memory. You have seen how I omitted to reserve the American rights in *Jekyll:* last winter I wrote and demanded, as an increase, a less sum than had already been agreed upon for a story that I gave to *Cassell's.* For once that my forgetfulness has, by a cursed fortune, seemed to gain, instead of lose, me money, it is painful indeed that I should produce so poor an impression on the mind of Mr. Scribner. But I beg you to believe, and if possible to make him believe, that I am in no degree or sense a *faiseur*, and that in matters of business my design, at least, is honest. Nor (bating bad memory and self-deception) am I untruthful in such affairs.

If Mr. Scribner shall have said nothing to you in the matter, please regard the above as unwritten, and believe me, yours very truly,

ROBERT LOUIS STEVENSON.

To E. L. BURLINGAME

[SARANAC LAKE, *November, 1887.*]

DEAR MR. BURLINGAME,—The revise seemed all right, so I did not trouble you with it; indeed, my demand

1887 ÆT. 37 for one was theatrical, to impress that obdurate dog, your reader. Herewith a third paper: it has been a cruel long time upon the road, but here it is, and not bad at last, I fondly hope. I was glad you liked *The Lantern Bearers;* I did, too. I thought it was a good paper, really contained some excellent sense, and was ingeniously put together. I have not often had more trouble than I have with these papers; thirty or forty pages of foul copy, twenty is the very least I have had. Well, you pay high; it is fit that I should have to work hard, it somewhat quiets my conscience.—Yours very truly, ROBERT LOUIS STEVENSON.

To J. A. Symonds

SARANAC LAKE, ADIRONDACK MOUNTAINS,
NEW YORK, U. S. A., *November 21, 1887.*

MY DEAR SYMONDS,—I think we have both meant and wanted to write to you any time these months; but we have been much tossed about, among new faces and old, and new scenes and old, and scenes (like this of Saranac) which are neither one nor other. To give you some clue to our affairs, I had best begin pretty well back. We sailed from the Thames in a vast bucket of iron that took seventeen days from shore to shore. I cannot describe how I enjoyed the voyage, nor what good it did me; but on the Banks I caught friend catarrh. In New York and then in Newport I was pretty ill; but on my return to New York, lying in bed most of the time, with St. Gaudens the sculptor sculping me, and my old friend Low around, I began to pick up once more. Now here we are in a kind of wilderness of hills and firwoods and boulders and snow and wooden houses. So far as we have gone the climate is grey and harsh, but hungry and somnolent; and although not charming like that of Davos, essentially bracing and briskening. The country is a kind of insane mixture of Scotland and a touch of Switzerland and a dash of America, and a thought of the British Channel in the skies. We have a decent house— 1887 ÆT. 37

December 6th.

—A decent house, as I was saying, sir, on a hill-top, with a look down a Scottish river in front, and on one hand a Perthshire hill; on the other, the beginnings and skirts of the village play hide-and-seek among other hills. We have been below zero, I know not how far (·10 at 8 A. M. once), and when it is cold it is delightful; but hitherto the cold has not held, and we have chopped in and out from frost to thaw, from snow to rain, from quiet air to the most disastrous north-westerly curdlers of the blood. After a week of practical thaw, the ice still bears in favoured places. So there is hope.

I wonder if you saw my book of verses? It went into a second edition, because of my name, I suppose, and its *prose* merits. I do not set up to be a poet. Only an all-round literary man: a man who talks, not one who sings. But I believe the very fact that it was only speech served the book with the public. Horace is much a speaker, and see how popular! most of Martial is only speech, and I cannot conceive a person who does not love his Martial; most of Burns, also, such as *The Louse, The Toothache, The Haggis,* and lots more

1887 ÆT. 37 of his best. Excuse this little apology for my house; but I don't like to come before people who have a note of song, and let it be supposed I do not know the difference.

To return to the more important — news. My wife again suffers in high and cold places; I again profit. She is off to-day to New York for a change, as heretofore to Berne, but I am glad to say in better case than then. Still it is undeniable she suffers, and you must excuse her (at least) if we both prove bad correspondents. I am decidedly better, but I have been terribly cut up with business complications: one disagreeable, as threatening loss; one, of the most intolerable complexion, as involving me in dishonour. The burthen of consistent carelessness: I have lost much by it in the past; and for once (to my damnation) I have gained. I am sure you will sympathise. It is hard work to sleep; it is hard to be told you are a liar, and have to hold your peace, and think, "Yes, by God, and a thief too!" You remember my lectures on Ajax, or the Unintentional Sin? Well, I know all about that now. Nothing seems so unjust to the sufferer: or is more just in essence. *Laissez passer la justice de Dieu.*

Lloyd has learned to use the typewriter, and has most gallantly completed upon that the draft of a tale, which seems to me not without merit and promise, it is so silly, so gay, so absurd, in spots (to my partial eyes) so genuinely humorous. It is true, he would not have written it but for *The New Arabian Nights;* but it is strange to find a young writer funny. Heavens, but I was depressing when I took the pen in hand! And now I doubt if I am sadder than my neighbours. Will this beginner move in the inverse direction? 1887 ÆT. 37

Let me have your news, and believe me, my dear Symonds, with genuine affection, yours,

ROBERT LOUIS STEVENSON.

To W. E. Henley

The following refers to a volume on the elder Dumas, which Mr. Henley was at this time preparing to write, and which he proposed to dedicate to his friend.

SARANAC LAKE [*December, 1887*].

MY DEAR LAD,—I was indeed overjoyed to hear of the Dumas. In the matter of the dedication, are not cross-dedications a little awkward? Lang and Rider Haggard did it, to be sure. Perpend. And if you should conclude against a dedication, there is a passage in *Memories and Portraits* written *at* you, when I was most desperate (to stir you up a bit), which might be quoted: something about Dumas still waiting his biographer. I have a decent time when the weather is fine; when it is grey, or windy, or wet (as it too often is), I am merely degraded to the dirt. I get some work done every day with a devil of a heave; not extra good ever; and I regret my engagement. Whiles I have had the most deplorable business annoyances too; have been threatened with having to refund money; got over that; and found myself in the worse scrape of being a kind of unintentional swindler. These have worried me a great deal; also old age with his stealing steps seems to have clawed me in his clutch to some tune.

Do you play All Fours? We are trying it; it is still

1887 all haze to me. Can the elder hand *beg* more than once?
ÆT. 37 The Port Admiral is at Boston mingling with millionaires. I am but a weed on Lethe wharf. The wife is only so-so. The Lord lead us all: if I can only get off the stage with clean hands, I shall sing Hosanna. "Put" is described quite differently from your version in a book I have; what are your rules? The Port Admiral is using a game of put in a tale of his, the first copy of which was gloriously finished about a fortnight ago, and the revise gallantly begun: *The Finsbury Tontine* it is named, and might fill two volumes, and is quite incredibly silly, and in parts (it seems to me) pretty humorous.—Love to all from

AN OLD, OLD MAN.

I say, Taine's *Origines de la France Contemporaine* is no end; it would turn the dead body of Charles Fox into a living Tory.

TO MRS. FLEEMING JENKIN

[SARANAC LAKE, *December, 1887.*]

MY DEAR MRS. JENKIN,—The Opal is very well; it is fed with glycerine when it seems hungry. I am very well, and get about much more than I could have hoped. My wife is not very well; there is no doubt the high level does not agree with her, and she is on the move for a holiday to New York. Lloyd is at Boston on a visit, and I hope has a good time. My mother is really first-rate; she and I, despairing of other games for two, now play All Fours out of a gamebook, and have not yet discovered its niceties, if any.

You will have heard, I dare say, that they made a great row over me here. They also offered me much money, a great deal more than my works are worth: I took some of it, and was greedy and hasty, and am now very sorry. I have done with big prices from now out. Wealth and self-respect seem, in my case, to be strangers. 1887 ÆT. 37

We were talking the other day of how well Fleeming managed to grow rich. Ah, that is a rare art; something more intellectual than a virtue. The book has not yet made its appearance here; the life alone, with a little preface, is to appear in the States; and the Scribners are to send you half the royalties. I should like it to do well, for Fleeming's sake.

Will you please send me the Greek water-carrier's song? I have a particular use for it.

Have I any more news, I wonder?—and echo wonders along with me. I am strangely disquieted on all political matters; and I do not know if it is "the signs of the times" or the sign of my own time of life. But to me the sky seems black both in France and England, and only partly clear in America. I have not seen it so dark in my time; of that I am sure.

Please let us have some news; and excuse me, for the sake of my well-known idleness; and pardon Fanny, who is really not very well, for this long silence.—Very sincerely your friend,

ROBERT LOUIS STEVENSON.

TO MISS ADELAIDE BOODLE

The lady at Bournemouth (the giver of the paper-knife) to whom the following letter is addressed had been trusted to keep an eye on

1887 Stevenson's interests in connection with his house (which had been let)
ÆT. 37 and other matters, and to report thereon from time to time. In their correspondence Stevenson is generally referred to as the Squire, and the lady as the Gamekeeper.

[SARANAC LAKE, *December, 1887.*]

MY DEAR MISS BOODLE,—I am so much afraid, our gamekeeper may weary of unacknowledged reports! Hence, in the midst of a perfect horror of detestable weathers of a quite incongruous strain, and with less desire for correspondence than —well, than —well, with no desire for correspondence, behold me dash into the breach. Do keep up your letters. They are most delightful to this exiled backwoods family; and in your next, we shall hope somehow or other to hear better news of you and yours — that in the first place — and to hear more news of our beasts and birds and kindly fruits of earth and those human tenants who are (truly) too much with us.

I am very well; better than for years: that is for good. But then my wife is no great shakes; the place does not suit her — it is my private opinion that no place does — and she is now away down to New York for a change, which (as Lloyd is in Boston) leaves my mother and me and Valentine alone in our wind-beleaguered hilltop hatbox of a house. You should hear the cows butt against the walls in the early morning while they feed; you should also see our back log when the thermometer goes (as it does go) away — away below zero, till it can be seen no more by the eye of man — not the thermometer, which is still perfectly visible, but the mercury, which curls up into the bulb like a hibernating bear; you should also see the lad who "does chores" for us, with his red stockings and his thirteen-year-old face, and his highly manly tramp into the room; and his two alternative answers to all questions about the weather: either "Cold," or with a really lyrical movement of the voice, "*Lovely*—raining!"

Will you take this miserable scrap for what it is worth? Will you also understand that I am the man to blame, and my wife is really almost too much out of health to write, or at least does n't write?—And believe me, with kind remembrances to Mrs. Boodle and your sisters, very sincerely yours,

ROBERT LOUIS STEVENSON.

TO CHARLES BAXTER

[SARANAC LAKE], *12th December, '87.*

Give us news of all your folk. A Merry Christmas from all of us.

MY DEAR CHARLES,—Will you please send £20 to —— for a Christmas gift from ——? Moreover, I cannot remember what I told you to send to ——; but as God has dealt so providentially with me this year, I now propose to make it £20.

I beg of you also to consider my strange position. I jined a club which it was said was to defend the Union; and I had a letter from the secretary, which his name I believe was Lord Warmingpan (or words to that effect), to say I am elected, and had better pay up a certain sum of money, I forget what. Now I cannae verra weel draw a blank cheque and send to—

LORD WARMINGPAN (or words to that effect),
London, England.

1887 ÆT. 37 And, man, if it was possible, I would be dooms glad to be out o' this bit scrapie. Mebbe the club was ca'd "The Union," but I wouldnae like to sweir; and mebbe it wasnae, or mebbe only words to that effec'—but I wouldnae care just exac'ly about sweirin'. Do ye no think Henley, or Pollick, or some o' they London fellies, micht mebbe perhaps find out for me? and just what the soom was? And that you would aiblins pay for me? For I thocht I was sae dam patriotic jinin', and it would be a kind o' a come-doun to be turned out again. Mebbe Lang would ken; or mebbe Rider Haggyard: they 're kind o' Union folks. But it 's my belief his name was Warmingpan whatever.—Yours,

THOMSON,

alias ROBERT LOUIS STEVENSON.

Could it be Warminster?[1]

To Miss Monroe

The play of *Deacon Brodie* was at this time being performed at Chicago, with Mr. E. J. Henley in the title-part.

SARANAC LAKE, NEW YORK [*December 19, 1887*].

DEAR MISS MONROE,—Many thanks for your letter and your good wishes. It was much my desire to get to Chicago: had I done—or if I yet do—so, I shall hope to see the original of my photograph, which is one of my show possessions; but the fates are rather contrary. My wife is far from well; I myself dread worse than almost any other imaginable peril, that miraculous and

[1] The secretary was really, I believe, Lord Pollington.

My dear Henry James

It may please you to know how our family has been employed. In the silence of the snow, the afternoon lamp has lighted an eager fireside group: my mother reading, Fanny, Lloyd and I devoted listeners; and the work was really one of the best works I ever heard; and its author is to be praised and honoured; and what do you suppose is the name of it? and have you ever read it yourself? and (I am bound I will get to the bottom of the page before I blow the gaff, if I have to fill it out on this line all summer; for if you have not to turn a leaf, there can be no suspense, the conspectory eye being swift to pick out proper names; and without suspense, there can be little pleasure in this world, to my mind at least) and in short the name of it is

Roderick Hudson. if you please. My dear James, it is very spirited, and very sound, and very noble too. Hudson, Mrs Hudson, Rowland. O, all first rate. Rowland a very fine fellow. Hudson as good as he can stick (did you know Hudson? I suspect you did) Mrs H his real born mother, a thing rarely managed in fiction.

We are all keeping pretty fit and pretty hearty: but this letter is not from me to you, it is from a reader of R. H to the author of the same, and it says nothing, and has nothing to say, but Thank you.

We are going to re-read Casamassima as a proper pendant. Sir, I think these two are your best; and care not who knows it.

May I beg you, the next time Roderick is printed off, to go over the.

skirts of the last few chapters, and strike out "immense" and "tremendous"? You have simply dropped them there like your pocket-handkerchief; all you have to do is to pick them up and pouch them, and your room — what do I say? — your cathedral! — will be swept and garnished.

I am, dear Sir,

Your delighted reader

Robert Louis Stevenson

P.S. Perhaps it is a pang of causeless honesty, perhaps I hope it will set a value on my praise of Roderick, perhaps it's a burst of the diabolic, but I must break out with the news that I can't bear the Portrait of a Lady. I read it all, and I wept too; but I can't stand your having written it; and I beg you will write no more of the like. Infra, sir; Below you: I can't help it – it may be your favourite work, but in my eyes it's BELOW YOU to write and me to read. I thought Roderick was going to be another such at the beginning; and I cannot describe my pleasure as I found it taking bones and blood, and looking out at me with a moved and human countenance, whose lineaments are written in my memory until my last of days.

R. L. S.

My wife begs your forgiveness. I believe for her silence.

really insane invention the American Railroad Car. Heaven help the man — may I add the woman — that sets foot in one! Ah, if it were only an ocean to cross, it would be a matter of small thought to me — and great pleasure. But the railroad car — every man has his weak point; and I fear the railroad car as abjectly as I do an earwig, and, on the whole, on better grounds. You do not know how bitter it is to have to make such a confession; for you have not the pretension nor the weakness of a man. If I do get to Chicago, you will hear of me: so much can be said. And do you never come east?

I was pleased to recognise a word of my poor old Deacon in your letter. It would interest me very much to hear how it went and what you thought of piece and actors; and my collaborator, who knows and respects the photograph, would be pleased too.—Still in the hope of seeing you, I am, yours very truly,

ROBERT LOUIS STEVENSON.

TO HENRY JAMES

SARANAC LAKE [*Winter, 1887–8*].

MY DEAR HENRY JAMES,— It may please you to know how our family has been employed. In the silence of the snow the afternoon lamp has lighted an eager fireside group: my mother reading, Fanny, Lloyd, and I devoted listeners; and the work was really one of the best works I ever heard; and its author is to be praised and honoured; and what do you suppose is the name of it? and have you ever read it yourself? and (I am

1887 Æt. 37 bound I will get to the bottom of the page before I blow the gaff, if I have to fight it out on this line all summer; for if you have not to turn a leaf, there can be no suspense, the conspectory eye being swift to pick out proper names; and without suspense, there can be little pleasure in this world, to my mind at least)—and, in short, the name of it is *Roderick Hudson*, if you please. My dear James, it is very spirited, and very sound, and very noble too. Hudson, Mrs. Hudson, Rowland, O, all first-rate: Rowland a very fine fellow; Hudson as good as he can stick (did you know Hudson? I suspect you did), Mrs. H. his real born mother, a thing rarely managed in fiction.

We are all keeping pretty fit and pretty hearty; but this letter is not from me to you, it is from a reader of *R. H.* to the author of the same, and it says nothing, and has nothing to say, but thank you.

We are going to re-read *Casamassima* as a proper pendant. Sir, I think these two are your best, and care not who knows it.

May I beg you, the next time *Roderick* is printed off, to go over the sheets of the last few chapters, and strike out "immense" and "tremendous"? You have simply dropped them there like your pocket-handkerchief; all you have to do is to pick them up and pouch them, and your room—what do I say?—your cathedral!—will be swept and garnished.—I am, dear sir, your delighted reader, ROBERT LOUIS STEVENSON.

P. S.—Perhaps it is a pang of causeless honesty, perhaps I hope it will set a value on my praise of *Roderick*, perhaps it 's a burst of the diabolic, but I must break out with the news that I can't bear the *Portrait of a Lady*. I read it all, and I wept too; but I can't stand your having written it; and I beg you will write no more of the like. *Infra*, sir; Below you: I can't help it—it may be your favourite work, but in my eyes it's BELOW YOU to write and me to read. I thought *Roderick* was going to be another such at the beginning; and I cannot describe my pleasure as I found it taking bones and blood, and looking out at me with a moved and human countenance, whose lineaments are written in my memory until my last of days. R. L. S.

1887 ÆT. 37

My wife begs your forgiveness; I believe for her silence.

TO SIDNEY COLVIN

SARANAC LAKE [*December, 1887*].

MY DEAR COLVIN,—This goes to say that we are all fit, and the place is very bleak and wintry, and up to now has shown no such charms of climate as Davos, but is a place where men eat and where the cattarh, catarrh (cattarrh, or cattarrhh) appears to be unknown. I walk in my verandy in the snaw, sir, looking down over one of those dabbled wintry landscapes that are (to be frank) so chilly to the human bosom, and up at a grey, English—nay, *mehercle*, Scottish—heaven; and I think it pretty bleak; and the wind swoops at me round the corner, like a lion, and fluffs the snow in my face; and I could aspire to be elsewhere; but yet I do not catch cold, and yet, when I come in, I eat. So that hitherto Saranac, if not deliriously delectable, has not

1887 ÆT. 37 been a failure; nay, from the mere point of view of the wicked body, it has proved a success. But I wish I could still get to the woods; alas, *nous n' irons plus au bois* is my poor song; the paths are buried, the dingles drifted full, a little walk is grown a long one; till spring comes, I fear the burthen will hold good.

I get along with my papers for *Scribner* not fast, nor so far specially well; only this last, the fourth one (which makes a third part of my whole task), I do believe is pulled off after a fashion. It is a mere sermon: "Smith opens out";[1] but it is true, and I find it touching and beneficial, to me at least; and I think there is some fine writing in it, some very apt and pregnant phrases. *Pulvis et Umbra*, I call it; I might have called it a Darwinian Sermon, if I had wanted. Its sentiments, although parsonic, will not offend even you, I believe. The other three papers, I fear, bear many traces of effort, and the ungenuine inspiration of an income at so much per essay, and the honest desire of the incomer to give good measure for his money. Well, I did my damndest anyway.

We have been reading H. James's *Roderick Hudson*, which I eagerly press you to get at once: it is a book of a high order—the last volume in particular. I wish Meredith would read it. It took my breath away.

[1] "Smith opens out his cauld harangues
On practice and on morals."

The Rev. George Smith of Galston, the minister thus referred to by Burns (in *The Holy Fair*), was a great-grandfather of Stevenson on the mother's side; and against Stevenson himself, in his didactic moods, the passage was often quoted by his friends when they wished to tease him.

I am at the seventh book of the *Æneid*, and quite amazed at its merits (also very often floored by its difficulties). The Circe passage at the beginning, and the sublime business of Amata with the simile of the boy's top—O Lord, what a happy thought!—have specially delighted me.—I am, dear sir, your respected friend, JOHN GREGG GILLSON, J.P., M.R.I.A., etc. 1887 ÆT. 37

TO SIDNEY COLVIN

The following narrates the beginning of the author's labours on *The Master of Ballantrae*. An unfinished paper written some years later in Samoa, and intended for *Scribner's Magazine*, tells how the story first took shape in his mind. See Thistle edition, *Sketches, Criticisms, etc.*, vol. xxii. p. 431.

[SARANAC LAKE, *December 24, 1887*.]

MY DEAR COLVIN,—Thank you for your explanations. I have done no more Virgil since I finished the seventh book, for I have first been eaten up with Taine, and next have fallen head over heels into a new tale, *The Master of Ballantrae*. No thought have I now apart from it, and I have got along up to page ninety-two of the draft with great interest. It is to me a most seizing tale: there are some fantastic elements; the most is a dead genuine human problem—human tragedy, I should say rather. It will be about as long, I imagine, as *Kidnapped*.

DRAMATIS PERSONÆ:

(1) My old Lord Durrisdeer.
(2) The Master of Ballantrae, *and*
(3) Henry Durie, *his sons*.

1887
ÆT. 37

(4) Clementina, *engaged to the first, married to the second.*

(5) Ephraim Mackellar, *land steward at Durrisdeer and narrator of the most of the book.*

(6) Francis Burke, Chevalier de St. Louis, *one of Prince Charlie's Irishmen and narrator of the rest.*

Besides these, many instant figures, most of them dumb or nearly so: Jessie Brown the whore, Captain Crail, Captain MacCombie, our old friend Alan Breck, our old friend Riach (both only for an instant), Teach the pirate (vulgarly Blackbeard), John Paul and Macconochie, servants at Durrisdeer. The date is from 1745 to '65 (about). The scene, near Kirkcudbright, in the States, and for a little moment in the French East Indies. I have done most of the big work, the quarrel, duel between the brothers, and announcement of the death to Clementina and my Lord — Clementina, Henry, and Mackellar (nicknamed Squaretoes) are really very fine fellows; the Master is all I know of the devil. I have known hints of him, in the world, but always cowards; he is as bold as a lion, but with the same deadly, causeless duplicity I have watched with so much surprise in my two cowards. 'T is true, I saw a hint of the same nature in another man who was not a coward; but he had other things to attend to; the Master has nothing else but his devilry. Here come my visitors — and have now gone, or the first relay of them; and I hope no more may come. For mark you, sir, this is our 'day' — Saturday, as ever was; and here we sit, my mother and I, before a large wood fire and await the enemy with the most steadfast courage; and without snow and greyness: and the woman Fanny in New York for her health, which is far from good; and the lad Lloyd at the inn in the village because he has a cold; and the handmaid Valentine abroad in a sleigh upon her messages; and to-morrow Christmas and no mistake. Such is human life: *la carrière humaine.* I will enclose, if I remember, the required autograph. 1887 ÆT. 37

I will do better, put it on the back of this page. Love to all, and mostly, my very dear Colvin, to yourself. For whatever I say or do, or don't say or do, you may be very sure I am,—Yours always affectionately,

R. L. S.

To Miss Adelaide Boodle

Saranac Lake, Adirondacks,
N. Y., U. S. A., *Christmas, 1887.*

MY DEAR MISS BOODLE,—And a very good Christmas to you all; and better fortune; and if worse, the more courage to support it—which I think is the kinder wish in all human affairs. Somewhile—I fear a good while—after this, you should receive our Christmas gift; we have no tact and no taste, only a welcome and (often) tonic brutality; and I dare say the present, even after my friend Baxter has acted on and reviewed my hints, may prove a White Elephant. That is why I dread presents. And therefore pray understand if any element of that hamper prove unwelcome, *it is to be exchanged.* I will not sit down under the name of a giver of White Elephants. I never had any elephant

1887 ÆT. 37 but one, and his initials were R. L. S.; and he trod on my foot at a very early age. But this is a fable, and not in the least to the point: which is that if, for once in my life, I have wished to make things nicer for anybody but the Elephant (see fable), do not suffer me to have made them ineffably more embarrassing, and exchange—ruthlessly exchange!

For my part, I am the most cockered up of any mortal being; and one of the healthiest, or thereabout, at some modest distance from the bull's eye. I am condemned to write twelve articles in *Scribner's Magazine* for the love of gain; I think I had better send you them; what is far more to the purpose, I am on the jump with a new story which has bewitched me—I doubt it may bewitch no one else. It is called *The Master of Ballantrae*—pronounce Băllăn-tray. If it is not good, well, mine will be the fault; for I believe it is a good tale.

The greetings of the season to you, and your mother, and your sisters. My wife heartily joins.—And I am, yours very sincerely, ROBERT LOUIS STEVENSON.

P.S.—You will think me an illiterate dog: I am, for the first time, reading *Robertson's Sermons*. I do not know how to express how much I think of them. If by any chance you should be as illiterate as I, and not know them, it is worth while curing the defect.

R. L. S.

TO CHARLES BAXTER

The following letter invites Mr. Baxter to allow himself (under an *alias*) and his office in Edinburgh to figure in a preface to the new story. Such a preface was drafted accordingly, but on second thoughts suppressed; to be, on renewed consideration, reinstated in the final editions. 1888 ÆT. 38

[SARANAC LAKE, *January, '88.*]

DEAR CHARLES,— You are the flower of Doers. . . . Will my doer collaborate thus much in my new novel? In the year 1794 or 5, Mr. Ephraim Mackellar, A.M., late steward on the Durrisdeer estates, completed a set of memoranda (as long as a novel) with regard to the death of the (then) late Lord Durrisdeer, and as to that of his attainted elder brother, called by the family courtesy title the Master of Ballantrae. These he placed in the hands of John Macbrair, W.S., the family agent, on the understanding they were to be sealed until 1862, when a century would have elapsed since the affair in the wilderness (my lord's death). You succeeded Mr. Macbrair's firm; the Durrisdeers are extinct; and last year, in an old green box, you found these papers with Macbrair's indorsation. It is that indorsation of which I want a copy; you may remember, when you gave me the papers, I neglected to take that, and I am sure you are a man too careful of antiquities to have let it fall aside. I shall have a little introduction descriptive of my visit to Edinburgh, arrival there, denner with yoursel', and first reading of the papers in your smoking-room: all of which, of course, you well remember.—Ever yours affectionately, R. L. S.

Your name is my friend Mr. Johnstone Thomson, W.S.!!!

1888
ÆT. 38

To E. L. Burlingame

[Saranac Lake, *Winter, 1887–8.*]

Dear Mr. Burlingame,—I am keeping the sermon to see if I can't add another. Meanwhile, I will send you very soon a different paper which may take its place. Possibly some of these days soon I may get together a talk on things current, which should go in (if possible) earlier than either. I am now less nervous about these papers; I believe I can do the trick without great strain, though the terror that breathed on my back in the beginning is not yet forgotten.

The Master of Ballantrae I have had to leave aside, as I was quite worked out. But in about a week I hope to try back and send you the first four numbers: these are all drafted, it is only the revision that has broken me down, as it is often the hardest work. These four I propose you should set up for me at once, and we 'll copyright 'em in a pamphlet. I will tell you the names of the *bona fide* purchasers in England.

The numbers will run from twenty to thirty pages of my manuscript. You can give me that much, can you not? It is a howling good tale—at least these first four numbers are; the end is a trifle more fantastic, but 't is all picturesque.

Don't trouble about any more French books; I am on another scent, you see, just now. Only the *French in Hindustan* I await with impatience, as that is for *Ballantrae.* The scene of that romance is Scotland—the States—Scotland—India—Scotland—and the States again; so it jumps like a flea. I have enough about the States now, and very much obliged I am; yet if Drake's *Tragedies of the Wilderness* is (as I gather) a collection of originals, I should like to purchase it. If it is a picturesque vulgarisation, I do not wish to look it in the face. Purchase, I say; for I think it would be well to have some such collection by me with a view to fresh works.—Yours very sincerely, 1888 ÆT. 38

ROBERT LOUIS STEVENSON.

P.S.—If you think of having *The Master* illustrated, I suggest that Hole would be very well up to the Scottish, which is the larger, part. If you have it done here, tell your artist to look at the hall of Craigievar in Billing's *Baronial and Ecclesiastical Antiquities*, and he will get a broad hint for the hall at Durrisdeer: it is, I think, the chimney of Craigievar and the roof of Pinkie, and perhaps a little more of Pinkie altogether; but I should have to see the book myself to be sure. Hole would be invaluable for this. I dare say if you had it illustrated, you could let me have one or two for the English edition. R. L. S.

TO WILLIAM ARCHER

The following refers to Mr. Bernard Shaw's novel *Cashel Byron's Profession*, which had been sent Stevenson to read by their common friend Mr. Archer.

[SARANAC LAKE, *Winter, 1887-88.*]

MY DEAR ARCHER,—What am I to say? I have read your friend's book with singular relish. If he has

1888 ÆT. 38 written any other, I beg you will let me see it; and if he has not, I beg him to lose no time in supplying the deficiency. It is full of promise; but I should like to know his age. There are things in it that are very clever, to which I attach small importance; it is the shape of the age. And there are passages, particularly the rally in presence of the Zulu king, that show genuine and remarkable narrative talent — a talent that few will have the wit to understand, a talent of strength, spirit, capacity, sufficient vision, and sufficient self-sacrifice, which last is the chief point in a narrator.

As a whole, it is (of course) a fever dream of the most feverish. Over Bashville the footman I howled with derision and delight; I dote on Bashville — I could read of him for ever; *de Bashville je suis le fervent* — there is only one Bashville, and I am his devoted slave; *Bashville est magnifique, mais il n'est guère possible.* He is the note of the book. It is all mad, mad and deliriously delightful; the author has a taste in chivalry like Walter Scott's or Dumas', and then he daubs in little bits of socialism; he soars away on the wings of the romantic griffon — even the griffon, as he cleaves air, shouting with laughter at the nature of the quest — and I believe in his heart he thinks he is labouring in a quarry of solid granite realism.

It is this that makes me — the most hardened adviser now extant — stand back and hold my peace. If Mr. Shaw is below five-and-twenty, let him go his path; if he is thirty, he had best be told that he is a romantic, and pursue romance with his eyes open; — or perhaps he knows it; — God knows! — my brain is softened.

It is HORRID FUN. All I ask is more of it. Thank you

for the pleasure you gave us, and tell me more of the inimitable author. 1888 ÆT. 38

(I say, Archer, my God, what women!)—Yours very truly, ROBERT LOUIS STEVENSON.

To WILLIAM ARCHER

[SARANAC LAKE, *February, 1888.*]

MY DEAR ARCHER,—Pretty sick in bed; but necessary to protest and continue your education.

Why was Jenkin an amateur in my eyes? You think because not amusing (I think he often was amusing). The reason is this: I never, or almost never, saw two pages of his work that I could not have put in one without the smallest loss of material. That is the only test I know of writing. If there is anywhere a thing said in two sentences that could have been as clearly and as engagingly and as forcibly said in one, then it 's amateur work. Then you will bring me up with old Dumas. Nay, the object of a story is to be long, to fill up hours; the story-teller's art of writing is to water out by continual invention, historical and technical, and yet not seem to water; seem on the other hand to practise that same wit of conspicuous and declaratory condensation which is the proper art of writing. That is one thing in which my stories fail: I am always cutting the flesh off their bones.

I would rise from the dead to preach!

Hope all well. I think my wife better, but she 's not allowed to write; and this (only wrung from me by

1888 desire to Boss and Parsonise and Dominate, strong in
ÆT. 38 sickness) is my first letter for days, and will likely be my last for many more. Not blame my wife for her silence: doctor's orders. All much interested by your last, and fragment from brother, and anecdotes of Tom-archer.—The sick but still Moral R. L. S.

Tell Shaw to hurry up: I want another.

To William Archer

In early days in Paris, Stevenson's chivalrous feelings were once shocked by the scene in the *Demi-Monde* of Dumas *fils* where Suzanne d'Auge is trapped by Olivier de Jalin. His correspondent had asked to know exactly what was the sequel.

[Saranac Lake, *Spring, 1888?*]

My dear Archer,—It happened thus. I came forth from that performance in a breathing heat of indignation. (Mind, at this distance of time and with my increased knowledge, I admit there is a problem in the piece; but I saw none then, except a problem in brutality; and I still consider the problem in that case not established.) On my way down the *Français* stairs, I trod on an old gentleman's toes, whereupon, with that suavity that so well becomes me, I turned about to apologise, and on the instant, repenting me of that intention, stopped the apology midway, and added something in French to this effect: No, you are one of the *lâches* who have been applauding that piece. I retract my apology. Said the old Frenchman, laying his hand on my arm, and with a smile that was truly heavenly in temperance, irony, good nature, and knowledge of the world, "Ah, monsieur, vous êtes bien jeune!"—Yours very truly, ROBERT LOUIS STEVENSON.

TO E. L. BURLINGAME

[SARANAC, *February, 1888*].

DEAR MR. BURLINGAME,—Will you send me (from the library) some of the works of my dear old G. P. R. James? With the following especially I desire to make or to renew acquaintance: *The Songster, The Gipsy, The Convict, The Stepmother, The Gentleman of the Old School, The Robber.*

Excusez du peu.

This sudden return to an ancient favourite hangs upon an accident. The "Franklin County Library" contains two works of his, *The Cavalier* and *Morley Ernstein.* I read the first with indescribable amusement—it was worse than I had feared, and yet somehow engaging; the second (to my surprise) was better than I had dared to hope: a good, honest, dull, interesting tale, with a genuine old-fashioned talent in the invention when not strained; and a genuine old-fashioned feeling for the English language. This experience awoke appetite, and you see I have taken steps to stay it. R. L. S.

TO E. L. BURLINGAME

[SARANAC LAKE, *February, 1888.*]

DEAR MR. BURLINGAME,—1. Of course then don't use it. Dear Man, I write these to please you, not myself,

1888 ÆT. 38 and you know a main sight better than I do what is good. In that case, however, I enclose another paper, and return the corrected proof of *Pulvis et Umbra*, so that we may be afloat.

2. I want to say a word as to *The Master*. (*The Master of Ballantrae* shall be the name by all means.) If you like and want it, I leave it to you to make an offer. You may remember I thought the offer you made when I was still in England too small; by which I did not at all mean, I thought it less than it was worth, but too little to tempt me to undergo the disagreeables of serial publication. This tale (if you want it) you are to have; for it is the least I can do for you; and you are to observe that the sum you pay me for my articles going far to meet my wants, I am quite open to be satisfied with less than formerly. I tell you I do dislike this battle of the dollars. I feel sure you all pay too much here in America; and I beg you not to spoil me any more. For I am getting spoiled: I do not want wealth, and I feel these big sums demoralise me.

My wife came here pretty ill; she had a dreadful bad night; to-day she is better. But now Valentine is ill; and Lloyd and I have got breakfast, and my hand somewhat shakes after washing dishes.—Yours very sincerely, ROBERT LOUIS STEVENSON.

P. S.—Please order me the *Evening Post* for two months. My subscription is run out. *The Mutiny* and *Edwardes* to hand.

To Sidney Colvin

[Saranac Lake, *March, 1888.*]

MY DEAR COLVIN,—Fanny has been very unwell. She is not long home, has been ill again since her return, but is now better again to a degree. You must not blame her for not writing, as she is not allowed to write at all, not even a letter. To add to our misfortunes, Valentine is quite ill and in bed. Lloyd and I get breakfast; I have now, 10.15, just got the dishes washed and the kitchen all clear, and sit down to give you as much news as I have spirit for, after such an engagement. Glass is a thing that really breaks my spirit: I do not like to fail, and with glass I cannot reach the work of my high calling—the artist's.

I am, as you may gather from this, wonderfully better: this harsh, grey, glum, doleful climate has done me good. You cannot fancy how sad a climate it is. When the thermometer stays all day below 10°, it is really cold; and when the wind blows, O commend me to the result. Pleasure in life is all delete; there is no red spot left, fires do not radiate, you burn your hands all the time on what seem to be cold stones. It is odd, zero is like summer heat to us now; and we like, when the thermometer outside is really low, a room at about 48°: 60° we find oppressive. Yet the natives keep their holes at 90° or even 100°.

This was interrupted days ago by household labours. Since then I have had and (I tremble to write it, but it does seem as if I had) beaten off an influenza. The cold is exquisite. Valentine still in bed. The proofs of the

1888 ÆT. 38 first part of *The Master of Ballantrae* begin to come in; soon you shall have it in the pamphlet form; and I hope you will like it. The second part will not be near so good; but there — we can but do as it 'll do with us. I have every reason to believe this winter has done me real good, so far as it has gone; and if I carry out my scheme for next winter, and succeeding years, I should end by being a tower of strength. I want you to save a good holiday for next winter; I hope we shall be able to help you to some larks. Is there any Greek Isle you would like to explore? or any creek in Asia Minor? — Yours ever affectionately, R. L. S.

To the Rev. Dr. Charteris

The Rev. Dr. Charteris, of Edinburgh, had been one of the most intimate and trusted friends of Stevenson's father, and R. L. S. turns to him accordingly for memories and impressions.

[Saranac Lake, *Winter, 1887–1888.*]

My dear Dr. Charteris, — I have asked Douglas and Foulis to send you my last volume, so that you may possess my little paper on my father in a permanent shape; not for what that is worth, but as a tribute of respect to one whom my father regarded with such love, esteem, and affection. Besides, as you will see, I have brought you under contribution, and I have still to thank you for your letter to my mother; so more than kind; in much, so just. It is my hope, when time and health permit, to do something more definite for my father's memory. You are one of the very few who can (if you will) help me. Pray believe that I lay on you no obligation; I know too well, you may believe me, how difficult it is to put even two sincere lines upon paper, where all, too, is to order. But if the spirit should ever move you, and you should recall something memorable of your friend, his son will heartily thank you for a note of it.—With much respect, believe me, yours sincerely, ROBERT LOUIS STEVENSON.

TO HENRY JAMES

[SARANAC LAKE, *March, 1888.*]

MY DEAR DELIGHTFUL JAMES,—To quote your heading to my wife, I think no man writes so elegant a letter, I am sure none so kind, unless it be Colvin, and there is more of the stern parent about him. I was vexed at your account of my admired Meredith: I wish I could go and see him; as it is, I will try to write. I read with indescribable admiration your *Emerson*. I begin to long for the day when these portraits of yours shall be collected: do put me in. But Emerson is a higher flight. Have you a *Tourgueneff?* You have told me many interesting things of him, and I seem to see them written, and forming a graceful and *bildend* sketch. My novel is a tragedy; four parts out of six or seven are written, and gone to Burlingame. Five parts of it are sound, human tragedy; the last one or two, I regret to say, not so soundly designed; I almost hesitate to write them; they are very picturesque, but they are fantastic; they shame, perhaps degrade, the beginning. I wish I

1888
ÆT. 38

knew; that was how the tale came to me, however. I got the situation; it was an old taste of mine: The older brother goes out in the '45, the younger stays; the younger, of course, gets title and estate and marries the bride designate of the elder — a family match, but he (the younger) had always loved her, and she had really loved the elder. Do you see the situation? Then the devil and Saranac suggested this *dénouement*, and I joined the two ends in a day or two of constant feverish thought, and began to write. And now — I wonder if I have not gone too far with the fantastic. The elder brother is an INCUBUS: supposed to be killed at Culloden, he turns up again and bleeds the family of money; on that stopping he comes and lives with them, whence flows the real tragedy, the nocturnal duel of the brothers (very naturally, and indeed, I think, inevitably arising), and second supposed death of the elder. Husband and wife now really make up, and then the cloven hoof appears. For the third supposed death and the manner of the third reappearance is steep; steep, sir. It is even very steep, and I fear it shames the honest stuff so far; but then it is highly pictorial, and it leads up to the death of the elder brother at the hands of the younger in a perfectly cold-blooded murder, of which I wish (and mean) the reader to approve. You see how daring is the design. There are really but six characters, and one of these episodic, and yet it covers eighteen years, and will be, I imagine, the longest of my works.—Yours ever, R. L. S.

Read Gosse's Raleigh. First-rate.—Yours ever,
R. L. S.

To the Rev. Dr. Charteris

Saranac Lake, Adirondacks,
New York, U. S. A., *Spring, 1888.*

My dear Dr. Charteris,—The funeral letter, your notes, and many other things, are reserved for a book, *Memorials of a Scottish Family*, if ever I can find time and opportunity. I wish I could throw off all else and sit down to it to-day. Yes, my father was a "distinctly religious man," but not a pious. The distinction painfully and pleasurably recalls old conflicts; it used to be my great gun—and you, who suffered for the whole Church, know how needful it was to have some reserve artillery! His sentiments were tragic; he was a tragic thinker. Now, granted that life is tragic to the marrow, it seems the proper function of religion to make us accept and serve in that tragedy, as officers in that other and comparable one of war. Service is the word, active service, in the military sense; and the religious man—I beg pardon, the pious man—is he who has a military joy in duty—not he who weeps over the wounded. We can do no more than try to do our best. Really, I am the grandson of the manse—I preach you a kind of sermon. Box the brat's ears!

My mother—to pass to matters more within my competence—finely enjoys herself. The new country, some new friends we have made, the interesting experiment of this climate—which (at least) is tragic—all have done her good. I have myself passed a better winter than for years, and now that it is nearly over

1888 ÆT. 38 have some diffident hopes of doing well in the summer and "eating a little more air" than usual.

I thank you for the trouble you are taking, and my mother joins with me in kindest regards to yourself and Mrs. Charteris.—Yours very truly,

ROBERT LOUIS STEVENSON.

To S. R. CROCKETT

[SARANAC LAKE, *Spring, 1888.*]

DEAR MINISTER OF THE FREE KIRK AT PENICUIK,—For O, man, I cannae read your name!—That I have been so long in answering your delightful letter sits on my conscience badly. The fact is I let my correspondence accumulate until I am going to leave a place; and then I pitch in, overhaul the pile, and my cries of penitence might be heard a mile about. Yesterday I despatched thirty-five belated letters: conceive the state of my conscience, above all as the Sins of Omission (see boyhood's guide, the Shorter Catechism) are in my view the only serious ones; I call it my view, but it cannot have escaped you that it was also Christ's. However, all that is not to the purpose, which is to thank you for the sincere pleasure afforded by your charming letter. I get a good few such; how few that please me at all, you would be surprised to learn—or have a singularly just idea of the dulness of our race; how few that please me as yours did, I can tell you in one word—*None.* I am no great kirkgoer, for many reasons—and the sermon 's one of them, and the first prayer another, but the chief and effectual reason is the stuffiness.

I am no great kirkgoer, says I, but when I read you letter of yours, I thought I would like to sit under ye. And then I saw ye were to send me a bit buik, and says I, I 'll wait for the bit buik, and then I 'll mebbe can read the man's name, and anyway I can kill twa birds wi' ae stane. And, man! the buik was ne'er heard tell o'!

That fact is an adminicle of excuse for my delay.

And now, dear minister of the illegible name, thanks to you, and greeting to your wife, and may you have good guidance in your difficult labours, and a blessing on your life. ROBERT LOUIS STEVENSON.

(No just so young sae young 's he was, though —
I 'm awfae near forty, man.)

ADDRESS c/o CHARLES SCRIBNER'S SONS,
743 BROADWAY, NEW YORK.

Don't put "N. B." in your paper: put *Scotland*, and be done with it. Alas, that I should be thus stabbed in the home of my friends! The name of my native land is not *North Britain*, whatever may be the name of yours. R. L. S.

TO MISS FERRIER

[SARANAC LAKE, *April, 1888.*]

MY DEAREST COGGIE,—I wish I could find the letter I began to you some time ago when I was ill; but I can't, and I don't believe there was much in it anyway. We have all behaved like pigs and beasts and barn-door poultry to you; but I have been sunk in work,

1888 ÆT. 38 and the lad is lazy and blind and has been working too; and as for Fanny, she has been (and still is) really unwell. I had a mean hope you might perhaps write again before I got up steam: I could not have been more ashamed of myself than I am, and I should have had another laugh.

They always say I cannot give news in my letters: I shall shake off that reproach. On Monday, if she is well enough, Fanny leaves for California to see her friends; it is rather an anxiety to let her go alone; but the doctor simply forbids it in my case, and she is better anywhere than here—a bleak, blackguard, beggarly climate, of which I can say no good except that it suits me and some others of the same or similar persuasions whom (by all rights) it ought to kill. It is a form of Arctic St. Andrews, I should imagine; and the miseries of forty degrees below zero, with a high wind, have to be felt to be appreciated. The greyness of the heavens here is a circumstance eminently revolting to the soul; I have near forgot the aspect of the sun—I doubt if this be news; it is certainly no news to us. My mother suffers a little from the inclemency of the place, but less on the whole than would be imagined. Among other wild schemes, we have been projecting yacht voyages; and I beg to inform you that Cogia Hassan was cast for the part of passenger. They may come off!—Again this is not news. The lad? Well, the lad wrote a tale this winter, which appeared to me so funny that I have taken it in hand, and some of these days you will receive a copy of a work entitled "*A Game of Bluff*, by Lloyd Osbourne and Robert Louis Stevenson."

Otherwise he (the lad) is much as usual. There remains, I believe, to be considered only R. L. S., the house-bond, prop, pillar, bread-winner, and bully of the establishment. Well, I do think him much better; he is making piles of money; the hope of being able to hire a yacht ere long dances before his eyes; otherwise he is not in very high spirits at this particular moment, though compared with last year at Bournemouth an angel of joy. 1888 ÆT. 38

And now is this news, Cogia, or is it not? It all depends upon the point of view, and I call it news. The devil of it is that I can think of nothing else, except to send you all our loves, and to wish exceedingly you were here to cheer us all up. But we 'll see about that on board the yacht.—Your affectionate friend,

ROBERT LOUIS STEVENSON.

TO SIDNEY COLVIN

The **Mutiny** novel here foreshadowed never got written.

[SARANAC LAKE], *April 9th !! 1888.*

MY DEAR COLVIN,—I have been long without writing to you, but am not to blame. I had some little annoyances quite for a private eye, but they ran me so hard that I could not write without lugging them in, which (for several reasons) I did not choose to do. Fanny is off to San Francisco, and next week I myself flit to New York: address Scribner's. Where we shall go I know not, nor (I was going to say) care; so bald and bad is my frame of mind. Do you know our—ahem!

1888 ÆT. 38 —fellow clubman, Colonel Majendie? I had such an interesting letter from him. Did you see my sermon? It has evoked the worst feeling: I fear people don't care for the truth, or else I don't tell it. Suffer me to wander without purpose. I have sent off twenty letters to-day, and begun and stuck at a twenty-first, and taken a copy of one which was on business, and corrected several galleys of proof, and sorted about a bushel of old letters; so if any one has a right to be romantically stupid it is I—and I am. Really deeply stupid, and at that stage when in old days I used to pour out words without any meaning whatever and with my mind taking no part in the performance. I suspect that is now the case. I am reading with extraordinary pleasure the life of Lord Lawrence: Lloyd and I have a mutiny novel—

(*Next morning, after twelve other letters*)—mutiny novel on hand—a tremendous work—so we are all at Indian books. The idea of the novel is Lloyd's: I call it a novel. 'T is a tragic romance, of the most tragic sort: I believe the end will be almost too much for human endurance—when the hero is thrown to the ground with one of his own (Sepoy) soldier's knees upon his chest, and the cries begin in the Beebeeghar. O truly, you know it is a howler! The whole last part is—well, the difficulty is that, short of resuscitating Shakespeare, I don't know who is to write it.

I still keep wonderful. I am a great performer before the Lord on the penny whistle.—Dear sir, sincerely yours,

ANDREW JACKSON.

To Miss Adelaide Boodle

[Saranac Lake, *April, 1888.*]
Address c/o Messrs. Scribner's Sons,
743 Broadway, N. Y.

My dear Gamekeeper,—Your p. c. (proving you a good student of Micawber) has just arrived, and it paves the way to something I am anxious to say. I wrote a paper the other day—*Pulvis et Umbra;*—I wrote it with great feeling and conviction: to me it seemed bracing and healthful, it is in such a world (so seen by me), that I am very glad to fight out my battle, and see some fine sunsets, and hear some excellent jests between whiles round the camp fire. But I find that to some people this vision of mine is a nightmare, and extinguishes all ground of faith in God or pleasure in man. Truth I think not so much of; for I do not know it. And I could wish in my heart that I had not published this paper, if it troubles folk too much: all have not the same digestion, nor the same sight of things. And it came over me with special pain that perhaps this article (which I was at the pains to send to her) might give dismalness to my *Gamekeeper at Home.* Well, I cannot take back what I have said; but yet I may add this. If my view be everything but the nonsense that it may be—to me it seems self-evident and blinding truth—surely of all things it makes this world holier. There is nothing in it but the moral side—but the great battle and the breathing times with their refreshments. I see no more and no less. And if you look again, it is not ugly, and it is filled with promise.

1888 ÆT. 38

Pray excuse a desponding author for this apology. My wife is away off to the uttermost parts of the States, all by herself. I shall be off, I hope, in a week; but where? Ah! that I know not. I keep wonderful, and my wife a little better, and the lad flourishing. We now perform duets on two D tin whistles; it is no joke to make the bass; I think I must really send you one, which I wish you would correct. . . . I may be said to live for these instrumental labours now; but I have always some childishness on hand.—I am, dear Gamekeeper, your indulgent but intemperate Squire,

ROBERT LOUIS STEVENSON.

TO CHARLES BAXTER

On the 16th of April, Stevenson and his party left Saranac. After spending a fortnight in New York, where, as always in cities, his health quickly flagged again, he went for the month of May into seaside quarters at Union House, Manasquan, on the New Jersey coast, for the sake of fresh air and boating. Here he enjoyed the occasional society of some of his New York friends, including Mr. St. Gaudens and Mr. W. H. Low, and was initiated in the congenial craft of cat-boat sailing. In the meantime, Mrs. Stevenson had gone to San Francisco to see her relatives, and holding that the climate of the Pacific was likely to be better for the projected cruise than that of the Atlantic, had inquired there whether a yacht was to be hired for such a purpose. The schooner *Casco*, Captain Otis, was found; Stevenson signified by telegraph his assent to the arrangement; determined to risk in the adventure the sum of £2000, of which his father's death had put him in possession, hoping to recoup himself by a series of letters recounting his experiences; and on the 2nd of June started with his mother and stepson for San Francisco, and thence for that island cruise from which he was destined never to return.

1888
ÆT. 38

UNION HOUSE, MANASQUAN, N. J.,
BUT ADDRESS TO SCRIBNER'S, *11th May, 1888.*

MY DEAR CHARLES,—I have found a yacht, and we are going the full pitch for seven months. If I cannot get my health back (more or less), 't is madness; but, of course, there is the hope, and I will play big. . . . If this business fails to set me up, well, £2000 is gone, and I know I can't get better. We sail from San Francisco, June 15th, for the South Seas in the yacht *Casco.*—With a million thanks for all your dear friendliness, ever yours affectionately,

ROBERT LOUIS STEVENSON.

TO HOMER ST. GAUDENS

The following is addressed from Manasquan to a boy, the son of the writer's friend, the sculptor St. Gaudens; for the rest, it explains itself.

MANASQUAN, NEW JERSEY, *27th May, 1888.*

DEAR HOMER ST. GAUDENS,—Your father has brought you this day to see me, and he tells me it is his hope you may remember the occasion. I am going to do what I can to carry out his wish; and it may amuse you, years after, to see this little scrap of paper and to read what I write. I must begin by testifying that you yourself took no interest whatever in the introduction, and in the most proper spirit displayed a single-minded ambition to get back to play, and this I thought an excellent and admirable point in your character. You were also (I use the past tense, with a view to the time when

1888 ÆT. 38 you shall read, rather than to that when I am writing) a very pretty boy, and (to my European views) startlingly self-possessed. My time of observation was so limited that you must pardon me if I can say no more: what else I marked, what restlessness of foot and hand, what graceful clumsiness, what experimental designs upon the furniture, was but the common inheritance of human youth. But you may perhaps like to know that the lean flushed man in bed, who interested you so little, was in a state of mind extremely mingled and unpleasant: harassed with work which he thought he was not doing well, troubled with difficulties to which you will in time succeed, and yet looking forward to no less a matter than a voyage to the South Seas and the visitation of savage and desert islands.—Your father's friend, ROBERT LOUIS STEVENSON.

TO HENRY JAMES

MANASQUAN (ahem!), NEW JERSEY,
May 28th, 1888.

MY DEAR JAMES,—With what a torrent it has come at last! Up to now, what I like best is the first number of *A London Life*. You have never done anything better, and I don't know if perhaps you have ever done anything so good as the girl's outburst: tip-top. I have been preaching your later works in your native land. I had to present the Beltraffio volume to Low, and it has brought him to his knees; he was *amazed* at the first part of Georgina's Reasons, although (like me) not so well satisfied with Part II. It is annoying to find the American public as stupid as the English, but they will waken up in time: I wonder what they will think of *Two Nations?* . . . 1888 ÆT. 38

This, dear James, is a valedictory. On June 15th the schooner yacht *Casco* will (weather and a jealous providence permitting) steam through the Golden Gates for Honolulu, Tahiti, the Galapagos, Guayaquil, and—I hope *not* the bottom of the Pacific. It will contain your obedient 'umble servant and party. It seems too good to be true, and is a very good way of getting through the green-sickness of maturity, which, with all its accompanying ills, is now declaring itself in my mind and life. They tell me it is not so severe as that of youth; if I (and the *Casco*) are spared, I shall tell you more exactly, as I am one of the few people in the world who do not forget their own lives.

Good-bye, then, my dear fellow, and please write us a word; we expect to have three mails in the next two months: Honolulu, Tahiti, and Guayaquil. But letters will be forwarded from Scribner's, if you hear nothing more definite directly. In 3 (three) days I leave for San Francisco.—Ever yours most cordially, R. L. S.

X

PACIFIC VOYAGES

(June, 1888–November, 1890)

X

PACIFIC VOYAGES

(June, 1888–November, 1890)

IT was on the 28th of June, 1888, that Stevenson started from the harbour of San Francisco on what was only intended to be a health and pleasure excursion of a few months' duration, but turned into a voluntary exile prolonged until the hour of his death. His company consisted, besides himself, of his wife, his mother, his stepson Mr. Lloyd Osbourne, and the servant Valentine Roch. They sailed on board the schooner yacht *Casco*, Captain Otis, and made straight for the Marquesas, dropping anchor on the 28th of July in Anaho Bay, the harbour of the island of Nukahiva. The magic effect of this first island landfall on his mind he has described in the opening chapter of his book *The South Seas*.

After spending six weeks in this group they sailed southeastwards, visiting (a somewhat perilous piece of navigation) several of the coral atolls of the Paumotus or Low Archipelago. Thence they arrived in the first week of October at the Tahitian group or "Society Islands." In these their longest stay was not at the chief town, Papeete, where Stevenson fell sharply ill, but in a more secluded and very beautiful station, Tautira, whither he went to recruit, and where they were detained by the necessity of remasting the schooner. Here Stevenson and one of the local chiefs, Ori a Ori, made special friends and parted with heartfelt mutual regret. Sailing thence due northwards through forty degrees of latitude, they arrived about Christmas at Honolulu, the more than semi-civilised capital of the Hawaiian group (Sandwich Islands) where they paid off the yacht *Casco* and made a stay of nearly six months. Here Stevenson finished *The Master of Ballantrae* and *The Wrong Box;* and hence his mother returned for a while to Scotland, to rejoin her son's household when it was fairly installed two years later at Vailima. From Honolulu Stevenson made several excursions, including one, which profoundly impressed him, to the leper settlement at Molokai, the scene of Father Damien's ministrations and death.

This first year of voyaging and residence among the Pacific Islands had resulted in so encouraging a renewal of health, with so keen a zest added to life by the restored capacity for outdoor activity and adventure, that Stevenson determined to prolong his experiences in yet more remote archipelagoes of the same ocean. He started accordingly from Honolulu in June, 1889, on a trading schooner, the *Equator*, bound to the Gilberts, one of the least visited and most primitively mannered of all the island groups of the Western Pacific; and emerged towards Christmas of the same year into semi-civilisation again at Samoa, where he wrote his first Polynesian story, the *Bottle Imp*. He stayed for six weeks, enchanted with the scenery and the people; bought a property, the future Vailima, on the mountain-side above Apia, with the notion of making it, if not a home, at least a place of rest and call on later projected excursions among the islands; and began to make collections for his studies in recent Samoan history. In February he went on to Sydney to find his correspondence and consider future plans. It was during this stay at Sydney that his righteous indignation was aroused by the publication of the letter against Father Damien by the Rev. Dr. Hyde of Honolulu. Here also he fell once more seriously ill, with a renewal of all his old symptoms; and the conclusion was forced upon him that he must make his home for the rest of his life in the tropics—though with occasional excursions, as he then hoped, at least half-way homewards to places where it might be possible for friends from England to meet him. In order to shake off the effects of this attack, he started with his party on a fresh sea voyage from Sydney, this time on a trading steamer, the *Janet Nicoll*, which took him by a very devious course among many remote islands during the months of April–August, 1890. During the voyage he began to put into shape the notes for a volume on the South Seas, which he had been compiling ever since he left San Francisco. Unfortunately he spoiled his work by trying to make it too impersonal and too full of information, or what he called "serious interest." On the return voyage of the *Janet Nicoll* he left her at New Caledonia, staying for some days at Noumea before he went on to Sydney, where he spent four or five weeks of later August and September.

Thence he returned in October to take up his abode for good on his Samoan property, where the work of clearing and planting had been going on busily during his absence. The letters in the following section are selected from those which reached his correspondents in England and the United States at intervals, necessarily somewhat rare, during these voyages.

To Sidney Colvin

Yacht "Casco," Anaho Bay, Nukahiva,
Marquesas Islands [*July, 1888*].

1888 Æt. 38

My dear Colvin,—From this somewhat (ahem!) out of the way place, I write to say how d' ye do. It is all a swindle: I chose these isles as having the most beastly population, and they are far better and far more civilised than we. I know one old chief Ko-o-amua, a great cannibal in his day, who ate his enemies even as he walked home from killing 'em, and he is a perfect gentleman and exceedingly amiable and simple-minded: no fool, though.

The climate is delightful; and the harbour where we lie one of the loveliest spots imaginable. Yesterday evening we had near a score of natives on board; lovely parties. We have a native god; very rare now. Very rare and equally absurd to view.

This sort of work is not favorable to correspondence: it takes me all the little strength I have to go about and see, and then come home and note, the strangeness around us. I should n't wonder if there came trouble here some day, all the same. I could name a nation

such races. My health has stood me splendidly; I am in for hours wading over the knees for shells; I have been five hours on horseback: I have been up pretty near all night waiting to see where the *Casco* would go ashore, and with my diary all ready—simply the most entertaining night of my life. Withal I still have colds; I have one now, and feel pretty sick too; but not as at home: instead of being in bed, for instance, I am at this moment sitting snuffling and writing in an undershirt and trousers; and as for colour, hands, arms, feet, legs, and face, I am browner than the berry: only my trunk and the aristocratic spot on which I sit retain the vile whiteness of the north. 1888 ÆT. 38

Please give my news and kind love to Henley, Henry James, and any whom you see of well-wishers. Accept from me the very best of my affection: and believe me ever yours, THE OLD MAN VIRULENT.

TAITI, *October 7th, 1888.*

Never having found a chance to send this off, I may add more of my news. My cold took a very bad turn, and I am pretty much out of sorts at this particular, living in a little bare one-twentieth-furnished house, surrounded by mangoes, etc. All the rest are well, and I mean to be soon. But these Taiti colds are very severe and, to children, often fatal; so they were not the thing for me. Yesterday the brigantine came in from San Francisco, so we can get our letters off soon. There are in Papeete at this moment, in a little wooden house with grated verandahs, two people who love you very much, and one of them is

ROBERT LOUIS STEVENSON.

1888
ÆT. 38

To Charles Baxter

Taiti, as ever was, *6th October, 1888.*

My dear Charles,— . . . You will receive a lot of mostly very bad proofs of photographs: the paper was so bad. Please keep them very private, as they are for the book. We send them, having learned so dread a fear of the sea, that we wish to put our eggs in different baskets. We have been thrice within an ace of being ashore: we were lost (!) for about twelve hours in the Low Archipelago, but by God's blessing had quiet weather all the time; and once, in a squall, we cam' so near gaun heels ower hurdies, that I really dinnae ken why we didnae athegither. Hence, as I say, a great desire to put our eggs in different baskets, particularly on the Pacific (aw-haw-haw!) Pacific Ocean.

You can have no idea what a mean time we have had, owing to incidental beastlinesses, nor what a glorious, owing to the intrinsic interest of these isles. I hope the book will be a good one; nor do I really very much doubt that — the stuff is so curious; what I wonder is, if the public will rise to it. A copy of my journal, or as much of it as is made, shall go to you also; it is, of course, quite imperfect, much being to be added and corrected; but O, for the eggs in the different baskets.

All the rest are well enough, and all have enjoyed the cruise so far, in spite of its drawbacks. We have had an awfae time in some ways, Mr. Baxter; and if I wasnae sic a verra patient man (when I ken that I *have* to be) there wad hae been a braw row; and ance if I hadnae happened to be on deck about three in the marnin', I *think* there would have been *murder* done. The American Mairchant Marine is a kent service; ye ll have heard its praise, I 'm thinkin'; an' if ye never did, ye can get *Twa Years Before the Mast*, by Dana, whaur forbye a great deal o' pleisure, ye 'll get a' the needcessary information. Love to your father and all the family.—Ever your affectionate friend, 1888 ÆT. 38

ROBERT LOUIS STEVENSON.

To Miss Adelaide Boodle

This lady, as we have seen, had made Mr. Stevenson a present of a paper-cutter when he left Bournemouth; and it is in the character of the paper-cutter that he now writes.

TAITI, *October 10th, 1888.*

DEAR GIVER,—I am at a loss to conceive your object in giving me to a person so locomotory as my proprietor. The number of thousand miles that I have travelled, the strange bed-fellows with which I have been made acquainted, I lack the requisite literary talent to make clear to your imagination. I speak of bedfellows; pocket-fellows would be a more exact expression, for the place of my abode is in my master's right-hand trouser-pocket; and there, as he waded on the resounding beaches of Nukahiva, or in the shallow tepid water on the reef of Fakarava, I have been overwhelmed by and buried among all manner of abominable South Sea shells, beautiful enough in their way, I make no doubt, but singular company for any

1888 ÆT. 38 self-respecting paper-cutter. He, my master—or as I more justly call him, my bearer; for although I occasionally serve him, does not he serve me daily and all day long, carrying me like an African potentate on my subject's legs?—*he* is delighted with these isles, and this climate, and these savages, and a variety of other things. He now blows a flageolet with singular effects: sometimes the poor thing appears stifled with shame, sometimes it screams with agony; he pursues his career with truculent insensibility. Health appears to reign in the party. I was very nearly sunk in a squall. I am sorry I ever left England, for here there are no books to be had, and without books there is no stable situation for, dear Giver, your affectionate

WOODEN PAPER-CUTTER.

A neighbouring pair of scissors snips a kiss in your direction.

TO SIDNEY COLVIN

The ballad referred to in the letter which follows is *The Feast of Famine*, published with others in the collection of 1890, "Ballads" (Chatto & Windus). I never very much admired his ballads for any quality except their narrative vigour, thinking them unequal and uncertain both in metre and style.

TAITI, *October 16th, 1888.*

MY DEAR COLVIN,—The cruiser for San Francisco departs to-morrow morning bearing you some kind of a scratch. This much more important packet will travel by way of Auckland. It contains a ballant; and I think a better ballant than I expected ever to do. I can imagine how you will wag your pow over it; and how ragged you will find it, etc., but has it not spirit all the same? and though the verse is not all your fancy painted it, has it not some life? And surely, as narrative, the thing has considerable merit! Read it, get a typewritten copy taken, and send me that and your opinion to the Sandwiches. I know I am only courting the most excruciating mortification; but the real cause of my sending the thing is that I could bear to go down myself, but not to have much MS. go down with me. To say truth, we are through the most dangerous; but it has left in all minds a strong sense of insecurity, and we are all for putting eggs in various baskets. 1888 ÆT. 38

We leave here soon, bound for Uahiva, Reiatea, Bora-Bora, and the Sandwiches.

O, how my spirit languishes
To step ashore on the Sanguishes;
For there my letters wait,
There shall I know my fate.
O, how my spirit languidges
To step ashore on the Sanguidges.

18th.—I think we shall leave here if all is well on Monday. I am quite recovered, astonishingly recovered. It must be owned these climates and this voyage have given me more strength than I could have thought possible. And yet the sea is a terrible place, stupefying to the mind and poisonous to the temper, the sea, the motion, the lack of space, the cruel publicity, the villainous tinned foods, the sailors, the captain, the passengers—but you are amply repaid when

1888 ÆT. 38 you sight an island, and drop anchor in a new world. Much trouble has attended this trip, but I must confess more pleasure. Nor should I ever complain, as in the last few weeks, with the curing of my illness indeed, as if that were the bursting of an abscess, the cloud has risen from my spirits and to some degree from my temper. Do you know what they call the *Casco* at Fakarava? The *Silver Ship*. Is that not pretty? Pray tell Mrs. Jenkin, *die silberne Frau*, as I only learned it since I wrote her. I think of calling the book by that name: *The Cruise of the Silver Ship*—so there will be one poetic page at least—the title. At the Sandwiches we shall say farewell to the *S. S.* with mingled feelings. She is a lovely creature: the most beautiful thing at this moment in Taiti.

Well, I will take another sheet, though I know I have nothing to say. You would think I was bursting: but the voyage is all stored up for the book, which is to pay for it, we fondly hope; and the troubles of the time are not worth telling; and our news is little.

Here I conclude (Oct. 24th, I think), for we are now stored, and the Blue Peter metaphorically flies.

R. L. S.

To William and Thomas Archer

Stevenson addresses part of this letter, as he does the whole of another later on, to a young son of Mr. Archer's, but rather to amuse himself than his nominal correspondent, who was then aged three.

Taiti, *October 17th, 1888.*

DEAR ARCHER,—Though quite unable to write letters, I nobly send you a line signifying nothing. The voyage has agreed well with all; it has had its pains, and its extraordinary pleasures; nothing in the world can equal the excitement of the first time you cast anchor in some bay of a tropical island, and the boats begin to surround you, and the tattooed people swarm aboard. Tell Tomarcher, with my respex, that hide-and-seek is not equal to it; no, nor hidee-in-the-dark; which, for the matter of that, is a game for the unskilful: the artist prefers daylight, a good-sized garden, some shrubbery, an open paddock, and — come on, Macduff. 1888 ÆT. 38

TOMARCHER, I am now a distinguished litterytour, but that was not the real bent of my genius. I was the best player of hide-and-seek going; not a good runner, I was up to every shift and dodge, I could jink very well, I could crawl without any noise through leaves, I could hide under a carrot plant, it used to be my favourite boast that I always *walked* into the den. You may care to hear, Tomarcher, about the children in these parts; their parents obey them, they do not obey their parents; and I am sorry to tell you (for I dare say you are already thinking the idea a good one) that it does not pay one halfpenny. There are three sorts of civilisation, Tomarcher: the real old-fashioned one, in which children either had to find out how to please their dear papas, or their dear papas cut their heads off. This style did very well, but is now out of fashion. Then the modern European style: in which children have to behave reasonably well, and go to school and say their prayers, or their dear papas *will know the reason why*. This does fairly well. Then there is the South Sea Island plan, which does not do one bit. The children beat their parents here; it

1888 ÆT. 38 does not make their parents any better; so do not try it.

Dear Tomarcher, I have forgotten the address of your new house, but will send this to one of your papa's publishers. Remember us all to all of you, and believe me, yours respectably,

ROBERT LOUIS STEVENSON.

TO CHARLES BAXTER

The stanzas which end this letter have already been printed, with one additional, in *Songs of Travel*, but gain effect, I think, from being given here in their place.

TAUTIRA (THE GARDEN OF THE WORLD), OTHERWISE CALLED HANS-CHRISTIAN-ANDERSEN-VILLE
[*November, 1888*].

MY DEAR CHARLES,—Whether I have a penny left in the wide world, I know not, nor shall know, till I get to Honolulu, where I anticipate a devil of an awakening. It will be from a mighty pleasant dream at least: Tautira being mere Heaven. But suppose, for the sake of argument, any money to be left in the hands of my painful doer, what is to be done with it? Save us from exile would be the wise man's choice, I suppose; for the exile threatens to be eternal. But yet I am of opinion—in case there should be *some* dibs in the hand of the P. D., *i.e.* painful doer; because if there be none, I shall take to my flageolet on the high-road, and work home the best way I can, having previously made away with my family—I am of opinion that if —— and his are in the customary state, and you are thinking of an offering, and there should be still some funds over, you would be a real good P. D. to put some in with yours and tak' the credit o't, like a wee man! I know it 's a beastly thing to ask; but it, after all, does no earthly harm, only that much good. And besides, like enough there 's nothing in the till, and there is an end. Yet I live here in the full lustre of millions; it is thought I am the richest son of man that has yet been to Tautira: I!—and I am secretly eaten with the fear of lying in pawn, perhaps for the remainder of my days, in San Francisco. As usual, my colds have much hashed my finances. 1888 ÆT. 38

Do tell Henley I write this just after having dismissed Ori the sub-chief, in whose house I live, Mrs. Ori, and Pairai, their adopted child, from the evening hour of music: during which I Publickly (with a *k*) Blow on the Flageolet. These are words of truth. Yesterday I told Ori about W. E. H., counterfeited his playing on the piano and the pipe, and succeeded in sending the six feet four there is of that sub-chief somewhat sadly to his bed; feeling that his was not the genuine article after all. Ori is exactly like a colonel in the Guards.—I am, dear Charles, ever yours affectionately,

R. L. S.

TAUTIRA, *10th November, '88.*

MY DEAR CHARLES,—Our mainmast is dry-rotten, and we are all to the devil; I shall lie in a debtor's jail. Never mind, Tautira is first chop. I am so besotted that I shall put on the back of this my attempt at words to *Wandering Willie;* if you can conceive at all the difficulty, you will also conceive the vanity with which

1888 I regard any kind of result; and whatever mine is like,
ÆT. 38 it has some sense, and Burns's has none.

Home no more home to me, whither must I wander?
  Hunger my driver, I go where I must.
Cold blows the winter wind over hill and heather;
  Thick drives the rain, and my roof is in the dust.
Loved of wise men was the shade of my roof-tree,
  The true word of welcome was spoken in the door—
Dear days of old, with the faces in the firelight,
  Kind folks of old, you come again no more.

Home was home then, my dear, full of kindly faces,
  Home was home then, my dear, happy for the child.
Fire and the windows bright glittered on the moorland;
  Song, tuneful song, built a palace in the wild.
Now, when day dawns on the brow of the moorland,
  Lone stands the house, and the chimney-stone is cold.
Lone let it stand, now the friends are all departed,
  The kind hearts, the true hearts, that loved the place
    of old.

R. L. S.

To J. A. Symonds

The following is the draft of a proposed dedication to the South Sea travel-book which was to be the fruit of the present voyages, as is explained in a note at the end.

November 11th, 1888.

One November night, in the village of Tautira, we sat at the high table in the hall of assembly, hearing the natives sing. It was dark in the hall, and very warm; though at times the land wind blew a little shrewdly through the chinks, and at times, through the larger openings, we could see the moonlight on the lawn. As the songs arose in the rattling Tahitian chorus, the chief translated here and there a verse. Farther on in the volume you shall read the songs themselves; and I am in hopes that not you only, but all who can find a savour in the ancient poetry of places, will read them with some pleasure. You are to conceive us, therefore, in strange circumstances and very pleasing; in a strange land and climate, the most beautiful on earth; surrounded by a foreign race that all travellers have agreed to be the most engaging; and taking a double interest in two foreign arts. 1888 ÆT. 38

We came forth again at last, in a cloudy moonlight, on the forest lawn which is the street of Tautira. The Pacific roared outside upon the reef. Here and there one of the scattered palm-built lodges shone out under the shadow of the wood, the lamplight bursting through the crannies of the wall. We went homeward slowly, Ori a Ori carrying behind us the lantern and the chairs, properties with which we had just been enacting our part of the distinguished visitor. It was one of those moments in which minds not altogether churlish recall the names and deplore the absence of congenial friends; and it was your name that first rose upon our lips. "How Symonds would have enjoyed this evening!" said one, and then another. The word caught in my mind; I went to bed, and it was still there. The glittering, frosty solitudes in which your days are cast, arose before me: I seemed to see you walking there in the late night, under the pine-trees and the stars; and I received the image with something like remorse.

1888
ÆT. 38

There is a modern attitude towards fortune; in this place I will not use a graver name. Staunchly to withstand her buffets and to enjoy with equanimity her favours was the code of the virtuous of old. Our fathers, it should seem, wondered and doubted how they had merited their misfortunes: we, rather how we have deserved our happiness. And we stand often abashed, and sometimes revolted, at those partialities of fate by which we profit most. It was so with me on that November night: I felt that our positions should be changed. It was you, dear Symonds, who should have gone upon that voyage and written this account. With your rich stores of knowledge, you could have remarked and understood a thousand things of interest and beauty that escaped my ignorance; and the brilliant colours of your style would have carried into a thousand sickrooms the sea air and the strong sun of tropic islands. It was otherwise decreed. But suffer me at least to connect you, if only in name and only in the fondness of imagination, with the voyage of the "Silver Ship."

ROBERT LOUIS STEVENSON.

DEAR SYMONDS,—I send you this (November 11th), the morning of its completion. If I ever write an account of this voyage, may I place this letter at the beginning? It represents—I need not tell you, for you too are an artist—a most genuine feeling, which kept me long awake last night; and though perhaps a little elaborate, I think it a good piece of writing. We are *in heaven here*. Do not forget R. L. S.

Please keep this: I have no perfect copy.
Tautira, on the peninsula of Tahiti.

To Thomas Archer

Tautira, Island of Tahiti [*November, 1888*].

Dear Tomarcher,—This is a pretty state of things! seven o'clock and no word of breakfast! And I was awake a good deal last night, for it was full moon, and they had made a great fire of cocoanut husks down by the sea, and as we have no blinds or shutters, this kept my room very bright. And then the rats had a wedding or a school-feast under my bed. And then I woke early, and I have nothing to read except Virgil's *Æneid*, which is not good fun on an empty stomach, and a Latin dictionary, which is good for naught, and by some humorous accident, your dear papa's article on Skerryvore. And I read the whole of that, and very impudent it is, but you must not tell your dear papa I said so, or it might come to a battle in which you might lose either a dear papa or a valued correspondent, or both, which would be prodigal. And still no breakfast; so I said "Let 's write to Tomarcher."

This is a much better place for children than any I have hitherto seen in these seas. The girls (and sometimes the boys) play a very elaborate kind of hopscotch. The boys play horses exactly as we do in Europe; and have very good fun on stilts, trying to knock each other down, in which they do not often succeed. The children of all ages go to church and are allowed to do what they please, running about the aisles, rolling balls, stealing mamma's bonnet and publicly sitting on it, and at last going to sleep in the middle of the floor. I forgot to say that the whips to play horses, and the balls

1888 ÆT. 38 to roll about the church — at least I never saw them used elsewhere — grow ready-made on trees; which is rough on toy-shops. The whips are so good that I wanted to play horses myself; but no such luck! my hair is grey, and I am a great, big, ugly man. The balls are rather hard, but very light and quite round. When you grow up and become offensively rich, you can charter a ship in the port of London, and have it come back to you entirely loaded with these balls; when you could satisfy your mind as to their character, and give them away when done with to your uncles and aunts. But what I really wanted to tell you was this: besides the tree-top toys (Hush-a-by, toy-shop, on the tree-top!), I have seen some real *made* toys, the first hitherto observed in the South Seas.

This was how. You are to imagine a four-wheeled gig; one horse; in the front seat two Tahiti natives, in their Sunday clothes, blue coat, white shirt, kilt (a little longer than the Scotch) of a blue stuff with big white or yellow flowers, legs and feet bare; in the back seat me and my wife, who is a friend of yours; under our feet, plenty of lunch and things: among us a great deal of fun in broken Tahitian, one of the natives, the sub-chief of the village, being a great ally of mine. Indeed we have exchanged names; so that he is now called Rui, the nearest they can come to Louis, for they have no *l* and no *s* in their language. Rui is six feet three in his stockings, and a magnificent man. We all have straw hats, for the sun is strong. We drive between the sea, which makes a great noise, and the mountains; the road is cut through a forest mostly of fruit trees, the very creepers, which take the place of our ivy, heavy with a great and delicious fruit, bigger than your head and far nicer, called Barbedine. Presently we came to a house in a pretty garden, quite by itself, very nicely kept, the doors and windows open, no one about, and no noise but that of the sea. It looked like a house in a fairy tale, and just beyond we must ford a river, and there we saw the inhabitants. Just in the mouth of the river, where it met the sea waves, they were ducking and bathing and screaming together like a covey of birds: seven or eight little naked brown boys and girls as happy as the day was long; and on the banks of the stream beside them, real toys—toy ships, full rigged, and with their sails set, though they were lying in the dust on their beam ends. And then I knew for sure they were all children in a fairy story, living alone together in that lonely house with the only toys in all the island; and that I had myself driven, in my four-wheeled gig, into a corner of the fairy story, and the question was, should I get out again? But it was all right; I guess only one of the wheels of the gig had got into the fairy story; and the next jolt the whole thing vanished, and we drove on in our sea-side forest as before, and I have the honour to be Tomarcher's valued correspondent, TERIITERA, which he was previously known as

ROBERT LOUIS STEVENSON.

TO SIDNEY COLVIN

YACHT "CASCO," AT SEA, *14th January, 1889.*

MY DEAR COLVIN,—Twenty days out from Papeete. Yes, sir, all that, and only (for a guess) in 4° north or

1889 ÆT. 39 at the best 4° 30′, though already the wind seems to smell a little of the North Pole. My handwriting you must take as you get, for we are speeding along through a nasty swell, and I can only keep my place at the table by means of a foot against the divan, the unoccupied hand meanwhile gripping the ink-bottle. As we begin (so very slowly) to draw near to seven months of correspondence, we are all in some fear; and I want to have letters written before I shall be plunged into that boiling pot of disagreeables which I constantly expect at Honolulu. What is needful can be added there.

We were kept two months at Tautira in the house of my dear old friend, Ori a Ori, till both the masts of this invaluable yacht had been repaired. It was all for the best: Tautira being the most beautiful spot, and its people the most amiable, I have ever found. Besides which, the climate suited me to the ground; I actually went sea-bathing almost every day, and in our feasts (we are all huge eaters in Taiarapu) have been known to apply four times for pig. And then again I got wonderful materials for my book, collected songs and legends on the spot; songs still sung in chorus by perhaps a hundred persons, not two of whom can agree on their translation; legends, on which I have seen half a dozen seniors sitting in conclave and debating what came next. Once I went a day's journey to the other side of the island to Tati, the high chief of the Tevas—*my* chief that is, for I am now a Teva and Teriitera, at your service—to collect more and correct what I had already. In the meanwhile I got on with my work, almost finished *The Master of Ballantrae*, which contains more human work than anything of mine but *Kidnapped*, and wrote the half of another ballad, *The Song of Rahéro*, on a Taiarapu legend of my own clan, sir—not so much fire as *The Feast of Famine*, but promising to be more even and correct. But the best fortune of our stay at Tautira was my knowledge of Ori himself, one of the finest creatures extant. The day of our parting was a sad one. We deduced from it a rule for travellers: not to stay two months in one place—which is to cultivate regrets. 1889 ÆT. 39

At last our contemptible ship was ready; to sea we went, bound for Honolulu and the letter-bag, on Christmas Day; and from then to now have experienced every sort of minor misfortune, squalls, calms, contrary winds and seas, pertinacious rains, declining stores, till we came almost to regard ourselves as in the case of Vanderdecken. Three days ago our luck seemed to improve, we struck a leading breeze, got creditably through the doldrums, and just as we looked to have the N. E. trades and a straight run, the rains and squalls and calms began again about midnight, and this morning, though there is breeze enough to send us along, we are beaten back by an obnoxious swell out of the north. Here is a page of complaint, when a verse of thanksgiving had perhaps been more in place. For all this time we must have been skirting past dangerous weather, in the tail and circumference of hurricanes, and getting only annoyance where we should have had peril, and ill-humour instead of fear.

I wonder if I have managed to give you any news this time, or whether the usual damn hangs over my letter? "The midwife whispered, Be thou dull!" or at

1889 ÆT. 39 least inexplicit. Anyway I have tried my best, am exhausted with the effort, and fall back into the land of generalities. I cannot tell you how often we have planned our arrival at the Monument: two nights ago, the 12th January, we had it all planned out, arrived in the lights and whirl of Waterloo, hailed a hansom, span up Waterloo Road, over the bridge, etc. etc., and hailed the Monument gate in triumph and with indescribable delight. My dear Custodian, I always think we are too sparing of assurances: Cordelia is only to be excused by Regan and Goneril in the same nursery; I wish to tell you that the longer I live, the more dear do you become to me; nor does my heart own any stronger sentiment. If the bloody schooner did n't send me flying in every sort of direction at the same time, I would say better what I feel so much; but really, if you were here, you would not be writing letters, I believe; and even I, though of a more marine constitution, am much perturbed by this bobbery and wish—O ye Gods, how I wish!—that it was done, and we had arrived, and I had Pandora's Box (my mail bag) in hand, and was in the lively hope of something eatable for dinner instead of salt horse, tinned mutton, duff without any plums, and pie fruit, which now make up our whole repertory. O Pandora's Box! I wonder what you will contain. As like as not you will contain but little money: if that be so, we shall have to retire to 'Frisco in the *Casco*, and thence by sea *via* Panama to Southampton, where we should arrive in April. I would like fine to see you on the tug: ten years older both of us than the last time you came to welcome Fanny and me to England. If we have money, however, we shall do a little differently: send the *Casco* away from Honolulu empty of its high-born lessees, for that voyage to 'Frisco is one long dead beat in foul and at last in cold weather; stay awhile behind, follow by steamer, cross the States by train, stay awhile in New York on business, and arrive probably by the German Line in Southampton. But all this is a question of money. We shall have to lie very dark awhile to recruit our finances: what comes from the book of the cruise, I do not want to touch until the capital is repaid. R. L. S.

To E. L. Burlingame

Honolulu [*January, 1889*].

MY DEAR BURLINGAME,—Here at last I have arrived. We could not get away from Tahiti till Christmas Day, and then had thirty days of calms and squalls, a deplorable passage. This has thrown me all out of gear in every way. I plunge into business.

1. *The Master:* Herewith go three more parts. You see he grows in bulk; this making ten already, and I am not yet sure if I can finish it in an eleventh; which shall go to you *quam primum*—I hope by next mail.

2. *Illustrations to M.* I totally forgot to try to write to Hole. It was just as well, for I find it impossible to forecast with sufficient precision. You had better throw off all this and let him have it at once. *Please do: all, and at once: see further;* and I should hope he would still be in time for the later numbers. The three pictures I have received are so truly good that I should bitterly regret having the volume imperfectly

1889 ÆT. 39 equipped. They are the best illustrations I have seen since I don't know when.

3. *Money*. To-morrow the mail comes in, and I hope it will bring me money either from you or home, but I will add a word on that point.

4. My address will be Honolulu — no longer Yacht *Casco*, which I am packing off — till probably April.

5. As soon as I am through with *The Master*, I shall finish the *Game of Bluff* — now rechristened *The Wrong Box*. This I wish to sell, cash down. It is of course copyright in the States; and I offer it to you for five thousand dollars. Please reply on this by return. Also please tell the typewriter who was so good as to be amused by our follies that I am filled with admiration for his piece of work.

6. *Master* again. Please see that I have n't the name of the Governor of New York wrong (1764 is the date) in part ten. I have no book of reference to put me right. Observe you now have up to August inclusive in hand, so you should begin to feel happy.

Is this all? I wonder, and fear not. Henry the Trader has not yet turned up: I hope he may to-morrow, when we expect a mail. Not one word of business have I received either from the States or England, nor anything in the shape of coin; which leaves me in a fine uncertainty and quite penniless on these islands. H. M.[1] (who is a gentleman of a courtly order and much tinctured with letters) is very polite; I may possibly ask for the position of palace doorkeeper. My voyage has been a singular mixture of good and ill fortune. As far as regards interest and material, the

[1] King Kalakaua.

fortune has been admirable; as far as regards time, money, and impediments of all kinds, from squalls and calms to rotten masts and sprung spars, simply detestable. I hope you will be interested to hear of two volumes on the wing. The cruise itself, you are to know, will make a big volume with appendices; some of it will first appear as (what they call) letters in some of M'Clure's papers. I believe the book when ready will have a fair measure of serious interest: I have had great fortune in finding old songs and ballads and stories, for instance, and have many singular instances of life in the last few years among these islands. 1889 ÆT. 39

The second volume is of ballads. You know *Ticonderoga*. I have written another: *The Feast of Famine*, a Marquesan story. A third is half done: *The Song of Rahéro*, a genuine Tahitian legend. A fourth dances before me. A Hawaiian fellow this, *The Priest's Drought*, or some such name. If, as I half suspect, I get enough subjects out of the islands, *Ticonderoga* shall be suppressed, and we 'll call the volume *South Sea Ballads*. In health, spirits, renewed interest in life, and, I do believe, refreshed capacity for work, the cruise has proved a wise folly. Still we 're not home, and (although the friend of a crowned head) are penniless upon these (as one of my correspondents used to call them) "lovely but *fatil* islands." By the way, who wrote *The Lion of the Nile?* My dear sir, that is Something Like. Overdone in bits, it has a true thought and a true ring of language. Beg the anonymous from me, to delete (when he shall republish) the two last verses, and end on "the lion of the Nile." One Lampman has a good sonnet on a "Winter Even-

1889 ÆT. 39 ing" in, I think, the same number: he seems ill named, but I am tempted to hope a man is not always answerable for his name.[1] For instance, you would think you knew mine. No such matter. It is—at your service and Mr. Scribner's and that of all of the faithful—Teriitera (pray pronounce Tayree-Tayra) or (*gallicé*) Téri-téra.

R. L. S.

More when the mail shall come.

I am an idiot. I want to be clear on one point. Some of Hole's drawings must of course be too late; and yet they seem to me so excellent I would fain have the lot complete. It is one thing for you to pay for drawings which are to appear in that soul-swallowing machine, your magazine: quite another if they are only to illustrate a volume. I wish you to take a brisk (even a fiery) decision on the point; and let Hole know. To resume my desultory song, I desire you would carry the same fire (hereinbefore suggested) into your decision on *The Wrong Box;* for in my present state of benighted ignorance as to my affairs for the last seven months—I know not even whether my house or my mother's house have been let—I desire to see something definite in front of me—outside the lot of palace doorkeeper. I believe the said *Wrong Box* is a real lark; in which, of course, I may be grievously deceived; but the typewriter is with me. I may also be deceived as to the numbers of *The Master* now going and already gone; but to me they seem First Chop, sir, First Chop. I hope I shall pull off that damned ending; but it still

[1] This is the Canadian poet Mr. Archibald Lampman, the news of whose death reaches England as these sheets are preparing for the press.

depresses me: this is your doing, Mr. Burlingame: you would have it there and then, and I fear it—I fear that ending. R. L. S. 1889 ÆT. 39

To Charles Baxter

Honolulu, *February 8th, 1889.*

My dear Charles,—Here we are at Honolulu, and have dismissed the yacht, and lie here till April anyway, in a fine state of haze, which I am yet in hopes some letter of yours (still on the way) may dissipate. No money, and not one word as to money! However, I have got the yacht paid off in triumph, I think; and though we stay here impignorate, it should not be for long, even if you bring us no extra help from home. The cruise has been a great success, both as to matter, fun, and health; and yet, Lord, man! we 're pleased to be ashore! Yon was a very fine voyage from Tahiti up here, but—the dry land 's a fine place too, and we don't mind squalls any longer, and eh, man, that 's a great thing. Blow, blow, thou wintry wind, thou hast done me no appreciable harm beyond a few grey hairs! Altogether, this foolhardy venture is achieved; and if I have but nine months of life and any kind of health, I shall have both eaten my cake and got it back again with usury. But, man, there have been days when I felt guilty, and thought I was in no position for the head of a house.

Your letter and accounts are doubtless at S. F., and will reach me in course. My wife is no great shakes; she is the one who has suffered most. My mother has had a Huge Old Time; Lloyd is first chop; I so well

1889 ÆT. 39 that I do not know myself—sea-bathing, if you please, and what is far more dangerous, entertaining and being entertained by His Majesty here, who is a very fine intelligent fellow, but O, Charles! what a crop for the drink! He carries it too like a mountain with a sparrow on its shoulders. We calculated five bottles of champagne in three hours and a half (afternoon), and the sovereign quite presentable, although perceptibly more dignified at the end. . . .

The extraordinary health I enjoy and variety of interests I find among these islands would tempt me to remain here; only for Lloyd, who is not well placed in such countries for a permanency; and a little for Colvin, to whom I feel I owe a sort of filial duty. And these two considerations will no doubt bring me back — to go to bed again—in England.—Yours ever affectionately,

R. L. S.

TO R. A. M. STEVENSON

HONOLULU, HAWAIIAN ISLANDS, *February, 1889.*

MY DEAR BOB, — My extremely foolhardy venture is practically over. How foolhardy it was I don't think I realised. We had a very small schooner, and, like most yachts, over-rigged and over-sparred, and like many American yachts on a very dangerous sail plan. The waters we sailed in are, of course, entirely unlighted, and very badly charted; in the Dangerous Archipelago, through which we were fools enough to go, we were perfectly in ignorance of where we were for a whole night and half the next day, and this in the midst of invisible islands and rapid and variable currents; and we were lucky when we found our whereabouts at last. We have twice had all we wanted in the way of squalls: once, as I came on deck, I found the green sea over the cockpit coamings and running down the companion like a brook to meet me; at that same moment the foresail sheet jammed and the captain had no knife; this was the only occasion on the cruise that ever I set a hand to a rope, but I worked like a Trojan, judging the possibility of hæmorrhage better than the certainty of drowning. Another time I saw a rather singular thing: our whole ship's company as pale as paper from the captain to the cook; we had a black squall astern on the port side and a white squall ahead to starboard; the complication passed off innocuous, the black squall only fetching us with its tail, and the white one slewing off somewhere else. Twice we were a long while (days) in the close vicinity of hurricane weather, but again luck prevailed, and we saw none of it. These are dangers incident to these seas and small craft. What was an amazement, and at the same time a powerful stroke of luck, both our masts were rotten, and we found it out —I was going to say in time, but it was stranger and luckier than that. The head of the mainmast hung over so that hands were afraid to go to the helm; and less than three weeks before—I am not sure it was more than a fortnight—we had been nearly twelve hours beating off the lee shore of Eimeo (or Moorea, next island to Tahiti) in half a gale of wind with a violent head sea: she would neither tack nor wear once, and had to be boxed off with the mainsail—you can imagine what an ungodly show of kites we carried—

1889 ÆT. 39 and yet the mast stood. The very day after that, in the southern bight of Tahiti, we had a near squeak, the wind suddenly coming calm; the reefs were close in with, my eye! what a surf! The pilot thought we were gone, and the captain had a boat cleared, when a lucky squall came to our rescue. My wife, hearing the order given about the boats, remarked to my mother, "Is n't that nice? We shall soon be ashore!" Thus does the female mind unconsciously skirt along the verge of eternity. Our voyage up here was most disastrous—calms, squalls, head sea, waterspouts of rain, hurricane weather all about, and we in the midst of the hurricane season, when even the hopeful builder and owner of the yacht had pronounced these seas unfit for her. We ran out of food, and were quite given up for lost in Honolulu: people had ceased to speak to Belle[1] about the *Casco,* as a deadly subject.

But the perils of the deep were part of the programme; and though I am very glad to be done with them for a while and comfortably ashore, where a squall does not matter a snuff to any one, I feel pretty sure I shall want to get to sea again ere long. The dreadful risk I took was financial, and double-headed. First, I had to sink a lot of money in the cruise, and if I did n't get health, how was I to get it back? I have got health to a wonderful extent; and as I have the most interesting matter for my book, bar accidents, I ought to get all I have laid out and a profit. But, second (what I own I never consider till too late), there

[1] Stevenson's stepdaughter, Mrs. Strong, who was at this time living at Honolulu, and joined his party and family for good when they continued their voyage from thence in the following June.

was the danger of collisions, of damages and heavy repairs, of disablement, towing, and salvage; indeed, the cruise might have turned round and cost me double. Nor will this danger be quite over till I hear the yacht is in San Francisco; for though I have shaken the dust of her deck from my feet, I fear (as a point of law) she is still mine till she gets there.

From my point of view, up to now the cruise has been a wonderful success. I never knew the world was so amusing. On the last voyage we had grown so used to sea-life that no one wearied, though it lasted a full month, except Fanny, who is always ill. All the time our visits to the islands have been more like dreams than realities: the people, the life, the beachcombers, the old stories and songs I have picked up, so interesting; the climate, the scenery, and (in some places) the women, so beautiful. The women are handsomest in Tahiti, the men in the Marquesas; both as fine types as can be imagined. Lloyd reminds me, I have not told you one characteristic incident of the cruise from a semi-naval point of view. One night we were going ashore in Anaho Bay; the most awful noise on deck; the breakers distinctly audible in the cabin; and there I had to sit below, entertaining in my best style a negroid native chieftain, much the worse for rum! You can imagine the evening's pleasure.

This naval report on cruising in the South Seas would be incomplete without one other trait. On our voyage up here I came one day into the dining-room, the hatch in the floor was open, the ship's boy was below with a baler, and two of the hands were carry-

1889 ÆT. 39 ing buckets as for a fire; this meant that the pumps had ceased working.

One stirring day was that in which we sighted Hawaii It blew fair, but very strong; we carried jib, foresail, and mainsail, all single-reefed, and she carried her lee rail under water and flew. The swell, the heaviest I have ever been out in — I tried in vain to estimate the height, *at least* fifteen feet — came tearing after us about a point and a half off the wind. We had the best hand — old Louis — at the wheel; and, really, he did nobly, and had noble luck, for it never caught us once. At times it seemed we must have it; Louis would look over his shoulder with the queerest look and dive down his neck into his shoulders; and then it missed us somehow, and only sprays came over our quarter, turning the little outside lane of deck into a mill race as deep as to the cockpit coamings. I never remember anything more delightful and exciting. Pretty soon after we were lying absolutely becalmed under the lee of Hawaii, of which we had been warned: and the captain never confessed he had done it on purpose, but when accused, he smiled. Really, I suppose he did quite right, for we stood committed to a dangerous race, and to bring her to the wind would have been rather a heart-sickening manœuvre.

R. L. S.

To Marcel Schwob

At Honolulu, Stevenson found awaiting him, among the accumulations of the mail-bag, two letters of friendly homage—the first, I think, he had received from any foreign *confrère*—addressed to him by a distinguished young French scholar and man of letters, M. Marcel Schwob.

HONOLULU, SANDWICH ISLANDS, 1889
February 8th, 1889. ÆT. 39

DEAR SIR,—I thank you—from the midst of such a flurry as you can imagine, with seven months' accumulated correspondence on my table—for your two friendly and clever letters. Pray write me again. I shall be home in May or June, and not improbably shall come to Paris in the summer. Then we can talk; or in the interval I may be able to write, which is to-day out of the question. Pray take a word from a man of crushing occupations, and count it as a volume. Your little *conte* is delightful. Ah yes, you are right, I love the eighteenth century; and so do you, and have not listened to its voice in vain.—The Hunted One, ROBERT LOUIS STEVENSON.

TO CHARLES BAXTER

HONOLULU, *8th March, 1889.*

MY DEAR CHARLES,—At last I have the accounts: the Doer has done excellently, and in the words of ——, "I reciprocate every step of your behaviour." . . . I send a letter for Bob in your care, as I don't know his Liverpool address, by which (for he is to show you part of it) you will see we have got out of this adventure—or hope to have—with wonderful fortune. I have the retrospective horrors on me when I think of the liabilities I incurred; but, thank God, I think I'm in port again, and I have found one climate in which I can enjoy life. Even Honolulu is too cold for me; but

1889 ÆT. 39 the south isles were a heaven upon earth to a puir, catarrhal party like Johns'one. We think, as Tahiti is too complete a banishment, to try Madeira. It 's only a week from England, good communications, and I suspect in climate and scenery not unlike our dear islands; in people, alas! there can be no comparison. But friends could go, and I could come in summer, so I should not be quite cut off.

Lloyd and I have finished a story, *The Wrong Box*. If it is not funny, I am sure I do not know what is. I have split over writing it. Since I have been here, I have been toiling like a galley slave: three numbers of *The Master* to rewrite, five chapters of *The Wrong Box* to write and rewrite, and about five hundred lines of a narrative poem to write, rewrite, and re-rewrite. Now I have *The Master* waiting me for its continuation, two numbers more; when that 's done, I shall breathe. This spasm of activity has been chequered with champagne parties: Happy and Glorious, Hawaii Ponoi paua: kou moi—(Native Hawaiians, dote upon your monarch!) Hawaiian God save the King. (In addition to my other labours, I am learning the language with a native moonshee.) Kalakaua is a terrible companion; a bottle of fizz is like a glass of sherry to him; he thinks nothing of five or six in an afternoon as a whet for dinner. You should see a photograph of our party after an afternoon with H. H. M.: my! what a crew!—Yours ever affectionately,

ROBERT LOUIS STEVENSON.

To Henry James

Honolulu [*March, 1889*].

MY DEAR JAMES,—Yes—I own up—I am untrue to friendship and (what is less, but still considerable) to civilisation. I am not coming home for another year. There it is, cold and bald, and now you won't believe in me at all, and serve me right (says you) and the devil take me. But look here, and judge me tenderly. I have had more fun and pleasure of my life these past months than ever before, and more health than any time in ten long years. And even here in Honolulu I have withered in the cold; and this precious deep is filled with islands, which we may still visit; and though the sea is a deathful place, I like to be there, and like squalls (when they are over); and to draw near to a new island, I cannot say how much I like. In short, I take another year of this sort of life, and mean to try to work down among the poisoned arrows, and mean (if it may be) to come back again when the thing is through, and converse with Henry James as heretofore; and in the meanwhile issue directions to H. J. to write to me once more. Let him address here at Honolulu, for my views are vague; and if it is sent here it will follow and find me, if I am to be found; and if I am not to be found, the man James will have done his duty, and we shall be at the bottom of the sea, where no post-office clerk can be expected to discover us, or languishing on a coral island, the philosophic drudges of some barbarian potentate: perchance, of an American Missionary. My wife has just sent to Mrs. Sitwell a translation (*tant bien que mal*) of a letter

1889 ÆT. 39 I have had from my chief friend in this part of the world: go and see her, and get a hearing of it; it will do you good; it is a better method of correspondence than even Henry James's.[1] I jest, but seriously it is a strange thing for a tough, sick middle-aged scrivener like R. L. S. to receive a letter so conceived from a man fifty years old, a leading politician, a crack orator, and the great wit of his village: boldly say, "the highly popular M. P. of Tautira." My nineteenth century strikes here, and lies alongside of something beautiful and ancient. I think the receipt of such a letter might humble, shall I say even ——? and for me, I would rather have received it than written *Redgauntlet* or the *Sixth Æneid.* All told, if my books have enabled or helped me to make this voyage, to know Rui, and to have received such a letter, they have (in the old pref-

[1] The following is the letter in question:—

"I make you to know my great affection. At the hour when you left us, I was filled with tears; my wife, Rui Telime, also, and all of my household. When you embarked I felt a great sorrow. It is for this that I went upon the road, and you looked from that ship, and I looked at you on the ship with great grief until you had raised the anchor and hoisted the sails. When the ship started I ran along the beach to see you still; and when you were on the open sea I cried out to you, 'Farewell, Louis'; and when I was coming back to my house I seemed to hear your voice crying, 'Rui, farewell.' Afterwards I watched the ship as long as I could until the night fell; and when it was dark I said to myself, 'If I had wings I should fly to the ship to meet you, and to sleep amongst you, so that I might be able to come back to shore and to tell Rui Telime, "I have slept upon the ship of Teriitera."' After that we passed that night in the impatience of grief. Towards eight o'clock I seemed to hear your voice, 'Teriitera—Rui—here is the hour for *putter* and *tiro*' [cheese and syrup]. I did not sleep that night, thinking continually of you, my very dear friend, until the

atorial expression) not been writ in vain. It would seem from this that I have been not so much humbled as puffed up; but, I assure you, I have in fact been both. A little of what that letter says is my own earning; not all, but yet a little; and the little makes me proud, and all the rest ashamed; and in the contrast, how much more beautiful altogether is the ancient man than him of to-day! 1889 ÆT. 39

Well, well, Henry James is pretty good, though he *is* of the nineteenth century, and that glaringly. And to curry favour with him, I wish I could be more explicit; but, indeed, I am still of necessity extremely vague, and cannot tell what I am to do, nor where I am to go for some while yet. As soon as I am sure, you shall hear. All are fairly well — the wife, your countrywoman, least of all; troubles are not entirely wanting; but on the whole we prosper, and we are all affectionately yours,

ROBERT LOUIS STEVENSON.

morning; being then still awake, I went to see Tapina Tutu on her bed, and alas, she was not there. Afterwards I looked into your rooms; they did not please me as they used to do. I did not hear your voice saying, 'Hail Rui'; I thought then that you had gone, and that you had left me. Rising up, I went to the beach to see your ship, and I could not see it. I wept, then, until the night, telling myself continually, 'Teriitera returns into his own country and leaves his dear Rui in grief, so that I suffer for him, and weep for him.' I will not forget you in my memory. Here is the thought: I desire to meet you again. It is my dear Teriitera makes the only riches I desire in this world. It is your eyes that I desire to see again. It must be that your body and my body shall eat together at one table: there is what would make my heart content. But now we are separated. May God be with you all. May His word and His mercy go with you, so that you may be well and we also, according to the words of Paul.

"ORI A ORI, that is to say, RUI."

1889
ÆT. 39

To Sidney Colvin

[Honolulu, *April 2nd, 1889.*]

MY DEAR COLVIN,—I am beginning to be ashamed of writing on to you without the least acknowledgment, like a tramp; but I do not care—I am hardened; and whatever be the cause of your silence, I mean to write till all is blue. I am outright ashamed of my news, which is that we are not coming home for another year. I cannot but hope it may continue the vast improvement of my health: I think it good for Fanny and Lloyd; and we have all a taste for this wandering and dangerous life. My mother I send home, to my relief, as this part of our cruise will be (if we can carry it out) rather difficult in places. Here is the idea: about the middle of June (unless the Boston Board objects) we sail from Honolulu in the missionary ship (barquentine auxiliary steamer) *Morning Star:* she takes us through the Gilberts and Marshalls, and drops us (this is my great idea) on Ponape, one of the volcanic islands of the Carolines. Here we stay marooned among a doubtful population, with a Spanish vice-governor and five native kings, and a sprinkling of missionaries all at loggerheads, on the chance of fetching a passage to Sydney in a trader, a labour ship, or (maybe, but this appears too bright) a ship of war. If we can't get the *Morning Star* (and the Board has many reasons that I can see for refusing its permission) I mean to try to fetch Fiji, hire a schooner there, do the Fijis and Friendlies, hit the course of the *Richmond* at Tonga Tabu, make back by Tahiti, and so to S. F., and home: perhaps in

June, 1890. For the latter part of the cruise will likely be the same in either case. You can see for yourself how much variety and adventure this promises, and that it is not devoid of danger at the best; but if we can pull it off in safety gives me a fine book of travel, and Lloyd a fine lecture and diorama, which should vastly better our finances. 1889 ÆT. 39

I feel as if I were untrue to friendship; believe me, Colvin, when I look forward to this absence of another year, my conscience sinks at thought of the Monument; but I think you will pardon me if you consider how much this tropical weather mends my health. Remember me as I was at home, and think of me sea-bathing and walking about, as jolly as a sandboy: you will own the temptation is strong; and as the scheme, bar fatal accidents, is bound to pay into the bargain, sooner or later, it seems it would be madness to come home now, with an imperfect book, no illustrations to speak of, no diorama, and perhaps fall sick again by autumn. I do not think I delude myself when I say the tendency to catarrh has visibly diminished.

It is a singular thing that as I was packing up old papers ere I left Skerryvore, I came on the prophecies of a drunken Highland sibyl, when I was seventeen. She said I was to be very happy, to visit America, and *to be much upon the sea.* It seems as if it were coming true with a vengeance. Also, do you remember my strong, old, rooted belief that I shall die by drowning? I don't want that to come true, though it is an easy death; but it occurs to me oddly, with these long chances in front. I cannot say why I like the sea; no man is more cynically and constantly alive to its perils; I regard it as the

1889 highest form of gambling; and yet I love the sea as
ÆT. 39 much as I hate gambling. Fine, clean emotions; a world all and always beautiful; air better than wine; interest unflagging: there is upon the whole no better life.—Yours ever, R. L. S.

To E. L. Burlingame

Honolulu [*April, 1889*].

MY DEAR BURLINGAME,—This is to announce the most prodigious change of programme. I have seen so much of the South Seas that I desire to see more, and I get so much health here that I dread a return to our vile climates. I have applied accordingly to the missionary folk to let me go round in the *Morning Star;* and if the Boston Board should refuse, I shall get somehow to Fiji, hire a trading schooner, and see the Fijis and Friendlies and Samoa. He would be a South Seayer, Mr. Burlingame. Of course, if I go in the *Morning Star,* I see all the eastern (or western?) islands.

Before I sail, I shall make out to let you have the last of *The Master:* though I tell you it sticks!—and I hope to have had some proofs forbye, of the verses anyway. And now to business.

I want (if you can find them) in the British sixpenny edition, if not, in some equally compact and portable shape—Seaside Library, for instance—the Waverley Novels entire, or as entire as you can get 'em, and the following of Marryat: *Phantom Ship, Peter Simple, Percival Keene, Privateersman, Children of the New Forest, Frank Mildmay, Newton Forster, Dog Fiend* (*Snarleyow*). Also *Midshipman Easy, Kingsburn,* Carlyle's *French Revolution,* Motley's *Dutch Republic,* Lang's *Letters on Literature,* a complete set of my works, *Jenkin,* in duplicate; also *Familiar Studies,* ditto. 1889 ÆT. 39

I have to thank you for the accounts, which are satisfactory indeed, and for the cheque for $1000. Another account will have come and gone before I see you. I hope it will be equally roseate in colour. I am quite worked out, and this cursed end of *The Master* hangs over me like the arm of the gallows; but it is always darkest before dawn, and no doubt the clouds will soon rise; but it is a difficult thing to write, above all in Mackellarese; and I cannot yet see my way clear. If I pull this off, *The Master* will be a pretty good novel or I am the more deceived; and even if I don't pull it off, it 'll still have some stuff in it.

We shall remain here until the middle of June anyway; but my mother leaves for Europe early in May. Hence our mail should continue to come here; but not hers. I will let you know my next address, which will probably be Sydney. If we get on the *Morning Star,* I propose at present to get marooned on Ponape, and take my chance of getting a passage to Australia. It will leave times and seasons mighty vague, and the cruise is risky; but I shall know something of the South Seas when it is done, or else the South Seas will contain all there is of me. It should give me a fine book of travels, anyway.

Low will probably come and ask some dollars of you. Pray let him have them, they are for outfit. O, another complete set of my books should go to Captain A. H. Otis, care of Dr. Merritt, Yacht *Casco,* Oakland, Cal. —In haste, R. L. S.

1889
ÆT. 39

To Miss Adelaide Boodle

HONOLULU, *April 6th, 1889.*

MY DEAR MISS BOODLE,—Nobody writes a better letter than my Gamekeeper: so gay, so pleasant, so engagingly particular, answering (by some delicate instinct) all the questions she suggests. It is a shame you should get such a poor return as I can make, from a mind essentially and originally incapable of the art epistolary. I would let the paper-cutter take my place; but I am sorry to say the little wooden seaman did after the manner of seamen, and deserted in the Societies. The place he seems to have stayed at—seems, for his absence was not observed till we were near the Equator—was Tautira, and, I assure you, he displayed good taste, Tautira being as "nigh hand heaven" as a paper-cutter or anybody has a right to expect.

I think all our friends will be very angry with us, and I give the grounds of their probable displeasure bluntly—we are not coming home for another year. My mother returns next month. Fanny, Lloyd, and I push on again among the islands on a trading schooner, the *Equator*—first for the Gilbert group, which we shall have an opportunity to explore thoroughly; then, if occasion serve, to the Marshalls and Carolines; and if occasion (or money) fail, to Samoa, and back to Tahiti. I own we are deserters, but we have excuses. You cannot conceive how these climates agree with the wretched house-plant of Skerryvore: he wonders to find himself sea-bathing, and cutting about the world loose, like a grown-up person. They agree with Fanny too, who does not suffer from her rheumatism, and with Lloyd also. And the interest of the islands is endless; and the sea, though I own it is a fearsome place, is very delightful. We had applied for places in the American missionary ship, the *Morning Star*, but this trading schooner is a far preferable idea, giving us more time and a thousandfold more liberty; so we determined to cut off the missionaries with a shilling.

The Sandwich Islands do not interest us very much; we live here, oppressed with civilisation, and look for good things in the future. But it would surprise you if you came out to-night from Honolulu (all shining with electric lights, and all in a bustle from the arrival of the mail, which is to carry you these lines) and crossed the long wooden causeway along the beach, and came out on the road through Kapiolani park, and seeing a gate in the palings, with a tub of gold-fish by the wayside, entered casually in. The buildings stand in three groups by the edge of the beach, where an angry little spitfire sea continually spirts and thrashes with impotent irascibility, the big seas breaking further out upon the reef. The first is a small house, with a very large summer parlour, or *lanai*, as they call it here, roofed, but practically open. There you will find the lamps burning and the family sitting about the table, dinner just done: my mother, my wife, Lloyd, Belle, my wife's daughter, Austin her child, and to-night (by way of rarity) a guest. All about the walls our South Sea curiosities, war clubs, idols, pearl shells, stone axes, etc.; and the walls are only a small part of a lanai, the rest being glazed or latticed windows, or mere open

1889
ÆT. 39
space. You will see there no sign of the Squire, however; and being a person of a humane disposition, you will only glance in over the balcony railing at the merrymakers in the summer parlour, and proceed further afield after the Exile. You look round, there is beautiful green turf, many trees of an outlandish sort that drop thorns — look out if your feet are bare; but I beg your pardon, you have not been long enough in the South Seas — and many oleanders in full flower. The next group of buildings is ramshackle, and quite dark; you make out a coach-house door, and look in — only some cocoanuts; you try round to the left and come to the sea front, where Venus and the moon are making luminous tracks on the water, and a great swell rolls and shines on the outer reef; and here is another door — all these places open from the outside — and you go in, and find photography, tubs of water, negatives steeping, a tap, and a chair and an inkbottle, where my wife is supposed to write; round a little further, a third door, entering which you find a picture upon the easel and a table sticky with paints; a fourth door admits you to a sort of court, where there is a hen sitting — I believe on a fallacious egg. No sign of the Squire in all this. But right opposite the studio door you have observed a third little house, from whose open door lamplight streams and makes hay of the strong moonlight shadows. You had supposed it made no part of the grounds, for a fence runs round it lined with oleander; but as the Squire is nowhere else, is it not just possible he may be here? It is a grim little wooden shanty; cobwebs bedeck it; friendly mice inhabit its recesses; the mailed cockroach walks upon the wall; so

also, I regret to say, the scorpion. Herein are two pallet beds, two mosquito curtains, strung to the pitch-boards of the roof, two tables laden with books and manuscripts, three chairs, and, in one of the beds, the Squire busy writing to yourself, as it chances, and just at this moment somewhat bitten by mosquitoes. He has just set fire to the insect powder, and will be all right in no time; but just now he contemplates large white blisters, and would like to scratch them, but knows better. The house is not bare; it has been inhabited by Kanakas, and—you know what children are!—the bare wood walls are pasted over with pages from the *Graphic*, *Harper's Weekly*, etc. The floor is matted, and I am bound to say the matting is filthy. There are two windows and two doors, one of which is condemned; on the panels of that last a sheet of paper is pinned up, and covered with writing. I cull a few plums:— 1889 ÆT. 39

"A duck-hammock for each person.
A patent organ like the commandant's at Taiohae.
Cheap and bad cigars for presents.
Revolvers.
Permanganate of potass.
Liniment for the head and sulphur.
Fine-tooth comb."

What do you think this is? Simply life in the South Seas foreshortened. These are a few of our desiderata for the next trip, which we jot down as they occur.

There, I have really done my best and tried to send something like a letter—one letter in return for all your dozens. Pray remember us all to yourself, Mrs. Boodle, and the rest of your house. I do hope your mother will be better when this comes. I shall write and give you a

1889 ÆT. 39 new address when I have made up my mind as to the most probable, and I do beg you will continue to write from time to time and give us airs from home. To-morrow—think of it—I must be off by a quarter to eight to drive into the palace and breakfast with his Hawaiian Majesty at 8.30: I shall be dead indeed. Please give my news to Scott, I trust he is better; give him my warm regards. To you we all send all kinds of things, and I am the absentee Squire,

ROBERT LOUIS STEVENSON.

TO CHARLES BAXTER

HONOLULU, *April, 1889.*

MY DEAR CHARLES,—As usual, your letter is as good as a cordial, and I thank you for it, and all your care, kindness, and generous and thoughtful friendship, from my heart. I was truly glad to hear a word of Colvin, whose long silence has terrified me; and glad to hear that you condoned the notion of my staying longer in the South Seas, for I have decided in that sense. The first idea was to go in the *Morning Star*, missionary ship; but now I have found a trading schooner, the *Equator*, which is to call for me here early in June and carry us through the Gilberts. What will happen then, the Lord knows. My mother does not accompany us: she leaves here for home early in May, and you will hear of us from her; but not, I imagine, anything more definite. We shall get dumped on Butaritari, and whether we manage to go on to the Marshalls and Carolines, or whether we fall back on Samoa, Heaven must decide; but I mean to fetch back into the course of the *Richmond*— (to think you don't know what the *Richmond* is!—*the* steamer of the Eastern South Seas, joining New Zealand, Tongatabu, the Samoas, Taheite, and Raratonga, and carrying by last advices sheep in the saloon!)—into the course of the *Richmond* and make Taheite again on the home track. Would I like to see the *Scots Observer?* Would n't I not? But whaur? I 'm direckit at space. They have nae post-offishes at the Gilberts, and as for the Car'lines! Ye see, Mr. Baxter, we 're no just in the punkshewal *centre* o' civ'lisation. But pile them up for me, and when I 've decided on an address, I 'll let you ken, and ye 'll can send them stavin' after me.—Ever your affectionate R. L. S. 1889 ÆT. 39

To Charles Baxter

The reference in the first paragraph is to the publication in the press, which Mr. Baxter had permitted, of one of Stevenson's letters written during the earlier part of his voyage. R. L. S. had remonstrated, always greatly disliking the publication of private letters during the writer's lifetime; and now writes to soften the effect of his remonstrance.

Honolulu, *10th May, 1889.*

My dear Charles,—I am appalled to gather from your last just to hand that you have felt so much concern about the letter. Pray dismiss it from your mind. But I think you scarce appreciate how disagreeable it is to have your private affairs and private unguarded expressions getting into print. It would soon sicken any one of writing letters. I have no doubt that letter was very

1889 ÆT. 39 wisely selected, but it just shows how things crop up. There was a raging jealousy between the two yachts; our captain was nearly in a fight over it. However, no more; and whatever you think, my dear fellow, do not suppose me angry with you or ——; although I was *annoyed at the circumstance*—a very different thing. But it is difficult to conduct life by letter, and I continually feel I may be drifting into some matter of offence, in which my heart takes no part.

I must now turn to a point of business. This new cruise of ours is somewhat venturesome; and I think it needful to warn you not to be in a hurry to suppose us dead. In these ill-charted seas, it is quite on the cards we might be cast on some unvisited, or very rarely visited, island; that there we might lie for a long time, even years, unheard of; and yet turn up smiling at the hinder end. So do not let me be "rowpit" till you get some certainty we have gone to Davie Jones in a squall, or graced the feast of some barbarian in the character of Long Pig.

I have just been a week away alone on the lee coast of Hawaii, the only white creature in many miles, riding five and a half hours one day, living with a native, seeing four lepers shipped off to Molokai, hearing native causes, and giving my opinion as *amicus curiæ* as to the interpretation of a statute in English; a lovely week among God's best—at least God's sweetest works—Polynesians. It has bettered me greatly. If I could only stay there the time that remains, I could get my work done and be happy; but the care of my family keeps me in vile Honolulu, where I am always out of sorts, amidst heat and cold and cesspools and beastly *haoles.*[1] What is a haole? You are one; and so, I am sorry to say, am I. After so long a dose of whites, it was a blessing to get among Polynesians again even for a week. 1889 ÆT. 39

Well, Charles, there are waur haoles than yoursel', I 'll say that for ye; and trust before I sail I shall get another letter with more about yourself.—Ever your affectionate friend,

R. L. S.

To W. H. Low

The allusions in the latter half of this letter are to the departure for Europe of the young Hawaiian princess Kaiulani (see the poem beginning "When from her land to mine she goes," in *Songs of Travel*, and to the circumstances of the great hurricane at Apia on March 15th, 1889.

HONOLULU, (*about*) *20th May, '89.*

MY DEAR LOW,— . . . The goods have come; many daughters have done virtuously, but thou excellest them all.—I have at length finished *The Master;* it has been a sore cross to me; but now he is buried, his body's under hatches,—his soul, if there is any hell to go to, gone to hell; and I forgive him: it is harder to forgive Burlingame for having induced me to begin the publication, or myself for suffering the induction.—Yes, I think Hole has done finely; it will be one of the most adequately illustrated books of our generation; he gets the note, he tells the story—*my* story: I know only one failure—the Master standing on the beach.—You must have a letter for me at Sydney—till further

[1] The Hawaiian name for white men.

1889 ÆT. 39 notice. Remember me to Mrs. Will H., the godlike sculptor, and any of the faithful. If you want to cease to be a republican, see my little Kaiulani, as she goes through — but she is gone already. You will die a red: I wear the colours of that little royal maiden, *Nous allons chanter à la ronde, si vous voulez!* only she is not blonde by several chalks, though she is but a half-blood, and the wrong half Edinburgh Scots like mysel'. But, O Low, I love the Polynesian: this civilisation of ours is a dingy, ungentlemanly business; it drops out too much of man, and too much of that the very beauty of the poor beast: who has his beauties in spite of Zola and Co. As usual, here is a whole letter with no news: I am a bloodless, inhuman dog; and no doubt Zola is a better correspondent.—Long live your fine old English admiral — yours, I mean — the U. S. A. one at Samoa; I wept tears and loved myself and mankind when I read of him: he is not too much civilised. And there was Gordon, too; and there are others, beyond question. But if you could live, the only white folk, in a Polynesian village; and drink that warm, light *vin du pays* of human affection, and enjoy that simple dignity of all about you — I will not gush, for I am now in my fortieth year, which seems highly unjust, but there it is, Mr. Low, and the Lord enlighten your affectionate

R. L. S.

To Mrs. R. L. Stevenson

The following two letters were written during and immediately after Stevenson's trip to the noted leper settlement, the scene of Father Damien's labours, at Molokai.

KALAWAO, MOLOKAI [*May, 1889*]. 1889 ÆT. 39

DEAR FANNY,—I had a lovely sail up. Captain Cameron and Mr. Gilfillan, both born in the States, yet the first still with a strong Highland, and the second still with a strong Lowland accent, were good company; the night was warm, the victuals plain but good. Mr. Gilfillan gave me his berth, and I slept well, though I heard the sisters sick in the next state-room, poor souls. Heavy rolling woke me in the morning; I turned in all standing, so went right on the upper deck. The da, was on the peep out of a low morning bank, and we were wallowing along under stupendous cliffs. As the lights brightened, we could see certain abutments and buttresses on their front where wood clustered and grass grew brightly. But the whole brow seemed quite impassable, and my heart sank at the sight. Two thousand feet of rock making 19° (the Captain guesses) seemed quite beyond my powers. However, I had come so far; and, to tell you the truth, I was so cowed with fear and disgust that I dared not go back on the adventure in the interests of my own self-respect. Presently we came up with the leper promontory: lowland, quite bare and bleak and harsh, a little town of wooden houses, two churches, a landing-stair, all unsightly, sour, northerly, lying athwart the sunrise, with the great wall of the pali cutting the world out on the south. Our lepers were sent on the first boat, about a dozen, one poor child very horrid, one white man, leaving a large grown family behind him in Honolulu, and then into the second stepped the sisters and myself. I do not know how it would have been with me had the sisters not been there. My horror of the horri-

1889 ÆT. 39 ble is about my weakest point; but the moral loveliness at my elbow blotted all else out; and when I found that one of them was crying, poor soul, quietly under her veil, I cried a little myself; then I felt as right as a trivet, only a little crushed to be there so uselessly. I thought it was a sin and a shame she should feel unhappy; I turned round to her, and said something like this: "Ladies, God Himself is here to give you welcome. I 'm sure it is good for me to be beside you; I hope it will be blessed to me; I thank you for myself and the good you do me." It seemed to cheer her up; but indeed I had scarce said it when we were at the landing-stairs, and there was a great crowd, hundreds of (God save us!) pantomime masks in poor human flesh, waiting to receive the sisters and the new patients.

Every hand was offered: I had gloves, but I had made up my mind on the boat's voyage *not* to give my hand, that seemed less offensive than the gloves. So the sisters and I went up among that crew, and presently I got aside (for I felt I had no business there) and set off on foot across the promontory, carrying my wrap and the camera. All horror was quite gone from me: to see these dread creatures smile and look happy was beautiful. On my way through Kalaupapa I was exchanging cheerful *alohas* with the patients coming galloping over on their horses; I was stopping to gossip at house-doors; I was happy, only ashamed of myself that I was here for no good. One woman was pretty, and spoke good English, and was infinitely engaging and (in the old phrase) towardly; she thought I was the new white patient; and when she found I was only a visitor, a curious change came in her face and voice—the only sad thing—morally sad, I mean—that I met that morning. But for all that, they tell me none want to leave. Beyond Kalaupapa the houses became rare; dry stone dykes, grassy, stony land, one sick pandanus; a dreary country; from overhead in the little clinging wood shogs of the pali chirruping of birds fell; the low sun was right in my face; the trade blew pure and cool and delicious; I felt as right as ninepence, and stopped and chatted with the patients whom I still met on their horses, with not the least disgust. About half-way over, I met the superintendent (a leper) with a horse for me, and O, was n't I glad! But the horse was one of those curious, dogged, cranky brutes that always dully want to go somewhere else, and my traffic with him completed my crushing fatigue. I got to the guest-house, an empty house with several rooms, kitchen, bath, etc. There was no one there, and I let the horse go loose in the garden, lay down on the bed, and fell asleep.

Dr. Swift woke me and gave me breakfast, then I came back and slept again while he was at the dispensary, and he woke me for dinner; and I came back and slept again, and he woke me about six for supper; and then in about an hour I felt tired again, and came up to my solitary guest-house, played the flageolet, and am now writing to you. As yet, you see, I have seen nothing of the settlement, and my crushing fatigue (though I believe that was moral and a measure of my cowardice) and the doctor's opinion make me think the pali hopeless. "You don't look a strong man," said the doctor; "but are you sound?" I told him the truth; then he said it was out of the question, and if I were to get up at all, I must be carried up. But, as it seems, men as well as horses continually fall on this ascent: the doctor goes up with a change of clothes—it is plain that to be carried would in itself be very fatiguing to both mind and body; and I should then be at the beginning of thirteen miles of mountain road to be ridden against time. How should I come through? I hope you will think me right in my decision: I mean to stay, and shall not be back in Honolulu till Saturday, June first. You must all do the best you can to make ready.

Dr. Swift has a wife and an infant son, beginning to toddle and run, and they live here as composed as brick and mortar—at least the wife does, a Kentucky German, a fine enough creature, I believe, who was quite amazed at the sisters shedding tears! How strange is mankind! Gilfillan too, a good fellow I think, and far from a stupid, kept up his hard Lowland Scottish talk in the boat while the sister was covering her face; but I believe he knew, and did it (partly) in embarrassment, and part perhaps in mistaken kindness. And that was one reason, too, why I made my speech to them. Partly, too, I did it, because I was ashamed to do so, and remembered one of my golden rules, "When you are ashamed to speak, speak up at once." But, mind you, that rule is only golden with strangers; with your own folks, there are other considerations. This is a strange place to be in. A bell has been sounded at intervals while I wrote, now all is still but a musical humming of the sea, not unlike the sound of telegraph wires; the night is quite cool and pitch dark, with a small fine rain; one light over in the leper settlement, one cricket whistling in the garden, my lamp here by my bedside, and my pen cheeping between my inky fingers. 1889 ÆT. 39

Next day, lovely morning, slept all night, 80° in the shade, strong, sweet Anaho trade-wind. LOUIS.

To Sidney Colvin

[HONOLULU, *May or June, 1889.*]

MY DEAR COLVIN,—I am just home after twelve days' journey to Molokai, seven of them at the leper settlement, where I can only say that the sight of so much courage, cheerfulness, and devotion strung me too high to mind the infinite pity and horror of the sights. I used to ride over from Kalawao to Kalaupapa (about three miles across the promontory, the cliff-wall, ivied with forest and yet inaccessible from steepness, on my left), go to the Sisters' home, which is a miracle of neatness, play a game of croquet with seven leper girls (90° in the shade), get a little old-maid meal served me by the Sisters, and ride home again, tired enough, but not too tired. The girls have all dolls, and love dressing them. You who know so many ladies delicately clad, and they who know so many dressmakers, please make it known it would be an acceptable gift to send scraps for doll dressmaking to the Reverend Sister Maryanne, Bishop Home, Kalaupapa, Molokai, Hawaiian Islands.

I have seen sights that cannot be told, and heard stories that cannot be repeated: yet I never admired my poor race so much, nor (strange as it may seem) loved life more than in the settlement. A horror of moral

1889 beauty broods over the place: that 's like bad Victor
ÆT. 39 Hugo, but it is the only way I can express the sense that lived with me all these days. And this even though it was in great part Catholic, and my sympathies flew never with so much difficulty as towards Catholic virtues. The pass-book kept with heaven stirs me to anger and laughter. One of the sisters calls the place "the ticket office to heaven." Well, what is the odds? They do their darg, and do it with kindness and efficiency incredible; and we must take folk's virtues as we find them, and love the better part. Of old Damien, whose weaknesses and worse perhaps I heard fully, I think only the more. It was a European peasant: dirty, bigotted, untruthful, unwise, tricky, but superb with generosity, residual candour and fundamental good-humour: convince him he had done wrong (it might take hours of insult) and he would undo what he had done and like his corrector better. A man, with all the grime and paltriness of mankind, but a saint and hero all the more for that. The place as regards scenery is grand, gloomy, and bleak. Mighty mountain walls descending sheer along the whole face of the island into a sea unusually deep; the front of the mountain ivied and furred with clinging forest, one viridescent cliff: about half-way from east to west, the low, bare, stony promontory edged in between the cliff and the ocean; the two little towns (Kalawao and Kalaupapa) seated on either side of it, as bare almost as bathing machines upon a beach; and the population—gorgons and chimæras dire. All this tear of the nerves I bore admirably; and the day after I got away, rode twenty miles along the opposite coast and up into the mountains: they call it

twenty, I am doubtful of the figures: I should guess it nearer twelve; but let me take credit for what residents allege; and I was riding again the day after, so I need say no more about health. Honolulu does not agree with me at all: I am always out of sorts there, with slight headache, blood to the head, etc. I had a good deal of work to do and did it with miserable difficulty; and yet all the time I have been gaining strength, as you see, which is highly encouraging. By the time I am done with this cruise I shall have the material for a very singular book of travels: names of strange stories and characters, cannibals, pirates, ancient legends, old Polynesian poetry,— never was so generous a farrago. I am going down now to get the story of a shipwrecked family, who were fifteen months on an island with a murderer: there is a specimen. The Pacific is a strange place; the nineteenth century only exists there in spots: all round, it is a no man's land of the ages, a stir-about of epochs and races, barbarisms and civilisations, virtues and crimes.

It is good of you to let me stay longer, but if I had known how ill you were, I should be now on my way home. I had chartered my schooner and made all arrangements before (at last) we got definite news. I feel highly guilty; I should be back to insult and worry you a little. Our address till further notice is to be c/o R. Towns and Co., Sydney. That is final: I only got the arrangement made yesterday; but you may now publish it abroad.—Yours ever, R. L. S.

1889
ÆT. 39

To James Payn

The following was written to his old friend of *Cornhill Magazine* days, Mr. James Payn, on receiving in Hawaii news of that gentleman's ill-health and gathering deafness.

Honolulu, H. I., *June 13th, 1889.*

MY DEAR JAMES PAYN,—I get sad news of you here at my offsetting for further voyages: I wish I could say what I feel. Sure there was never any man less deserved this calamity; for I have heard you speak time and again, and I remember nothing that was unkind, nothing that was untrue, nothing that was not helpful, from your lips. It is the ill-talkers that should hear no more. God knows, I know no word of consolation; but I do feel your trouble. You are the more open to letters now; let me talk to you for two pages. I have nothing but happiness to tell; and you may bless God you are a man so sound-hearted that (even in the freshness of your calamity) I can come to you with my own good fortune unashamed and secure of sympathy. It is a good thing to be a good man, whether deaf or whether dumb; and of all our fellow craftsmen (whom yet they count a jealous race), I never knew one but gave you the name of honesty and kindness: come to think of it gravely, this is better than the finest hearing. We are all on the march to deafness, blindness, and all conceivable and fatal disabilities; we shall not all get there with a report so good. My good news is a health astonishingly reinstated. This climate; these voyagings; these landfalls at dawn; new islands peaking from the morning bank; new forested harbours; new passing alarms of squalls and surf; new interests of gentle natives,—the whole tale of my life is better to me than any poem. 1889 ÆT. 39

I am fresh just now from the leper settlement of Molokai, playing croquet with seven leper girls, sitting and yarning with old, blind, leper beachcombers in the hospital, sickened with the spectacle of abhorrent suffering and deformation amongst the patients, touched to the heart by the sight of lovely and effective virtues in their helpers: no stranger time have I ever had, nor any so moving. I do not think it a little thing to be deaf, God knows, and God defend me from the same!—but to be a leper, or one of the self-condemned, how much more awful! and yet there 's a way there also. "There are Molokais everywhere," said Mr. Dutton, Father Damien's dresser; you are but new landed in yours; and my dear and kind adviser, I wish you, with all my soul, that patience and courage which you will require. Think of me meanwhile on a trading schooner, bound for the Gilbert Islands, thereafter for the Marshalls, with a diet of fish and cocoanut before me; bound on a cruise of—well, of investigation to what islands we can reach, and to get (some day or other) to Sydney, where a letter addressed to the care of R. Towns & Co. will find me sooner or later; and if it contain any good news, whether of your welfare or the courage with which you bear the contrary, will do me good.—Yours affectionately (although so near a stranger),

ROBERT LOUIS STEVENSON.

1889
ÆT. 39

TO SIDNEY COLVIN

Stevenson and his party sailed accordingly on the trading schooner *Equator*, "on a certain bright June day in 1889," for the Gilbert Islands, a scattered group of atolls in the Western Pacific. Their expectation was to come back into civilisation again by way of the Carolines, Manila, and the China ports; but instead of this, circumstances which occurred to change the trader's course took them southwards to Samoa, where they arrived in December of the same year. Their second voyage was thus of six months' duration; in the course of it they spent two periods of about six weeks each on land, first at one and then at another of the two island capitals, Butaritari and Apemama. The following letter is the first which reached Stevenson's friends from this part of his voyage, and was written in two instalments, the first from on board the *Equator* in the lagoon of the island of Apaiang; the second, six weeks later, from the settlement on shore at Apemama, which the king, his friend Tembinoka, allowed him and his party to occupy during their stay. The account of this stay at Apemama and of the character of the king, Tembinoka, is far the most interesting and attractive part of the volume called *The South Seas* (Vol. XIX of the Thistle edition), which was the literary result — and on the whole, despite the high hopes he had built on it, an unsuccessful result — of these voyages.

SCHOONER "EQUATOR," APAIANG LAGOON,
August 22nd, 1889.

MY DEAR COLVIN,—The missionary ship is outside the reef trying (vainly) to get in; so I may have a chance to get a line off. I am glad to say I shall be home by June next for the summer, or we shall know the reason why. For God's sake be well and jolly for the meeting. I shall be, I believe, a different character from what you have seen this long while. This cruise is up to now a huge success, being interesting, pleasant, and profitable. The beachcomber is perhaps the most interesting character here; the natives are very different, on the whole, from Polynesians: they are moral, standoffish (for good reasons), and protected by a dark tongue. It is delightful to meet the few Hawaiians (mostly missionaries) that are dotted about, with their Italian *brio* and their ready friendliness. The whites are a strange lot, many of them good, kind, pleasant fellows; others quite the lowest I have ever seen even in the slums of cities. I wish I had time to narrate to you the doings and character of three white murderers (more or less proven) I have met. One, the only undoubted assassin of the lot, quite gained my affection in his big home out of a wreck, with his New Hebrides wife in her savage turban of hair and yet a perfect lady, and his three adorable little girls in Rob Roy Macgregor dresses, dancing to the hand organ, performing circus on the floor with startling effects of nudity, and curling up together on a mat to sleep, three sizes, three attitudes, three Rob Roy dresses, and six little clenched fists: the murderer meanwhile brooding and gloating over his chicks, till your whole heart went out to him; and yet his crime on the face of it was dark: disembowelling, in his own house, an old man of seventy, and him drunk.

It is lunch-time, I see, and I must close up with my warmest love to you. I wish you were here to sit upon me when required. Ah! if you were but a good sailor! I will never leave the sea, I think; it is only there that a Briton lives: my poor grandfather, it is from him I inherit the taste, I fancy, and he was round many islands in his day; but I, please God, shall beat him at that before the recall is sounded. Would you

1889 Æт. 39 be surprised to learn that I contemplate becoming a shipowner? I do, but it is a secret. Life is far better fun than people dream who fall asleep among the chimney stacks and telegraph wires.

Love to Henry James and others near.—Ever yours, my dear fellow, ROBERT LOUIS STEVENSON.

EQUATOR TOWN, APEMAMA, *October, 1889.*

No *Morning Star* came, however; and so now I try to send this to you by the schooner *J. L. Tiernan.* We have been about a month ashore, camping out in a kind of town the king set up for us: on the idea that I was really a "big chief" in England. He dines with us sometimes, and sends up a cook for a share of our meals when he does not come himself. This sounds like high living! alas, undeceive yourself. Salt junk is the mainstay; a low island, except for cocoanuts, is just the same as a ship at sea: brackish water, no supplies, and very little shelter. The king is a great character—a thorough tyrant, very much of a gentleman, a poet, a musician, a historian, or perhaps rather more a genealogist—it is strange to see him lying in his house among a lot of wives (nominal wives) writing the History of Apemama in an account-book; his description of one of his own songs, which he sang to me himself, as "about sweethearts, and trees, and the sea—and no true, all-the-same lie," seems about as compendious a definition of lyric poetry as a man could ask. Tembinoka is here the great attraction: all the rest is heat and tedium and villainous dazzle, and yet more villainous mosquitoes. We are like to be here, however, many a long week before we get away, and then whither? A strange trade this voyaging: so vague, so bound-down, so helpless. Fanny has been planting some vegetables, and we have actually onions and radishes coming up: ah, onion-despiser, were you but awhile in a low island, how your heart would leap at sight of a coster's barrow! I think I could shed tears over a dish of turnips. No doubt we shall all be glad to say farewell to low islands—I had near said for ever. They are very tame; and I begin to read up the directory, and pine for an island with a profile, a running brook, or were it only a well among the rocks. The thought of a mango came to me early this morning and set my greed on edge; but you do not know what a mango is, so——. 1889 ÆT. 39

I have been thinking a great deal of you and the Monument of late, and even tried to get my thoughts into a poem, hitherto without success. God knows how you are: I begin to weary dreadfully to see you—well, in nine months, I hope; but that seems a long time. I wonder what has befallen me too, that flimsy part of me that lives (or dwindles) in the public mind; and what has befallen *The Master*, and what kind of a Box the Merry Box has been found. It is odd to know nothing of all this. We had an old woman to do devil-work for you about a month ago, in a Chinaman's house on Apaiang (August 23rd or 24th). You should have seen the crone with a noble masculine face, like that of an old crone [*sic*], a body like a man's (naked all but the feathery female girdle), knotting cocoanut leaves and muttering spells: Fanny and I, and the good captain of the *Equator*, and the Chinaman and his native wife and sister-in-law, all squatting on

1889 ÆT. 39 the floor about the sibyl; and a crowd of dark faces watching from behind her shoulder (she sat right in the doorway) and tittering aloud with strange, appalled, embarrassed laughter at each fresh adjuration. She informed us you were in England, not travelling and now no longer sick; she promised us a fair wind the next day, and we had it, so I cherish the hope she was as right about Sidney Colvin. The shipownering has rather petered out since I last wrote, and a good many other plans beside.

Health? Fanny very so-so; I pretty right upon the whole, and getting through plenty work: I know not quite how, but it seems to me not bad and in places funny.

South Sea Yarns:

1. *The Wrecker*		R. L. S.
2. *The Pearl Fisher*	by	and
3. *The Beachcombers*		Lloyd O.

The Pearl Fisher, part done, lies in Sydney. It is *The Wrecker* we are now engaged upon: strange ways of life, I think, they set forth: things that I can scarce touch upon, or even not at all, in my travel book; and the yarns are good, I do believe. *The Pearl Fisher* is for the *New York Ledger:* the yarn is a kind of Monte Cristo one. *The Wrecker* is the least good as a story, I think; but the characters seem to me good. *The Beachcombers* is more sentimental. These three scarce touch the outskirts of the life we have been viewing; a hot-bed of strange characters and incidents: Lord, how different from Europe or the Pallid States! Farewell. Heaven knows when this will get to you. I burn to be in Sydney and have news. R. L. S.

To Sidney Colvin

The following, written in the last days of the sail southwards from the Gilberts to Samoa, contains the full plan of the *South Seas* book as it had now been conceived. The verses at the end have already been printed (*Songs of Travel*, p. 58); but I give them here with the context, as in similar instances above. The allusion to the two colossal images from the Easter Islands, which used to stand under the portico to the right hand of the visitor entering the Museum, has partly lost its point since they have been moved.

Schooner "Equator," at sea. 190 miles off Samoa.
Monday, December 2nd, 1889.

MY DEAR COLVIN,—We are just nearing the end of our long cruise. Rain, calms, squalls, bang—there 's the foretopmast gone; rain, calm, squalls, away with the staysail; more rain, more calm, more squalls; a prodigious heavy sea all the time, and the *Equator* staggering and hovering like a swallow in a storm; and the cabin, a great square, crowded with wet human beings, and the rain avalanching on the deck, and the leaks dripping everywhere: Fanny, in the midst of fifteen males, bearing up wonderfully. But such voyages are at the best a trial. We had one particularity: coming down on Winslow Reef, p. d. (position doubtful): two positions in the directory, a third (if you cared to count that) on the chart; heavy sea running, and the night due. The boats were cleared, bread put on board, and we made up our packets for a boat voyage of four or five hundred miles, and turned in, expectant of a crash. Needless to say it did not come, and no doubt we were far to leeward. If we only had twopenceworth of wind, we might be at dinner in Apia to-morrow evening; but no

1889 ÆT. 39 such luck: here we roll, dead before a light air—and that is no point of sailing at all for a fore and aft schooner—the sun blazing overhead, thermometer 88°, four degrees above what I have learned to call South Sea temperature; but for all that, land so near, and so much grief being happily astern, we are all pretty gay on board, and have been photographing and draught-playing and sky-larking like anything. I am minded to stay not very long in Samoa and confine my studies there (as far as any one can forecast) to the history of the late war. My book is now practically modelled: if I can execute what is designed, there are few better books now extant on this globe, bar the epics, and the big tragedies, and histories, and the choice lyric poetics and a novel or so—none. But it is not executed yet; and let not him that putteth on his armour, vaunt himself. At least, nobody has had such stuff; such wild stories, such beautiful scenes, such singular intimacies, such manners and traditions, so incredible a mixture of the beautiful and horrible, the savage and civilised. I will give you here some idea of the table of contents, which ought to make your mouth water. I propose to call the book *The South Seas:* it is rather a large title, but not many people have seen more of them than I, perhaps no one—certainly no one capable of using the material.

Part I. General. "Of schooners, islands, and maroons."

CHAPTER I. Marine.
" II. Contraband (smuggling, barratry, labour traffic).
" III. The Beachcomber.

1889 ÆT. 39

CHAPTER XVIII. ii. A Ride in the Forest. iii. A Law Case. iv. The City of Refuge. v. The Lepers.

" XIX. Molokai. i. A Week in the Precinct. ii. History of the Leper Settlement. iii. The Mokolii. iv. The Free Island.

Part VI. The Gilberts.

" XX. The Group. ii. Position of Woman. iii. The Missions. iv. Devil-work. v. Republics.

" XXI. Rule and Misrule on Makin. i. Butaritari, its King and Court. ii. History of Three Kings. iii. The Drink Question.

" XXII. A Butaritarian Festival.

" XXIII. The King of Apemama. i. First Impressions. ii. Equator Town and the Palace. iii. The Three Corselets.

Part VII. Samoa.

which I have not yet reached.

Even as so sketched it makes sixty chapters, not less than 300 *Cornhill* pages; and I suspect not much under 500. Samoa has yet to be accounted for: I think it will be all history, and I shall work in observations on Samoan manners, under the similar heads in other Polynesian islands. It is still possible, though unlikely, that I may add a passing visit to Fiji or Tonga, or even both; but I am growing impatient to see yourself, and I do not want to be later than June of coming to England. Anyway, you see it will be a large work, and as it will be copiously illustrated, the Lord knows what it will cost. We shall return, God willing, by Sydney, Ceylon, Suez and, I guess, Marseilles the many-masted (copyright epithet). I shall likely pause a day or two in Paris, but all that is too far ahead — although now it begins to look near — so near, and I can hear the rattle of the hansom up Endell Street, and see the gates swing back, and feel myself jump out upon the Monument steps — Hosanna! — home again. My dear fellow, now that my father is done with his troubles, and 17 Heriot Row no more than a mere shell, you and that gaunt old Monument in Bloomsbury are all that I have in view when I use the word home; some passing thoughts there may be of the rooms at Skerryvore, and the blackbirds in the chine on a May morning; but the essence is S. C. and the Museum. Suppose, by some damned accident, you were no more: well, I should return just the same, because of my mother and Lloyd, whom I now think to send to Cambridge; but all the spring would have gone out of me, and ninety per cent. of the attraction lost. I will copy for you here a copy of verses made in Apemama.

I heard the pulse of the besieging sea
Throb far away all night. I heard the wind
Fly crying, and convulse tumultuous palms.
I rose and strolled. The isle was all bright sand,
And flailing fans and shadows of the palm:
The heaven all moon, and wind, and the blind vault—
The keenest planet slain, for Venus slept.
The King, my neighbour, with his host of wives,
Slept in the precinct of the palisade:

1889
ÆT. 39

Where single, in the wind, under the moon,
Among the slumbering cabins, blazed a fire,
Sole street-lamp and the only sentinel.
To other lands and nights my fancy turned,
To London first, and chiefly to your house,
The many-pillared and the well-beloved.
There yearning fancy lighted; there again
In the upper room I lay and heard far off
The unsleeping city murmur like a shell;
The muffled tramp of the Museum guard
Once more went by me; I beheld again
Lamps vainly brighten the dispeopled street;
Again I longed for the returning morn,
The awaking traffic, the bestirring birds,
The consentaneous trill of tiny song
That weaves round monumental cornices
A passing charm of beauty: most of all,
For your light foot I wearied, and your knock
That was the glad reveillé of my day.
Lo, now, when to your task in the great house
At morning through the portico you pass,
One moment glance where, by the pillared wall,
Far-voyaging island gods, begrimed with smoke,
Sit now unworshipped, the rude monument
Of faiths forgot and races undivined;
Sit now disconsolate, remembering well
The priest, the victim, and the songful crowd,
The blaze of the blue noon, and that huge voice
Incessant, of the breakers on the shore.
As far as these from their ancestral shrine,
So far, so foreign, your divided friends
Wander, estranged in body, not in mind. R. L. S.

1889
ÆT. 39

To E. L. Burlingame

Schooner "Equator," at sea,
Wednesday, 4th December, 1889.

MY DEAR BURLINGAME,—We are now about to rise, like whales, from this long dive, and I make ready a communication which is to go to you by the first mail from Samoa. How long we shall stay in that group I cannot forecast; but it will be best still to address at Sydney, where I trust, when I shall arrive, perhaps in one month from now, more probably in two or three, to find all news.

Business.—Will you be likely to have a space in the Magazine for a serial story, which should be ready, I believe, by April, at latest by autumn? It is called *The Wrecker;* and in book form will appear as number I of *South Sea Yarns* by R. L. S. and Lloyd Osbourne. Here is the table as far as fully conceived, and indeed executed.[1] . . .

The story is founded on fact, the mystery I really believe to be insoluble; the purchase of a wreck has never been handled before, no more has San Francisco. These seem all elements of success. There is, besides, a character, Jim Pinkerton, of the advertising American, on whom we build a good deal; and some sketches of the American merchant marine, opium smuggling in Honolulu, etc. It should run to (about) three hundred pages of my MS. I would like to know if this tale smiles upon you, if you will have a vacancy, and what

[1] Table of chapter headings follows

1889 ÆT. 39 you will be willing to pay. It will of course be copyright in both the States and England. I am a little anxious to have it tried serially, as it tests the interest of the mystery.

Pleasure.—We have had a fine time in the Gilbert group, though four months on low islands, which involves low diet, is a largish order; and my wife is rather down. I am myself, up to now, a pillar of health, though our long and vile voyage of calms, squalls, cataracts of rain, sails carried away, foretopmast lost, boats cleared and packets made on the approach of a p. d. reef, etc., has cured me of salt brine, and filled me with a longing for beefsteak and mangoes not to be depicted. The interest has been immense. Old King Tembinoka of Apemama, the Napoleon of the group, poet, tyrant, altogether a man of mark, gave me the woven corselets of his grandfather, his father and his uncle, and what pleased me more, told me their singular story, then all manner of strange tales, facts and experiences for my South Sea book, which should be a Tearer, Mr. Burlingame: no one at least has had such stuff.

We are now engaged in the hell of a dead calm, the heat is cruel — it is the only time when I suffer from heat: I have nothing on but a pair of serge trousers, and a singlet without sleeves of Oxford gauze — O, yes, and a red sash about my waist; and yet as I sit here in the cabin, sweat streams from me. The rest are on deck under a bit of awning; we are not much above a hundred miles from port, and we might as well be in Kamchatka. However, I should be honest: this is the first calm I have endured without the added bane of a heavy swell, and the intoxicated blue-bottle wallowings and knockings of the helpless ship. 1889 ÆT. 39

I wonder how you liked the end of *The Master;* that was the hardest job I ever had to do; did I do it?

My wife begs to be remembered to yourself and Mrs. Burlingame. Remember all of us to all friends, particularly Low, in case I don't get a word through for him.—I am, yours very sincerely,

ROBERT LOUIS STEVENSON.

TO CHARLES BAXTER

The following was written soon after the termination of the voyage of the *Equator* and Stevenson's first landing in Samoa, where he was engaged in collecting materials for the account (then intended to be the concluding part of his great projected South Sea book) of the war and hurricane of the previous year.

SAMOA [*December, 1889*].

MY DEAR BAXTER,— . . . I cannot return until I have seen either Tonga or Fiji or both: and I must not leave here till I have finished my collections on the war—a very interesting bit of history, the truth often very hard to come at, and the search (for me) much complicated by the German tongue, from the use of which I have desisted (I suppose) these fifteen years. The last two days I have been mugging with a dictionary from five to six hours a day; besides this, I have to call upon, keep sweet, and judiciously interview all sorts of persons—English, American, German, and Samoan. It makes a hard life; above all, as after every interview I have to come and get my notes straight on the nail. I

1889 ÆT. 39 believe I should have got my facts before the end of January, when I shall make for Tonga or Fiji. I am down right in the hurricane season; but they had so bad a one last year, I don't imagine there will be much of an edition this. Say that I get to Sydney some time in April, and I shall have done well, and be in a position to write a very singular and interesting book, or rather two; for I shall begin, I think, with a separate opuscule on the Samoan Trouble, about as long as *Kidnapped*, not very interesting, but valuable—and a thing proper to be done. And then, hey! for the big South Sea book: a devil of a big one, and full of the finest sport.

This morning as I was going along to my breakfast a little before seven, reading a number of *Blackwood's Magazine*, I was startled by a soft *talofa, alii* (note for my mother: they are quite courteous here in the European style, quite unlike Tahiti) right in my ear: it was Mataafa coming from early mass in his white coat and white linen kilt, with three fellows behind him. Mataafa is the nearest thing to a hero in my history, and really a fine fellow; plenty sense, and the most dignified, quiet, gentle manners. Talking of *Blackwood*—a file of which I was lucky enough to find here in the lawyer's—Mrs. Oliphant seems in a staggering state: from *The Wrong Box* to *The Master* I scarce recognise either my critic or myself. I gather that *The Master* should do well, and at least that notice is agreeable reading. I expect to be home in June: you will have gathered that I am pretty well. In addition to my labours, I suppose I walk five or six miles a day, and almost every day I ride up and see Fanny and Lloyd, who are in a house in the bush with Ah Fu. I live in Apia for history's sake with Moors, an American trader. Day before yesterday I was arrested and fined for riding fast in the street, which made my blood bitter, as the wife of the manager of the German Firm has twice almost ridden me down, and there seems none to say her nay. The Germans have behaved pretty badly here, but not in all ways so ill as you may have gathered: they were doubtless much provoked; and if the insane Knappe had not appeared upon the scene, might have got out of the muddle with dignity. I write along without rhyme or reason, as things occur to me. 1889 ÆT. 39

I hope from my outcries about printing you do not think I want you to keep my news or letters in a Bluebeard closet. I like all friends to hear of me; they all should if I had ninety hours in the day, and strength for all of them; but you must have gathered how hard worked I am, and you will understand I go to bed a pretty tired man.

29th December [*1889*].

To-morrow (Monday, I won't swear to my day of the month; this is the Sunday between Christmas and New Year) I go up the coast with Mr. Clarke, one of the London Society missionaries, in a boat to examine schools, see Tamasese, etc. Lloyd comes to photograph. Pray Heaven we have good weather; this is the rainy season; we shall be gone four or five days; and if the rain keep off, I shall be glad of the change; if it rain, it will be beastly. This explains still further how hard pressed I am, as the mail will be gone ere I return, and I have thus lost the days I meant to write in. I

1889 ÆT. 39 have a boy, Henry, who interprets and copies for me, and is a great nuisance. He said he wished to come to me in order to learn "long explessions." Henry goes up along with us; and as I am not fond of him, he may before the trip is over hear some "stlong explessions." I am writing this on the back balcony at Moors', palms and a hill like the hill of Kinnoull looking in at me; myself lying on the floor, and (like the parties in Handel's song) "clad in robes of virgin white"; the ink is dreadful, the heat delicious, a fine going breeze in the palms, and from the other side of the house the sudden angry splash and roar of the Pacific on the reef, where the warships are still piled from last year's hurricane, some under water, one high and dry upon her side, the strangest figure of a ship was ever witnessed; the narrow bay there is full of ships; the men-of-war covered with sail after the rains, and (especially the German ship, which is fearfully and awfully top heavy) rolling almost yards in, in what appears to be calm water.

Samoa, Apia at least, is far less beautiful than the Marquesas or Tahiti: a more gentle scene, gentler acclivities, a tamer face of nature; and this much aided, for the wanderer, by the great German plantations with their countless regular avenues of palms. The island has beautiful rivers, of about the bigness of our waters in the Lothians, with pleasant pools and waterfalls and overhanging verdure, and often a great volume of sound, so that once I thought I was passing near a mill, and it was only the voice of the river. I am not specially attracted by the people; but they are courteous; the women very attractive, and dress lovely; the men purposelike, well set up, tall, lean, and dignified. As I write, the breeze is brisking up, doors are beginning to slam, and shutters; a strong draught sweeps round the balcony; it looks doubtful for to-morrow. Here I shut up.—Ever your affectionate 1890 ÆT. 40

R. L. STEVENSON.

TO DR. SCOTT

This gentleman is the physician to whose assiduous care and kindness, as recorded in the dedication to *Underwoods*, Stevenson owed so much during his invalid years at Bournemouth.

APIA, SAMOA, *January 20th, 1890.*

MY DEAR SCOTT,—Shameful indeed that you should not have heard from me before! I have now been some twenty months in the South Seas, and am (up to date) a person whom you would scarce know. I think nothing of long walks and rides: I was four hours and a half gone the other day, partly riding, partly climbing up a steep ravine. I have stood a six months' voyage on a copra schooner with about three months ashore on coral atolls, which means (except for cocoanuts to drink) no change whatever from ship's food. My wife suffered badly—it was too rough a business altogether—Lloyd suffered—and, in short, I was the only one of the party who "kept my end up."

I am so pleased with this climate that I have decided to settle; have even purchased a piece of land from three to four hundred acres, I know not which till the survey is completed, and shall only return next summer to wind up my affairs in England; thenceforth I mean to be a subject of the High Commissioner.

1890 ÆT. 40 Now you would have gone longer yet without news of your truant patient, but that I have a medical discovery to communicate. I find I can (almost immediately) fight off a cold with liquid extract of coca; two or (if obstinate) three teaspoonfuls in the day for a variable period of from one to five days sees the cold generally to the door. I find it at once produces a glow, stops rigour, and though it makes one very uncomfortable, prevents the advance of the disease. Hearing of this influenza, it occurred to me that this might prove remedial; and perhaps a stronger exhibition — injections of cocaine, for instance—still better.

If on my return I find myself let in for this epidemic, which seems highly calculated to nip me in the bud, I shall feel very much inclined to make the experiment. See what a gulf you may save me from if you shall have previously made it on *anima vili*, on some less important sufferer, and shall have found it worse than useless.

How is Miss Boodle and her family? Greeting to your brother and all friends in Bournemouth.—Yours very sincerely, ROBERT LOUIS STEVENSON.

TO CHARLES BAXTER

After a stay of four or five weeks at Apia, during which he had fallen more and more in love with Samoa and the Samoans, and bought the property on which he afterwards settled, Stevenson took steamer again, this time for Sydney, where he had ordered his letters to await him. This and the two following letters were written during the passage. I again print in their original place a set of verses which have already appeared in *Songs of Travel*.

Februar den Zen, 1890. 1890 ÆT. 40

DAMPFER "LÜBECK" ZWISCHEN APIA UND SYDNEY.

MY DEAR CHARLES,—I have got one delightful letter from you, and heard from my mother of your kindness in going to see her. Thank you for that: you can in no way more touch and serve me. . . . Ay, ay, it is sad to sell 17; sad and fine were the old days: when I was away in Apemama, I wrote two copies of verse about Edinburgh and the past, so ink black, so golden bright. I will send them, if I can find them, for they will say something to you, and indeed one is more than half addressed to you. This is it—

TO MY OLD COMRADES

Do you remember—can we e'er forget?—
How, in the coiled perplexities of youth,
In our wild climate, in our scowling town,
We gloomed and shivered, sorrowed, sobbed, and
feared?
The belching winter wind, the missile rain,
The rare and welcome silence of the snows,
The laggard morn, the haggard day, the night,
The grimy spell of the nocturnal town,
Do you remember?—Ah, could one forget!
As when the fevered sick that all night long
Listed the wind intone, and hear at last
The ever-welcome voice of the chanticleer
Sing in the bitter hour before the dawn,—
With sudden ardour, these desire the day:

(Here a squall sends all flying.)

1890
ÆT. 40

So sang in the gloom of youth the bird of hope;
So we, exulting, hearkened and desired.
For lo! as in the palace porch of life
We huddled with chimæras, from within —
How sweet to hear! — the music swelled and fell,
And through the breach of the revolving doors
What dreams of splendour blinded us and fled!
I have since then contended and rejoiced;
Amid the glories of the house of life
Profoundly entered, and the shrine beheld:
Yet when the lamp from my expiring eyes
Shall dwindle and recede, the voice of love
Fall insignificant on my closing ears,
What sound shall come but the old cry of the wind
In our inclement city? what return
But the image of the emptiness of youth,
Filled with the sound of footsteps and that voice
Of discontent and rapture and despair?
So, as in darkness, from the magic lamp,
The momentary pictures gleam and fade
And perish, and the night resurges — these
Shall I remember, and then all forget.

They 're pretty second-rate, but felt. I can't be bothered to copy the other.

I have bought 314½ acres of beautiful land in the bush behind Apia; when we get the house built, the garden laid, and cattle in the place, it will be something to fall back on for shelter and food; and if the island could stumble into political quiet, it is conceivable it might even bring a little income. . . . We range from 600 to 1500 feet, have five streams, waterfalls, precipices, profound ravines, rich tablelands, fifty head of cattle on the ground (if any one could catch them), a great view of forest, sea, mountains, the warships in the haven: really a noble place. Some day you are to take a long holiday and come and see us: it has been all planned. 1890 ÆT. 40

With all these irons in the fire, and cloudy prospects, you may be sure I was pleased to hear a good account of business. I believed *The Master* was a sure card: I wonder why Henley thinks it grimy; grim it is, God knows, but sure not grimy, else I am the more deceived. I am sorry he did not care for it; I place it on the line with *Kidnapped* myself. We 'll see as time goes on whether it goes above or falls below.

R. L. S.

To E. L. Burlingame

The editor of *Scribner's Magazine* had written asking him for fresh contributions, and he sends the set of verses afterwards reprinted in *Songs of Travel*, beginning "Let us who part like brothers part like bards."

SS. "Lübeck" [between Apia and Sydney, *February*], *1890.*

My dear Burlingame,—I desire nothing better than to continue my relation with the Magazine, to which it pleases me to hear I have been useful. The only thing I have ready is the enclosed barbaric piece. As soon as I have arrived in Sydney I shall send you some photographs, a portrait of Tembinoka, perhaps a view of the palace or of the "matted men" at their singing; also

1890 ÆT. 40 T.'s flag, which my wife designed for him: in a word, what I can do best for you. It will be thus a foretaste of my book of travels. I shall ask you to let me have, if I wish it, the use of the plates made, and to make up a little tract of the verses and illustrations, of which you might send six copies to H. M. Tembinoka, King of Apemama, *via* Butaritari, Gilbert Islands. It might be best to send it by Crawford and Co., S. F. There is no postal service; and schooners must take it, how they may and when. Perhaps some such note as this might be prefixed:

At my departure from the island of Apemama, for which you will look in vain in most atlases, the king and I agreed, since we both set up to be in the poetical way, that we should celebrate our separation in verse. Whether or not his Majesty has been true to his bargain, the laggard posts of the Pacific may perhaps inform me in six months, perhaps not before a year. The following lines represent my part of the contract, and it is hoped, by their pictures of strange manners, they may entertain a civilised audience. Nothing throughout has been invented or exaggerated; the lady herein referred to as the author's Muse, has confined herself to stringing into rhyme facts and legends that I saw or heard during two months' residence upon the island.

R. L. S.

You will have received from me a letter about *The Wrecker*. No doubt it is a new experiment for me, being disguised so much as a study of manners, and the interest turning on a mystery of the detective sort. I think there need be no hesitation about beginning it in the fall of the year. Lloyd has nearly finished his part, and I shall hope to send you very soon the MS. of about the first four-sevenths. At the same time, I have been employing myself in Samoa, collecting facts about the recent war; and I propose to write almost at once and to publish shortly a small volume, called I know not what—the War in Samoa, the Samoa Trouble, an Island War, the War of the Three Consuls, I know not—perhaps you can suggest. It was meant to be a part of my travel book; but material has accumulated on my hands until I see myself forced into volume form, and I hope it may be of use, if it come soon. I have a few photographs of the war, which will do for illustrations. It is conceivable you might wish to handle this in the Magazine, although I am inclined to think you won't, and to agree with you. But if you think otherwise, there it is. The travel letters (fifty of them) are already contracted for in papers; these I was quite bound to let M'Clure handle, as the idea was of his suggestion, and I always felt a little sore as to one trick I played him in the matter of the end-papers. The war volume will contain some very interesting and picturesque details: more I can't promise for it. Of course the fifty newspaper letters will be simply patches chosen from the travel volume (or volumes) as it gets written.

But you see I have in hand:—

Say half done.	1. *The Wrecker.*
Lloyd's copy half done, mine not touched.	2. *The Pearl Fisher* (a novel promised to the *Ledger*, and which will form, when it comes in book

1890
ÆT. 40

	form, No. 2 of our *South Sea Yarns*).
Not begun, but all material ready.	3. *The War Volume.*
Ditto.	4. *The Big Travel Book*, which includes the letters.
You know how they stand.	5. *The Ballads.*

Excusez du peu! And you see what madness it would be to make any fresh engagement. At the same time, you have *The Wrecker* and the *War Volume*, if you like either — or both — to keep my name in the Magazine.

It begins to look as if I should not be able to get any more ballads done this somewhile. I know the book would sell better if it were all ballads; and yet I am growing half tempted to fill up with some other verses. A good few are connected with my voyage, such as the *Home of Tembinoka* sent herewith, and would have a sort of slight affinity to the *South Sea Ballads.* You might tell me how that strikes a stranger.

In all this, my real interest is with the travel volume, which ought to be of a really extraordinary interest.

I am sending you *Tembinoka* as he stands; but there are parts of him that I hope to better, particularly in stanzas III. and II. I scarce feel intelligent enough to try just now; and I thought at any rate you had better see it, set it up if you think well, and let me have a proof; so, at least, we shall get the bulk of it straight. I have spared you Teñkoruti, Tenbaitcke, Tembinatake, and other barbarous names, because I thought the dentists in the States had work enough without my assistance; but my chief's name is TEMBINOKA, pronounced, according to the present quite modern habit in the Gilberts, Tembinok'. Compare in the margin Tengkorootch; a singular new trick, setting at defiance all South Sea analogy, for nowhere else do they show even the ability, far less the will, to end a word upon a consonant. Loia is Lloyd's name, ship becomes shipé, teapot, tipoté, etc. Our admirable friend Herman Melville, of whom, since I could judge, I have thought more than ever, had no ear for languages whatever: his Hapar tribe should be Hapaa, etc.

But this is of no interest to you: suffice it, you see how I am as usual up to the neck in projects, and really all likely bairns this time. When will this activity cease? Too soon for me, I dare to say. R. L. S.

TO JAMES PAYN

February 4th, 1890, SS. "LÜBECK."

MY DEAR JAMES PAYN,—In virtue of confessions in your last, you would at the present moment, if you were along of me, be sick; and I will ask you to receive that as an excuse for my hand of write. Excuse a plain seaman if he regards with scorn the likes of you pore landlubbers ashore now. (Reference to nautical ditty.) Which I may however be allowed to add that when eight months' mail was laid by my side one evening in Apia, and my wife and I sat up the most of the night to peruse the same—(precious indisposed we were

1890 ÆT. 40 next day in consequence) — no letter, out of so many, more appealed to our hearts than one from the pore, stick-in-the-mud, land-lubbering, common (or garden) Londoner, James Payn. Thank you for it; my wife says, "Can't I see him when we get back to London?" I have told her the thing appeared to me within the spear of practical politix. (Why can't I spell and write like an honest, sober, God-fearing litry gent? I think it 's the motion of the ship.) Here I was interrupted to play chess with the chief engineer; as I grow old, I prefer the "athletic sport of cribbage," of which (I am sure I misquote) I have just been reading in your delightful *Literary Recollections*. How you skim along, you and Andrew Lang (different as you are), and yet the only two who can keep a fellow smiling every page, and ever and again laughing out loud. I joke wi' deeficulty, I believe; I am not funny; and when I am, Mrs. Oliphant says I 'm vulgar, and somebody else says (in Latin) that I 'm a whore, which seems harsh and even uncalled for: I shall stick to weepers; a 5*s.* weeper, 2*s.* 6*d.* laugher, 1*s.* shocker.

My dear sir, I grow more and more idiotic; I cannot even feign sanity. Sometime in the month of June a stalwart weather-beaten man, evidently of seafaring antecedents, shall be observed wending his way between the Athenæum Club and Waterloo Place. Arrived off No. 17. he shall be observed to bring his head sharply to the wind, and tack into the outer haven. "Captain Payn in the harbour?"—"Ay, ay, sir. What ship?" —"Barquentine R. L. S., nine hundred and odd days out from the port of Bournemouth, homeward bound, with yarns and curiosities."

Who was it said, "For God's sake, don't speak of it!" about Scott and his tears? He knew what he was saying. The fear of that hour is the skeleton in all our cupboards; that hour when the pastime and the livelihood go together; and—I am getting hard of hearing myself; a pore young child of forty, but new come frae my Mammy, O! 1890 ÆT. 40

Excuse these follies, and accept the expression of all my regards.—Yours affectionately,

R. L. STEVENSON.

TO CHARLES BAXTER

Stevenson had not been long at Sydney—just long enough to write and print the famous *Letter to Dr. Hyde* in defence of Father Damien—when, to his heavy disappointment, he fell ill again with one of his old bad attacks of fever and hæmorrhage from the lungs. It was this experience which finally determined him to settle for good on his new island property in Samoa, which at first he had thought of rather as an occasional refuge and resting-place in the intervals between future projected yachting voyages.

UNION CLUB, SYDNEY, *March 7th, 1890.*

MY DEAR CHARLES,—I did not send off the enclosed before from laziness; having gone quite sick, and being a blooming prisoner here in the club, and indeed in my bedroom. I was in receipt of your letters and your ornamental photo, and was delighted to see how well you looked, and how reasonably well I stood. . . . I am sure I shall never come back home except to die; I may do it, but shall always think of the move as suicidal, unless a great change comes over me, of which as

1890 ÆT. 40 yet I see no symptom. This visit to Sydney has smashed me handsomely; and yet I made myself a prisoner here in the club upon my first arrival. This is not encouraging for further ventures; Sydney winter—or, I might almost say, Sydney spring, for I came when the worst was over—is so small an affair, comparable to our June depression at home in Scotland. . . . The pipe is right again; it was the springs that had rusted, and ought to have been oiled. Its voice is now that of an angel; but, Lord! here in the club I dare not wake it! Conceive my impatience to be in my own backwoods and raise the sound of minstrelsy. What pleasures are to be compared with those of the Unvirtuous Virtuoso?—Yours ever affectionately, the Unvirtuous Virtuoso, ROBERT LOUIS STEVENSON.

TO SIDNEY COLVIN

To try and recover from the effects of his illness at Sydney, Stevenson determined to take another voyage; and started accordingly in April with his party on a trading steamer, the *Janet Nicoll*, which took him by a long and devious course among many groups of islands that he had not yet visited, returning to Sydney in August by way of New Caledonia. On the first night out of Auckland harbour the voyage nearly came to a premature end through the blowing up of some trade fireworks, or materials for fireworks, which had been packed in the stateroom.

SS. "JANET NICOLL," OFF UPOLU [*Spring, 1890*].

MY DEAREST COLVIN,—I was sharply ill at Sydney, cut off, right out of bed, in this steamer on a fresh island cruise, and have already reaped the benefit. We are excellently found this time, on a spacious vessel, with an excellent table; the captain, supercargo, our one fellow passenger, etc., very nice; and the charterer, Mr. Henderson, the very man I could have chosen. The truth is, I fear, this life is the only one that suits me; so long as I cruise in the South Seas, I shall be well and happy — alas, no, I do not mean that, and *absit omen!*— I mean that, so soon as I cease from cruising, the nerves are strained, the decline commences, and I steer slowly but surely back to bedward. We left Sydney, had a cruel rough passage to Auckland, for the *Janet* is the worst roller I was ever aboard of. I was confined to my cabin, ports closed, self shied out of the berth, stomach (pampered till the day I left on a diet of perpetual egg-nog) revolted at ship's food and ship eating, in a frowsy bunk, clinging with one hand to the plate, with the other to the glass, and using the knife and fork (except at intervals) with the eyelid. No matter: I picked up hand over hand. After a day in Auckland, we set sail again; were blown up in the main cabin with calcium fires, as we left the bay. Let no man say I am unscientific: when I ran, on the alert, out of my state-room, and found the main cabin incarnadined with the glow of the last scene of a pantomime, I stopped dead: "What is this?" said I. "This ship is on fire, I see that; but why a pantomime?" And I stood and reasoned the point, until my head was so muddled with the fumes that I could not find the companion. A few seconds later, the captain had to enter crawling on his belly, and took days to recover (if he has recovered) from the fumes. By singular good fortune, we got the hose down in time and saved the ship, but Lloyd lost most of his clothes and a great part of our photographs

1890
ÆT. 40

1890 ÆT. 40 was destroyed. Fanny saw the native sailors tossing overboard a blazing trunk; she stopped them in time, and behold, it contained my manuscripts. Thereafter we had three (or two) days fine weather: then got into a gale of wind, with rain and a vexatious sea. As we drew into our anchorage in a bight of Savage Island, a man ashore told me afterwards the sight of the *Janet Nicoll* made him sick; and indeed it was rough play, though nothing to the night before. All through this gale I worked four to six hours per diem, spearing the ink-bottle like a flying fish, and holding my papers together as I might. For of all things, what I was at was history — the Samoan business — and I had to turn from one to another of these piles of manuscript notes, and from one page to another in each, until I should have found employment for the hands of Briareus. All the same, this history is a godsend for a voyage; I can put in time getting events co-ordinated and the narrative distributed, when my much-heaving numskull would be incapable of finish or fine style. At Savage we met the missionary barque *John Williams.* I tell you it was a great day for Savage Island: the path up the cliffs was crowded with gay islandresses (I like that feminine plural) who wrapped me in their embraces, and picked my pockets of all my tobacco, with a manner something between a whore and a child, which a touch would have made revolting, but as it was, was simply charming like the Golden Age. One pretty, little, stalwart minx, with a red flower behind her ear, had searched me with extraordinary zeal; and when, soon after, I missed my matches, I accused her (she still following us) of being the thief. After some delay, and with a subtle smile, she produced the box, gave me *one match*, and put the rest away again. Too tired to add more.—Your most affectionate R. L. S. 1890 ÆT. 40

To E. L. Burlingame

SS. "Janet Nicoll," off Peru Island,
Kingsmills Group, *July 13th, '90*.

MY DEAR BURLINGAME,—I am moved to write to you in the matter of the end papers. I am somewhat tempted to begin them again. Follow the reasons *pro* and *con*:—

1st. I must say I feel as if something in the nature of the end paper were a desirable finish to the number, and that the substitutes of occasional essays by occasional contributors somehow fail to fill the bill. Should you differ with me on this point, no more is to be said. And what follows must be regarded as lost words.

2nd. I am rather taken with the idea of continuing the work. For instance, should you have no distaste for papers of the class called *Random Memories*, I should enjoy continuing them (of course at intervals), and when they were done I have an idea they might make a readable book. On the other hand, I believe a greater freedom of choice might be taken, the subjects more varied and more briefly treated, in somewhat approaching the manner of Andrew Lang in the *Sign of the Ship;* it being well understood that the broken sticks[1] method is one not very suitable (as Colonel Burke would say) to my genius, and not very likely to be pushed far in

[1] French *bâtons rompus*: disconnected thoughts or studies.

1890 ÆT. 40 my practice. Upon this point I wish you to condense your massive brain. In the last lot I was promised, and I fondly expected to receive, a vast amount of assistance from intelligent and genial correspondents. I assure you, I never had a scratch of a pen from any one above the level of a village idiot, except once, when a lady sowed my head full of grey hairs by announcing that she was going to direct her life in future by my counsels. Will the correspondents be more copious and less irrelevant in the future? Suppose that to be the case, will they be of any use to me in my place of exile? Is it possible for a man in Samoa to be in touch with the great heart of the People? And is it not perhaps a mere folly to attempt, from so hopeless a distance, anything so delicate as a series of papers? Upon these points, perpend, and give me the results of your perpensions.

3rd. The emolument would be agreeable to your humble servant.

I have now stated all the *pros*, and the most of the *cons* are come in by the way. There follows, however, one immense Con (with a capital "C"), which I beg you to consider particularly. I fear that, to be of any use for your magazine, these papers should begin with the beginning of a volume. Even supposing my hands were free, this would be now impossible for next year. You have to consider whether, supposing you have no other objection, it would be worth while to begin the series in the middle of a volume, or desirable to delay the whole matter until the beginning of another year.

Now supposing that the *cons* have it, and you refuse

my offer, let me make another proposal, which you will be very inclined to refuse at the first off-go, but which I really believe might in time come to something. You know how the penny papers have their answers to correspondents. Why not do something of the same kind for the "culchawed"? Why not get men like Stimson, Brownell, Professor James, Goldwin Smith, and others who will occur to you more readily than to me, to put and to answer a series of questions of intellectual and general interest, until at last you should have established a certain standard of matter to be discussed in this part of the Magazine? 1890 ÆT. 40

I want you to get me bound volumes of the Magazine from its start. The Lord knows I have had enough copies; where they are I know not. A wandering author gathers no magazines.

The Wrecker is in no forrader state than in last reports. I have indeed got to a period when I cannot well go on until I can refresh myself on the proofs of the beginning. My respected collaborator, who handles the machine which is now addressing you, has indeed carried his labours farther, but not, I am led to understand, with what we used to call a blessing; at least, I have been refused a sight of his latest labours. However, there is plenty of time ahead, and I feel no anxiety about the tale, except that it may meet with your approval.

All this voyage I have been busy over my *Travels*, which, given a very high temperature and the saloon of a steamer usually going before the wind, and with the cabins in front of the engines, has come very near to prostrating me altogether. You will therefore un-

1890 derstand that there are no more poems. I wonder
ÆT. 40 whether there are already enough, and whether you think that such a volume would be worth the publishing? I shall hope to find in Sydney some expression of your opinion on this point. Living as I do among—not the most cultured of mankind ("splendidly educated and perfect gentlemen when sober")—I attach a growing importance to friendly criticisms from yourself.

I believe that this is the most of our business. As for my health, I got over my cold in a fine style, but have not been very well of late. To my unaffected annoyance, the blood-spitting has started again. I find the heat of a steamer decidedly wearing and trying in these latitudes, and I am inclined to think the superior expedition rather dearly paid for. Still, the fact that one does not even remark the coming of a squall, nor feel relief on its departure, is a mercy not to be acknowledged without gratitude. The rest of the family seem to be doing fairly well; both seem less run down than they were on the *Equator*, and Mrs. Stevenson very much less so. We have now been three months away, have visited about thirty-five islands, many of which were novel to us, and some extremely entertaining; some also were old acquaintances, and pleasant to revisit. In the meantime, we have really a capital time aboard ship, in the most pleasant and interesting society, and with (considering the length and nature of the voyage) an excellent table. Please remember us all to Mr. Scribner, the young chieftain of the house, and the lady, whose health I trust is better. To Mrs. Burlingame we all desire to be remembered, and I hope you will give our news to Low, St. Gaudens, Faxon, and others of the faithful in the city. I shall probably return to Samoa direct, having given up all idea of returning to civilisation in the meanwhile. There, on my ancestral acres, which I purchased six months ago from a blind Scots blacksmith, you will please address me until further notice. The name of the ancestral acres is going to be Vailima; but as at the present moment nobody else knows the name, except myself and the co-patentees, it will be safer, if less ambitious, to address R. L. S., Apia, Samoa. The ancestral acres run to upwards of three hundred; they enjoy the ministrations of five streams, whence the name. They are all at the present moment under a trackless covering of magnificent forest, which would be worth a great deal if it grew beside a railway terminus. To me, as it stands, it represents a handsome deficit. Obliging natives from the Cannibal Islands are now cutting it down at my expense. You would be able to run your magazine to much greater advantage if the terms of authors were on the same scale with those of my cannibals. We have also a house about the size of a manufacturer's lodge. 'T is but the egg of the future palace, over the details of which on paper Mrs. Stevenson and I have already shed real tears; what it will be when it comes to paying for it, I leave you to imagine. But if it can only be built as now intended, it will be with genuine satisfaction and a growunded pride that I shall welcome you at the steps of my Old Colonial Home, when you land from the steamer on a long-merited holiday. I speak much at my ease; yet I do not know, I may be now an outlaw, a bankrupt, the abhorred of all

1890 ÆT. 40 good men. I do not know, you probably do. Has Hyde[1] turned upon me? Have I fallen, like Danvers Carew?

It is suggested to me that you might like to know what will be my future society. Three consuls, all at loggerheads with one another, or at the best in a clique of two against one; three different sets of missionaries, not upon the best of terms; and the Catholics and Protestants in a condition of unhealable ill-feeling as to whether a wooden drum ought or ought not to be beaten to announce the time of school — the pertinacity of this dispute and the importance attached to it by the Catholics is something not to be conceived. The native population, very genteel, very songful, very agreeable, very good-looking, chronically spoiling for a fight (a circumstance not to be entirely neglected in the design of the palace). As for the white population of (technically, "The Beach"), I don't suppose it is possible for any person not thoroughly conversant with the South Seas to form the smallest conception of such a society, with its grog-shops, its apparently unemployed hangers-on, its merchants of all degrees of respectability and the reverse. The paper, of which I must really send you a copy — if yours were really a live magazine, you would have an exchange with the editor: I assure you, it has of late contained a great deal of matter about one of your contributors — rejoices in the name of *Samoa Times and South Sea Advertiser*. The advertisements in the *Advertiser* are permanent, being simply subsidies for its existence. A dashing warfare of newspaper

[1] The Rev. Dr. Hyde, of Honolulu: in reference to Stevenson's letter on Father Damien.

correspondence goes on between the various residents, who are rather fond of recurring to one another's antecedents. But when all is said, there are a lot of very nice, pleasant people, and I don't know that Apia is very much worse than half a hundred towns that I could name. ROBERT LOUIS STEVENSON. 1890 ÆT. 40

TO CHARLES BAXTER

As above indicated, on the way between Samoa and Sydney Stevenson left the *Janet Nicoll* for a week's stay in New Caledonia, during which he was hospitably received by the French officials.

HOTEL SEBASTOPOL, NOUMEA, *August, 1890.*

MY DEAR CHARLES,—I have stayed here a week while Lloyd and my wife continue to voyage in the *Janet Nicoll;* this I did, partly to see the convict system, partly to shorten my stay in the extreme cold—hear me with my extreme! *moi qui suis originaire d'Edimbourg*—of Sydney at this season. I am feeling very seedy, utterly fatigued, and overborne with sleep. I have a fine old gentleman of a doctor, who attends and cheers and entertains, if he does not cure me; but even with his ministrations I am almost incapable of the exertion sufficient for this letter; and I am really, as I write, falling down with sleep. What is necessary to say, I must try to say shortly. Lloyd goes to clear out our establishments: pray keep him in funds, if I have any; if I have not, pray try to raise them. Here is the idea: to install ourselves, at the risk of bankruptcy, in Samoa. It is not the least likely it will pay (although it may); but it is almost certain it will support life, with

1890 ÆT. 40 very few external expenses. If I die, it will be an endowment for the survivors, at least for my wife and Lloyd; and my mother, who might prefer to go home, has her own. Hence I believe I shall do well to hurry my installation. The letters are already in part done; in part done is a novel for Scribner; in the course of the next twelve months I should receive a considerable amount of money. I am aware I had intended to pay back to my capital some of this. I am now of opinion I should act foolishly. Better to build the house and have a roof and farm of my own; and thereafter, with a livelihood assured, save and repay. . . . There is my livelihood, all but books and wine, ready in a nutshell; and it ought to be more easy to save and to repay afterwards. Excellent, say you, but will you save and will you repay? I do not know, said the Bell of Old Bow. . . . It seems clear to me. . . . The deuce of the affair is that I do not know when I shall see you and Colvin. I guess you will have to come and see me: many a time already we have arranged the details of your visit in the yet unbuilt house on the mountain. I shall be able to get decent wine from Noumea. We shall be able to give you a decent welcome, and talk of old days. *Apropos* of old days, do you remember still the phrase we heard in Waterloo Place? I believe you made a piece for the piano on that phrase. Pray, if you remember it, send it me in your next. If you find it impossible to write correctly, send it me *à la recitative*, and indicate the accents. Do you feel (you must) how strangely heavy and stupid I am? I must at last give up and go sleep; I am simply a rag.

The morrow: I feel better, but still dim and groggy. To-night I go to the governor's; such a lark — no dress clothes — twenty-four hours' notice — able-bodied Polish tailor — suit made for a man with the figure of a puncheon — same hastily altered for self with the figure of a bodkin — sight inconceivable. Never mind; dress clothes, "which nobody can deny"; and the officials have been all so civil that I liked neither to refuse nor to appear in mufti. Bad dress clothes only prove you are a grisly ass; no dress clothes, even when explained, indicate a want of respect. I wish you were here with me to help me dress in this wild raiment, and to accompany me to M. Noel-Pardon's. I cannot say what I would give if there came a knock now at the door and you came in. I guess Noel-Pardon would go begging, and we might burn the fr. 200 dress clothes in the back garden for a bonfire; or what would be yet more expensive and more humorous, get them once more expanded to fit you, and when that was done, a second time cut down for my gossamer dimensions. 1890 ÆT. 40

I hope you never forget to remember me to your father who has always a place in my heart, as I hope I have a little in his. His kindness helped me infinitely when you and I were young; I recall it with gratitude and affection in this town of convicts at the world's end. There are very few things, my dear Charles, worth mention: on a retrospect of life, the day's flash and colour, one day with another, flames, dazzles, and puts to sleep; and when the days are gone, like a fast-flying thaumatrope, they make but a single pattern. Only a few things stand out; and among these — most

1890 ÆT. 40 plainly to me—Rutland Square.—Ever, my dear Charles, your affectionate friend,

ROBERT LOUIS STEVENSON.

P. S.—Just returned from trying on the dress clo'. Lord, you should see the coat! It stands out at the waist like a bustle, the flaps cross in front, the sleeves are like bags.

TO E. L. BURLINGAME

The next letter is in acknowledgment of proofs received from Messrs. Scribner of a proposed volume of verse to contain, besides *Ticonderoga* and the two ballads on Marquesan and Tahitian legends, a number of the other miscellaneous verses which he had written in the course of his travels. In the end, the ballads only stood for publication at this time; the other verses were reserved, and have been posthumously published under the title *Songs of Travel.*

UNION CLUB, SYDNEY [*August, 1890*].

MY DEAR BURLINGAME,—

Ballads.

The deuce is in this volume. It has cost me more botheration and dubiety than any other I ever took in hand. On one thing my mind is made up: the verses at the end have no business there, and throw them down. Many of them are bad, many of the rest want nine years' keeping, and the remainder are not relevant—throw them down; some I never want to hear of more, others will grow in time towards decent items in a second *Underwoods*—and in the meanwhile, down with them! At the same time, I have a sneaking idea the ballads are not altogether without merit—I don't know if they 're poetry, but they 're good narrative, or I 'm deceived. (You 've never said one word about them, from which I astutely gather you are dead set against: "he was a diplomatic man" —extract from epitaph of E. L. B.—"and remained on good terms with Minor Poets.") You will have to judge: one of the Gladstonian trinity of paths must be chosen. (1st) Either publish the five ballads, such as they are, in a volume called *Ballads;* in which case pray send sheets at once to Chatto and Windus. Or (2nd) write and tell me you think the book too small, and I 'll try and get into the mood to do some more. Or (3rd) write and tell me the whole thing is a blooming illusion; in which case draw off some twenty copies for my private entertainment, and charge me with the expense of the whole dream. 1890 ÆT. 40

In the matter of rhyme no man can judge himself; I am at the world's end, have no one to consult, and my publisher holds his tongue. I call it unfair and almost unmanly. I do indeed begin to be filled with animosity; Lord, wait till you see the continuation of *The Wrecker,* when I introduce some New York publishers. . . . It 's a good scene; the quantities you drink and the really hideous language you are represented as employing may perhaps cause you one tithe of the pain you have inflicted by your silence on, sir, The Poetaster,

R. L. S.

Lloyd is off home; my wife and I dwell sundered: she in lodgings, preparing for the move; I here in the

1890 club, and at my old trade—bedridden. Naturally, the
ÆT. 40 visit home is given up; we only wait our opportunity to get to Samoa, where, please, address me.

Have I yet asked you to despatch the books and papers left in your care to me at Apia, Samoa? I wish you would, *quam primum*. R. L. S.

TO HENRY JAMES

Proceeding from New Caledonia to Sydney, Stevenson again made a stay there of about a month, before going to settle in his new island home and superintend the operations of planning and building.

UNION CLUB, SYDNEY, *August, 1890.*

MY DEAR HENRY JAMES,—Kipling is too clever to live. The *Bête Humaine* I had already perused in Noumea, listening the while to the strains of the convict band. He is a Beast; but not human, and, to be frank, not very interesting. "Nervous maladies: the homicidal ward," would be the better name: O, this game gets very tedious.

Your two long and kind letters have helped to entertain the old familiar sickbed. So has a book called *The Bondman*, by Hall Caine; I wish you would look at it. I am not half-way through yet. Read the book, and communicate your views. Hall Caine, by the way, appears to take Hugo's view of History and Chronology. (*Later;* the book does n't keep up; it gets very wild.)

I must tell you plainly—I can't tell Colvin—I do not think I shall come to England more than once, and then it 'll be to die. Health I enjoy in the tropics; even here, which they call sub- or semi-tropical, I come only to catch cold. I have not been out since my arrival; live here in a nice bedroom by the fireside, and read books and letters from Henry James, and send out to get his *Tragic Muse*, only to be told they can't be had as yet in Sydney; and have altogether a placid time. But I can't go out! The thermometer was nearly down to 50° the other day—no temperature for me, Mr. James: how should I do in England? I fear not at all. Am I very sorry? I am sorry about some seven or eight people in England, and one or two in the States. And outside of that, I simply prefer Samoa. These are the words of honesty and soberness. (I am fasting from all but sin, coughing, *The Bondman*, a couple of eggs and a cup of tea.) I was never fond of towns, houses, society, or (it seems) civilisation. Nor yet it seems was I ever very fond of (what is technically called) God's green earth. The sea, islands, the islanders, the island life and climate, make and keep me truly happier. These last two years I have been much at sea, and I have *never wearied;* sometimes I have indeed grown impatient for some destination; more often I was sorry that the voyage drew so early to an end; and never once did I lose my fidelity to blue water and a ship. It is plain, then, that for me my exile to the place of schooners and islands can be in no sense regarded as a calamity.

Good-bye just now: I must take a turn at my proofs.

N. B.—Even my wife has weakened about the sea. She wearied, the last time we were ashore, to get afloat again.—Yours ever,
R. L. S.

1890
ÆT. 40

To Marcel Schwob

UNION CLUB, SYDNEY, *August 19th, 1890.*

MY DEAR MR. SCHWOB,—*Mais, alors, vous avez tous les bonheurs, vous!* More about Villon; it seems incredible: when it is put in order, pray send it me.

You wish to translate the *Black Arrow:* dear sir, you are hereby authorised; but I warn you, I do not like the work. Ah, if you, who know so well both tongues, and have taste and instruction—if you would but take a fancy to translate a book of mine that I myself admired—for we sometimes admire our own—or I do—with what satisfaction would the authority be granted! But these things are too much to expect. *Vous ne détestez pas alors mes bonnes femmes? moi, je les déteste.* I have never pleased myself with any women of mine save two character parts, one of only a few lines—the Countess of Rosen, and Madame Desprez in *The Treasure of Franchard.*

I had indeed one moment of pride about my poor *Black Arrow:* Dickon Crookback I did, and I do, think is a spirited and possible figure. Shakespeare's—O, if we can call that cocoon Shakespeare!—Shakespeare's is spirited—one likes to see the untaught athlete butting against the adamantine ramparts of human nature, head down, breach up; it reminds us how trivial we are to-day, and what safety resides in our triviality. For spirited it may be, but O, sure not possible! I love Dumas and I love Shakespeare: you will not mistake me when I say that the Richard of the one reminds me of the Porthos of the other; and if by any sacrifice of my own literary baggage I could clear the *Vicomte de Bragelonne* of Porthos, *Jekyll* might go, and *The Master*, and the *Black Arrow*, you may be sure, and I should think my life not lost for mankind if half a dozen more of my volumes must be thrown in. 1890 ÆT. 40

The tone of your pleasant letters makes me egotistical; you make me take myself too gravely. Comprehend how I have lived much of my time in France, and loved your country, and many of its people, and all the time was learning that which your country has to teach — breathing in rather that atmosphere of art which can only there be breathed; and all the time knew — and raged to know — that I might write with the pen of angels or of heroes, and no Frenchman be the least the wiser! And now steps in M. Marcel Schwob, writes me the most kind encouragement, and reads and understands, and is kind enough to like my work.

I am just now overloaded with work. I have two huge novels on hand — *The Wrecker* and *The Pearl Fisher*, in collaboration with my stepson: the latter, *The Pearl Fisher*, I think highly of, for a black, ugly, trampling, violent story, full of strange scenes and striking characters. And then I am about waist-deep in my big book on the South Seas: *the* big book on the South Seas it ought to be, and shall. And besides, I have some verses in the press, which, however, I hesitate to publish. For I am no judge of my own verse; self-deception is there so facile. All this and the cares of an impending settlement in Samoa keep me very busy, and a cold (as usual) keeps me in bed.

Alas, I shall not have the pleasure to see you yet

1890 ÆT. 40 awhile, if ever. You must be content to take me as a wandering voice, and in the form of occasional letters from recondite islands; and address me, if you will be good enough to write, to Apia, Samoa. My stepson, Mr. Osbourne, goes home meanwhile to arrange some affairs; it is not unlikely he may go to Paris to arrange about the illustrations to my *South Seas;* in which case I shall ask him to call upon you, and give you some word of our outlandish destinies. You will find him intelligent, I think; and I am sure, if (*par hasard*) you should take any interest in the islands, he will have much to tell you.—Herewith I conclude, and am your obliged and interested correspondent,

ROBERT LOUIS STEVENSON.

P. S.—The story you refer to has got lost in the post.

TO ANDREW LANG

UNION CLUB, SYDNEY [*August, 1890*].

MY DEAR LANG,—I observed with a great deal of surprise and interest that a controversy in which you have been taking sides at home, in yellow London, hinges in part at least on the Gilbert Islanders and their customs in burial. Nearly six months of my life has been passed in the group: I have revisited it but the other day; and I make haste to tell you what I know. The upright stones—I enclose you a photograph of one on Apemama—are certainly connected with religion; I do not think they are adored. They stand usually on the windward shore of the islands, that is to say, apart from habitation (on enclosed islands, where the people live on the sea side, I do not know how it is, never having lived on one). I gathered from Tembinoka, Rex Apemamæ, that the pillars were supposed to fortify the island from invasion: spiritual martellos. I think he indicated they were connected with the cult of Tenti — pronounce almost as chintz in English, the *t* being explosive; but you must take this with a grain of salt, for I know no word of Gilbert Island; and the King's English, although creditable, is rather vigorous than exact. Now, here follows the point of interest to you: such pillars, or standing stones, have no connection with graves. The most elaborate grave that I have ever seen in the group — to be certain — is in the form of a *raised border* of gravel, usually strewn with broken glass. One — of which I cannot be sure that it was a grave, for I was told by one that it was, and by another that it was not — consisted of a mound about breast-high in an excavated taro swamp, on the top of which was a child's house, or rather *maniapa* — that is to say, shed, or open house, such as is used in the group for social or political gatherings — so small that only a child could creep under its eaves. I have heard of another great tomb on Apemama, which I did not see; but here again, by all accounts, no sign of a standing stone. My report would be — no connection between standing stones and sepulture. I shall, however, send on the terms of the problem to a highly intelligent resident trader, who knows more than perhaps any one living, white or native, of the Gilbert group; and you shall have the result. In Samoa, whither I return for

1890 good, I shall myself make inquiries; up to now, I
ÆT. 40 have neither seen nor heard of any standing stones in that group.—Yours, R. L. STEVENSON.

TO MRS. CHARLES FAIRCHILD

UNION CLUB, SYDNEY [*September, 1890*].

MY DEAR MRS. FAIRCHILD,—I began a letter to you on board the *Janet Nicoll* on my last cruise, wrote, I believe, two sheets, and ruthlessly destroyed the flippant trash. Your last has given me great pleasure and some pain, for it increased the consciousness of my neglect. Now, this must go to you, whatever it is like.

. . . You are quite right; our civilisation is a hollow fraud, all the fun of life is lost by it; all it gains is that a larger number of persons can continue to be contemporaneously unhappy on the surface of the globe. O, unhappy! — there is a big word and a false — continue to be not nearly — by about twenty per cent.— so happy as they might be: that would be nearer the mark.

When — observe that word, which I will write again and larger — WHEN you come to see us in Samoa, you will see for yourself a healthy and happy people.

You see, you are one of the very few of our friends rich enough to come and see us; and when my house is built, and the road is made, and we have enough fruit planted and poultry and pigs raised, it is undeniable that you must come — must is the word; that is the way in which I speak to ladies. You and Fairchild, anyway — perhaps my friend Blair — we 'll arrange de-a heavy strain for a disappointing result); to compose his *Foot-note to History*—an appeal to the European powers, and especially to Germany, for a wiser handling of Samoan difficulties, but an appeal which for the time being failed of its effect—and at the same time to produce a masterly piece of Polynesian fiction in *The Beach of Falesá*, and all but the best of his Scottish romances in *Catriona*.

To E. L. Burlingame

The opening sentences of the following refer, of course, to *The Wrecker*. 1890 ÆT. 40

VAILIMA, APIA, SAMOA, *Nov. 7, 1890.*

I WISH you to add to the words at the end of the prologue; they run, I think, thus, "And this is the yarn of Loudon Dodd"; add, "not as he told, but as he wrote it afterwards for his diversion." This becomes the more needful, because, when all is done, I shall probably revert to Tai-o-hae, and give final details about the characters in the way of a conversation between Dodd and Havers. These little snippets of information and *faits-divers* have always a disjointed, broken-backed appearance; yet, readers like them. In this book we have introduced so many characters, that this kind of epilogue will be looked for; and I rather hope, looking far ahead, that I can lighten it in dialogue.

We are well past the middle now. How does it strike you? and can you guess my mystery? It will make a fattish volume!

I say, have you ever read *The Highland Widow*? I never had till yesterday: I am half inclined, bar a trip

1890 ÆT. 40 or two, to think it Scott's masterpiece; and it has the name of a failure! Strange things are readers.

I expect proofs and revises in duplicate.

We have now got into a small barrack at our place. We see the sea six hundred feet below filling the end of two vales of forest. On one hand the mountain runs above us some thousand feet higher; great trees stand round us in our clearing; there is an endless voice of birds; I have never lived in such a heaven; just now, I have fever, which mitigates but not destroys my gusto in my circumstances.—You may envy

ROBERT LOUIS STEVENSON.

. . . O, I don't know if I mentioned that having seen your new tail to the magazine, I cried off interference, at least for this trip. Did I ask you to send me my books and papers, and all the bound volumes of the mag.? *quorum pars.* I might add that were there a good book or so—new—I don't believe there is—such would be welcome.

I desire—I positively begin to awake—to be remembered to Scribner, Low, St. Gaudens, Russell Sullivan. Well, well, you fellows have the feast of reason and the flow of soul; I have a better-looking place and climate: you should hear the birds on the hill now! The day has just wound up with a shower; it is still light without, though I write within here at the cheek of a lamp; my wife and an invaluable German are wrestling about bread on the back verandah; and how the birds and the frogs are rattling, and piping, and hailing from the woods! Here and there a throaty chuckle; here and there, cries like those of jolly children who have lost

FIRST HOUSE AT VAILIMA, WITH VAEA MOUNTAIN IN THE BACKGROUND.

their way; here and there, the ringing sleigh-bell of the tree frog. Out and away down below me on the sea it is still raining; it will be wet under foot on schooners, and the house will leak; how well I know that! Here the showers only patter on the iron roof, and sometimes roar; and within, the lamp burns steady on the tafa-covered walls, with their dusky tartan patterns, and the book-shelves with their thin array of books; and no squall can rout my house or bring my heart into my mouth.—The well-pleased South Sea Islander, 1890 ÆT. 40

R. L. S.

To E. L. Burlingame

The intention here announced was only carried out to the extent of finishing one paper, "My First Book," and beginning a few others—"Genesis of the Master of Ballantrae," "Rosa Quo Locorum," etc. (see Thistle edition, *Miscellanies*, vol. xx.). The "long experience of gambling places" is a phrase which must not be misunderstood. Stevenson loved risk, but hated gambling for money, and had known the tables only as a looker-on during holiday or invalid travels as a boy and young man. "Tamate" is the native (Raratongan) word for trader, used especially as a name for the famous missionary pioneer, the Rev. James Chalmers.

[Vailima, *December, 1890.*]

My dear Burlingame,—By some diabolical accident, I have mislaid your last. What was in it? I know not, and here I am caught unexpectedly by the American mail, a week earlier than by computation. The computation, not the mail, is supposed to be in error. The vols. of *Scribner's* have arrived, and present a noble appearance in my house, which is not a noble structure

1890 at present. But by autumn we hope to be sprawling
ÆT. 40 in our verandah, twelve feet, sir, by eighty-eight in front, and seventy-two on the flank; view of the sea and mountains, sunrise, moonrise, and the German fleet at anchor three miles away in Apia harbour. I hope some day to offer you a bowl of kava there, or a slice of a pineapple, or some lemonade from my own hedge. "I know a hedge where the lemons grow"—*Shakespeare.* My house at this moment smells of them strong; and the rain, which a while ago roared there, now rings in minute drops upon the iron roof. I have no *Wrecker* for you this mail, other things having engaged me. I was on the whole rather relieved you did not vote for regular papers, as I feared the traces. It is my design from time to time to write a paper of a reminiscential (beastly word) description; some of them I could scarce publish from different considerations; but some of them—for instance, my long experience of gambling places—Homburg, Wiesbaden, Baden-Baden, old Monaco, and new Monte Carlo—would make good magazine padding, if I got the stuff handled the right way. I never could fathom why verse was put in magazines; it has something to do with the making-up, has it not? I am scribbling a lot just now; if you are taken badly that way, apply to the South Seas. I could send you some, I believe, anyway, only none of it is thoroughly ripe. If you have kept back the volume of ballads, I 'll soon make it of a respectable size if this fit continue. By the next mail you may expect some more *Wrecker*, or I shall be displeased. Probably no more than a chapter, however, for it is a hard one, and I am denuded of my proofs, my collaborator having walked away

with them to England; hence some trouble in catching the just note. 1890 ÆT. 40

I am a mere farmer: my talk, which would scarce interest you on Broadway, is all of fuafua and tuitui, and black boys, and planting and weeding, and axes and cutlasses; my hands are covered with blisters and full of thorns; letters are, doubtless, a fine thing, so are beer and skittles, but give me farmering in the tropics for real interest. Life goes in enchantment; I come home to find I am late for dinner; and when I go to bed at night, I could cry for the weariness of my loins and thighs. Do not speak to me of vexation, the life brims with it, but with living interest fairly.

Christmas I go to Auckland, to meet Tamate, the New Guinea missionary, a man I love. The rest of my life is a prospect of much rain, much weeding and making of paths, a little letters, and devilish little to eat.—I am, my dear Burlingame, with messages to all whom it may concern, very sincerely yours,

ROBERT LOUIS STEVENSON.

To Henry James

Mr. La Farge, mentioned below, is of course the distinguished painter and decorator in stained glass, whose collection of drawings made in Samoa was exhibited in Paris in 1895. Mr. Henry Adams is the historian. The pinch in the matter of eatables only lasted for a little while, until Mrs. Stevenson had taken her bearings and made her arrangements in the matter of marketing, etc.

VAILIMA, APIA, SAMOA, *December 29th, 1890.*

MY DEAR HENRY JAMES,—It is terrible how little everybody writes, and how much of that little disappears in

1890 ÆT. 40 the capacious maw of the Post Office. Many letters, both from and to me, I now know to have been lost in transit: my eye is on the Sydney Post Office, a large ungainly structure with a tower, as being not a hundred miles from the scene of disappearance; but then I have no proof. The *Tragic Muse* you announced to me as coming; I had already ordered it from a Sydney bookseller: about two months ago he advised me that his copy was in the post; and I am still tragically museless.

News, news, news. What do we know of yours? What do you care for ours? We are in the midst of the rainy season, and dwell among alarms of hurricanes, in a very unsafe little two-storied wooden box 650 feet above and about three miles from the sea-beach. Behind us, till the other slope of the island, desert forest, peaks, and loud torrents; in front green slopes to the sea, some fifty miles of which we dominate. We see the ships as they go out and in to the dangerous roadstead of Apia; and if they lie far out, we can even see their topmasts while they are at anchor. Of sounds of men, beyond those of our own labourers, there reach us, at very long intervals, salutes from the warships in harbour, the bell of the cathedral church, and the low of the conch-shell calling the labour boys on the German plantations. Yesterday, which was Sunday—the *quantième* is most likely erroneous; you can now correct it — we had a visitor — Baker of Tonga. Heard you ever of him? He is a great man here: he is accused of theft, rape, judicial murder, private poisoning, abortion, misappropriation of public moneys — oddly enough, not forgery, nor arson: you would be amused if you knew how thick the accusations fly in this South

Sea world. I make no doubt my own character is something illustrious; or if not yet, there is a good time coming. 1890 ÆT. 40

But all our resources have not of late been Pacific. We have had enlightened society: La Farge the painter, and your friend Henry Adams: a great privilege—would it might endure. I would go oftener to see them, but the place is awkward to reach on horseback. I had to swim my horse the last time I went to dinner; and as I have not yet returned the clothes I had to borrow, I dare not return in the same plight: it seems inevitable—as soon as the wash comes in, I plump straight into the American consul's shirt or trousers! They, I believe, would come oftener to see me but for the horrid doubt that weighs upon our commissariat department; we have *often* almost nothing to eat; a guest would simply break the bank; my wife and I have dined on one avocado pear; I have several times dined on hard bread and onions. What would you do with a guest at such narrow seasons?—eat him? or serve up a labour boy fricasseed?

Work? work is now arrested, but I have written, I should think, about thirty chapters of the South Sea book; they will all want rehandling, I dare say. Gracious, what a strain is a long book! The time it took me to design this volume, before I could dream of putting pen to paper, was excessive; and then think of writing a book of travels on the spot, when I am continually extending my information, revising my opinions, and seeing the most finely finished portions of my work come part by part in pieces. Very soon I shall have no opinions left. And without an opinion,

1890 how to string artistically vast accumulations of fact?
ÆT. 40 Darwin said no one could observe without a theory; I suppose he was right; 't is a fine point of metaphysic; but I will take my oath, no man can write without one—at least the way he would like to—and my theories melt, melt, melt, and as they melt the thaw-waters wash down my writing, and leave unideal tracts—wastes instead of cultivated farms.

Kipling is by far the most promising young man who has appeared since—ahem—I appeared. He amazes me by his precocity and various endowment. But he alarms me by his copiousness and haste. He should shield his fire with both hands "and draw up all his strength and sweetness in one ball." ("Draw all his strength and all His sweetness up into one ball"? I cannot remember Marvell's words.) So the critics have been saying to me; but I was never capable of—and surely never guilty of—such a debauch of production. At this rate his works will soon fill the habitable globe; and surely he was armed for better conflicts than these succinct sketches and flying leaves of verse? I look on, I admire, I rejoice for myself; but in a kind of ambition we all have for our tongue and literature I am wounded. If I had this man's fertility and courage, it seems to me I could heave a pyramid.

Well, we begin to be the old fogies now; and it was high time *something* rose to take our places. Certainly Kipling has the gifts; the fairy godmothers were all tipsy at his christening: what will he do with them?

Good-bye, my dear James; find an hour to write to us, and register your letter.—Yours affectionately,

R. L. S.

To Rudyard Kipling

In 1890, on first becoming acquainted with Mr. Kipling's *Soldiers Three*, Stevenson had written off his congratulations red-hot. "Well and indeed, Mr. Mulvaney," so ran the first sentences of his note, "but it 's as good as meat to meet in with you, sir. They tell me it was a man of the name of Kipling made ye; but indeed and they can't fool me; it was the Lord God Almighty that made you." Taking the cue thus offered, Mr. Kipling had written back in the character of his own Irishman, Thomas Mulvaney, addressing Stevenson's Highlander, Alan Breck Stewart. In the following letter, which belongs to an uncertain date in 1891, Alan Breck is made to reply. "The gentleman I now serve with" means, of course, R. L. S. himself.

[Vailima, *1891.*]

Sir,—I cannot call to mind having written you, but I am so throng with occupation this may have fallen aside. I never heard tell I had any friends in Ireland, and I am led to understand you are come of no considerable family. The gentleman I now serve with assures me, however, you are a very pretty fellow and your letter deserves to be remarked. It 's true he is himself a man of a very low descent upon the one side; though upon the other he counts cousinship with a gentleman, my very good friend, the late Mr. Balfour of the Shaws, in the Lothian; which I should be wanting in good fellowship to forget. He tells me besides you are a man of your hands; I am not informed of your weapon; but if all be true it sticks in my mind I would be ready to make exception in your favour, and meet you like one gentleman with another. I suppose this 'll

1891 ÆT. 41 be your purpose in your favour, which I could very ill make out; it 's one I would be sweir to baulk you of. It seems, Mr. McIlvaine, which I take to be your name, you are in the household of a gentleman of the name of Coupling: for whom my friend is very much engaged. The distances being very uncommodious, I think it will be maybe better if we leave it to these two to settle all that 's necessary to honour. I would have you to take heed it 's a very unusual condescension on my part, that bear a King's name; and for the matter of that I think shame to be mingled with a person of the name of Coupling, which is doubtless a very good house but one I never heard tell of, any more than Stevenson. But your purpose being laudable, I would be sorry (as the word goes) to cut off my nose to spite my face.—I am, sir, your humble servant,

A. STEWART,
Chevalier de St. Louis.

TO MARCEL SCHWOB

SYDNEY, *January 19th, 1891.*

MY DEAR SIR,—*Sapristi, comme vous y allez! Richard III.* and Dumas, with all my heart; but not *Hamlet. Hamlet* is great literature; *Richard III.* a big, black, gross, sprawling melodrama, writ with infinite spirit but with no refinement or philosophy by a man who had the world, himself, mankind, and his trade still to learn. I prefer the *Vicomte de Brage-*

lonne to *Richard III.;* it is better done of its kind: I simply do not mention the *Vicomte* in the same part of the building with *Hamlet*, or *Lear*, or *Othello*, or any of those masterpieces that Shakespeare survived to give us. 1891 ÆT. 41

Also, *comme vous y allez* in my commendation! I fear my *solide éducation classique* had best be described, like Shakespeare's, as "little Latin and no Greek," and I was educated, let me inform you, for an engineer. I shall tell my bookseller to send you a copy of *Memories and Portraits*, where you will see something of my descent and education, as it was, and hear me at length on my dear Vicomte. I give you permission gladly to take your choice out of my works, and translate what you shall prefer, too much honoured that so clever a young man should think it worth the pains. My own choice would lie between *Kidnapped* and *The Master of Ballantrae*. Should you choose the latter, pray do not let Mrs. Henry thrust the sword up to the hilt in the frozen ground—one of my inconceivable blunders, an exaggeration to stagger Hugo. Say "she sought to thrust it in the ground." In both these works you should be prepared for Scotticisms used deliberately.

I fear my stepson will not have found time to get to Paris; he was overwhelmed with occupation, and is already on his voyage back. We live here in a beautiful land, amid a beautiful and interesting people. The life is still very hard: my wife and I live in a two-roomed cottage, about three miles and six hundred and fifty feet above the sea;

1891 ÆT. 41 we have had to make the road to it; our supplies are very imperfect; in the wild weather of this (the hurricane) season we have much discomfort: one night the wind blew in our house so outrageously that we must sit in the dark; and as the sound of the rain on the roof made speech inaudible, you may imagine we found the evening long. All these things, however, are pleasant to me. You say *l'artiste inconscient* set off to travel: you do not divide me right. 0.6 of me is artist; 0.4, adventurer. First, I suppose, come letters; then adventure; and since I have indulged the second part, I think the formula begins to change: 0.55 of an artist, 0.45 of the adventurer were nearer true. And if it had not been for my small strength, I might have been a different man in all things.

Whatever you do, do not neglect to send me what you publish on Villon: I look forward to that with lively interest. I have no photograph at hand, but I will send one when I can. It would be kind if you would do the like, for I do not see much chance of our meeting in the flesh: and a name, and a handwriting, and an address, and even a style? I know about as much of Tacitus, and more of Horace; it is not enough between contemporaries, such as we still are. I have just remembered another of my books, which I re-read the other day, and thought in places good—*Prince Otto.* It is not as good as either of the others; but it has one recommendation—it has female parts, so it might perhaps please better in France.

I will ask Chatto to send you, then—*Prince Otto,*

Memories and Portraits, Underwoods, and *Ballads,* 1891
none of which you seem to have seen. They will be ÆT. 41
too late for the New Year: let them be an Easter present.

You must translate me soon; you will soon have better to do than to transvase the work of others.—Yours very truly,

ROBERT LOUIS STEVENSON,
With the worst pen in the South Pacific.

TO CHARLES BAXTER

SS. "LÜBECK," AT SEA [*on the return voyage from Sydney, March, 1891*].

MY DEAR CHARLES,—Perhaps in my old days I do grow irascible; "the old man virulent" has long been my pet name for myself. Well, the temper is at least all gone now; time is good at lowering these distemperatures; far better is a sharp sickness, and I am just (and scarce) afoot again after a smoking hot little malady at Sydney. And the temper being gone, I still think the same. . . . We have not our parents for ever; we are never very good to them; when they go and we have lost our front-file man, we begin to feel all our neglects mighty sensibly. I propose a proposal. My mother is here on board with me; to-day for once I mean to make her as happy as I am able, and to do that which

1891 ÆT. 41 I know she likes. You, on the other hand, go and see your father, and do ditto, and give him a real good hour or two. We shall both be glad hereafter.—Yours ever, R. L. S.

To H. B. Baildon

Mr. H. Bellyse Baildon, at present Lecturer on English Literature at the University of Vienna, had been an old schoolmate and fellow aspirant in literature with Stevenson at Edinburgh. "Chalmers," of course, is the Rev. James Chalmers of Raratonga and New Guinea already referred to above, the admirable missionary, explorer, and administrator, whom Stevenson sometimes expressed a desire to survive, for the sake only of writing his life.

Vailima, Upolu [*Undated, but written in 1891*].

My dear Baildon,—This is a real disappointment. It was so long since we had met, I was anxious to see where time had carried and stranded us. Last time we saw each other—it must have been all ten years ago, as we were new to the thirties—it was only for a moment, and now we 're in the forties, and before very long we shall be in our graves. Sick and well, I have had a splendid life of it, grudge nothing, regret very little—and then only some little corners of misconduct for which I deserve hanging, and must infallibly be damned—and, take it all over, damnation and all, would hardly change with any man of my time, unless perhaps it were Gordon or our friend Chalmers: a man I admire for his virtues, love for his faults, and envy for the really A 1 life he has, with everything heart—my heart, I mean—could wish. It is curious to think you will read this in the grey metropolis; go the first grey, east-windy day into the Caledonian Station, if it looks at all as it did of yore: I met Satan there. And then go and stand by the cross, and remember the other one—him that went down—my brother, Robert Fergusson. It is a pity you had not made me out, and seen me as patriarch and planter. I shall look forward to some record of your time with Chalmers: you can't weary me of that fellow, he is as big as a house and far bigger than any church, where no man warms his hands. Do you know anything of Thomson? Of A——, B——, C——, D——, E——, F——, at all? As I write C's name mustard rises to my nose; I have never forgiven that weak, amiable boy a little trick he played me when I could ill afford it: I mean that whenever I think of it, some of the old wrath kindles, not that I would hurt the poor soul, if I got the world with it. And Old X—— ? Is he still afloat? Harmless barque! I gather you ain't married yet, since your sister, to whom I ask to be remembered, goes with you. Did you see a silly tale, *John Nicholson's Predicament*,[1] or some such name, in which I made free with your home at Murrayfield? There is precious little sense in it, but it might amuse. Cassell's published it in a thing called *Yule-Tide* years ago, and nobody that ever I heard of read or has ever seen *Yule-Tide*. It is addressed to a class we never met—readers of Cassell's series and that class of conscientious chaff, and my tale was dull, though I don't recall that it was

1891 ÆT. 41

[1] *The Misadventures of John Nicholson.*

1891 ÆT. 41 conscientious. Only, there 's the house at Murrayfield and a dead body in it. Glad the *Ballads* amused you. They failed to entertain a coy public, at which I wondered, not that I set much account by my verses, which are the verses of Prosator; but I do know how to tell a yarn, and two of the yarns are great. *Rahéro* is for its length a perfect folk-tale: savage and yet fine, full of tailforemost morality, ancient as the granite rocks; if the historian, not to say the politician, could get that yarn into his head, he would have learned some of his A B C. But the average man at home cannot understand antiquity; he is sunk over the ears in Roman civilisation; and a tale like that of *Rahéro* falls on his ears inarticulate. The *Spectator* said there was no psychology in it; that interested me much: my grandmother (as I used to call that able paper, and an able paper it is, and a fair one) cannot so much as observe the existence of savage psychology when it is put before it. I am at bottom a psychologist and ashamed of it; the tale seized me one-third because of its picturesque features, two-thirds because of its astonishing psychology, and the *Spectator* says there 's none. I am going on with a lot of island work, exulting in the knowledge of a new world, "a new created world" and new men; and I am sure my income will DECLINE and FALL off; for the effort of comprehension is death to the intelligent public, and sickness to the dull.

I do not know why I pester you with all this trash, above all as you deserve nothing. I give you my warm *talofa* (" my love to you," Samoan salutation). Write me again when the spirit moves you. And some day, if I still live, make out the trip again and let us hob-a-nob with our grey pows on my verandah.—Yours sincerely, ROBERT LOUIS STEVENSON. 1891 ÆT. 41

To W. CRAIBE ANGUS

Mr. Craibe Angus of Glasgow was one of the chief organizers of the Burns Exhibition in that city, and had proposed to send out to Samoa a precious copy of the *Jolly Beggars* to receive the autograph of R. L. S. and be returned for the purposes of that Exhibition. The line quoted, "But still our hearts are true," etc., should, it appears, run, "But still the blood is strong, the heart is Highland." The author of the *Canadian Boat Song* which opens thus was Hugh, twelfth Earl of Eglinton. The first quotation is, of course, from Burns.

VAILIMA, SAMOA, *April, 1891.*

DEAR MR. ANGUS,—Surely I remember you! It was W. C. Murray who made us acquainted, and we had a pleasant crack. I see your poet is not yet dead. I remember even our talk—or you would not think of trusting that invaluable *Jolly Beggars* to the treacherous posts, and the perils of the sea, and the carelessness of authors. I love the idea, but I could not bear the risk. However—

"Hale be your heart, hale be your fiddle—"

it was kindly thought upon.

My interest in Burns is, as you suppose, perennial. I would I could be present at the exhibition, with the purpose of which I heartily sympathise; but the *Nancy* has not waited in vain for me, I have followed my chest, the anchor is weighed long ago, I have said my last farewell to the hills and the heather and the lynns: like Leyden, I have gone into far lands to die, not

1891 ÆT. 41 stayed like Burns to mingle in the end with Scottish soil. I shall not even return like Scott for the last scene. Burns Exhibitions are all over. 'T is a far cry to Lochow from tropical Vailima.

> "But still our hearts are true, our hearts are Highland,
> And we in dreams behold the Hebrides."

When your hand is in, will you remember our poor Edinburgh Robin? Burns alone has been just to his promise; follow Burns, he knew best, he knew whence he drew fire — from the poor, white-faced, drunken, vicious boy that raved himself to death in the Edinburgh madhouse. Surely there is more to be gleaned about Fergusson, and surely it is high time the task was set about. I may tell you (because your poet is not dead) something of how I feel: we are three Robins who have touched the Scots lyre this last century. Well, the one is the world's, he did it, he came off, he is for ever; but I and the other — ! what bonds we have — born in the same city; both sickly; both pestered, one nearly to madness, one to the madhouse, with a damnatory creed; both seeing the stars and the dawn, and wearing shoe-leather on the same ancient stones, under the same pends, down the same closes, where our common ancestors clashed in their armour, rusty or bright. And the old Robin, who was before Burns and the flood, died in his acute, painful youth, and left the models of the great things that were to come; and the new, who came after, outlived his greensickness, and has faintly tried to parody the finished work. If you will collect the strays of Robin Fergusson, fish for material, collect any last re-echoing of gossip, command me to do what you prefer—to write the preface 1891 — to write the whole if you prefer: anything, so that ÆT. 41 another monument (after Burns's) be set up to my unhappy predecessor on the causey of Auld Reekie. You will never know, nor will any man, how deep this feeling is: I believe Fergusson lives in me. I do, but tell it not in Gath; every man has these fanciful superstitions, coming, going, but yet enduring; only most men are so wise (or the poet in them so dead) that they keep their follies for themselves.—I am, yours very truly, ROBERT LOUIS STEVENSON.

TO EDMUND GOSSE

VAILIMA, *April, 1891.*

MY DEAR GOSSE,—I have to thank you and Mrs. Gosse for many mementos, chiefly for your *Life* of your father. There is a very delicate task, very delicately done. I noted one or two carelessnesses, which I meant to point out to you for another edition; but I find I lack the time, and you will remark them for yourself against a new edition. There were two, or perhaps three, flabbinesses of style which (in your work) amazed me. Am I right in thinking you were a shade bored over the last chapters? or was it my own fault that made me think them susceptible of a more athletic compression? (The flabbinesses were not there, I think, but in the more admirable part, where they showed the bigger.) Take it all together, the book struck me as if you had been hurried at the last, but particularly hurried over the proofs, and could still

1891 Æт. 41 spend a very profitable fortnight in earnest revision and (towards the end) heroic compression. The book, in design, subject, and general execution, is well worth the extra trouble. And even if I were wrong in thinking it specially wanted, it will not be lost; for do we not know, in Flaubert's dread confession, that "prose is never done"? What a medium to work in, for a man tired, perplexed among different aims and subjects, and spurred by the immediate need of "siller"! However, it's mine for what it's worth; and it's one of yours, the devil take it; and you know, as well as Flaubert, and as well as me, that it is *never done;* in other words, it is a torment of the pit, usually neglected by the bards who (lucky beggars!) approached the Styx in measure. I speak bitterly at the moment, having just detected in myself the last fatal symptom, three blank verses in succession—and I believe, God help me, a hemistich at the tail of them; hence I have deposed the labourer, come out of hell by my private trap, and now write to you from my little place in purgatory. But I prefer hell: would I could always dig in those red coals—or else be at sea in a schooner, bound for isles unvisited: to be on shore and not to work is emptiness—suicidal vacancy.

I was the more interested in your *Life* of your father, because I meditate one of mine, or rather of my family. I have no such materials as you, and (our objections already made) your attack fills me with despair; it is direct and elegant, and your style is always admirable to me—lenity, lucidity, usually a high strain of breeding, an elegance that has a pleasant air of the accidental. But beware of purple passages. I wonder if you think as well of your purple passages as I do of mine? I wonder if you think as ill of mine as I do of yours? I wonder; I can tell you at least what is wrong with yours—they are treated in the spirit of verse. The spirit—I don't mean the measure, I don't mean you fall into bastard cadences; what I mean is that they seem vacant and smoothed out, ironed, if you like. And in a style which (like yours) aims more and more successfully at the academic, one purple word is already much; three—a whole phrase—is inadmissible. Wed yourself to a clean austerity: that is your force. Wear a linen ephod, splendidly candid. Arrange its folds, but do not fasten it with any brooch. I swear to you, in your talking robes, there should be no patch of adornment; and where the subject forces, let it force you no further than it must; and be ready with a twinkle of your pleasantry. Yours is a fine tool, and I see so well how to hold it; I wonder if you see how to hold mine? But then I am to the neck in prose, and just now in the "dark *interstylar* cave," all methods and effects wooing me, myself in the midst impotent to follow any. I look for dawn presently, and a full flowing river of expression, running whither it wills. But these useless seasons, above all, when a man *must* continue to spoil paper, are infinitely weary.

We are in our house after a fashion; without furniture, 't is true, camping there, like the family after a sale. But the bailiff has not yet appeared; he will probably come after. The place is beautiful beyond dreams; some fifty miles of the Pacific spread in front;

1891 ÆT. 41 deep woods all round; a mountain making in the sky a profile of huge trees upon our left; about us, the little island of our clearing, studded with brave old gentlemen (or ladies, or "the twa o' them") whom we have spared. It is a good place to be in; night and morning, we have Theodore Rousseaus (always a new one) hung to amuse us on the walls of the world; and the moon—this is our good season, we have a moon just now—makes the night a piece of heaven. It amazes me how people can live on in the dirty north; yet if you saw our rainy season (which is really a caulker for wind, wet, and darkness—howling showers, roaring winds, pit-blackness at noon) you might marvel how we could endure that. And we can't. But there 's a winter everywhere; only ours is in the summer. Mark my words: there will be a winter in heaven—and in hell. *Cela rentre dans les procédés du bon Dieu; et vous verrez!* There 's another very good thing about Vailima, I am away from the little bubble of the literary life. It is not all beer and skittles, is it? By the by, my *Ballads* seem to have been dam bad; all the crickets sing so in their crickety papers; and I have no ghost of an idea on the point myself: verse is always to me the unknowable. You might tell me how it strikes a professional bard: not that it really matters, for, of course, good or bad, I don't think I shall get into *that* galley any more. But I should like to know if you join the shrill chorus of the crickets. The crickets are the devil in all to you: 't is a strange thing, they seem to rejoice like a strong man in their injustice. I trust you got my letter about your Browning book. In case it missed, I wish to say again that your publication of Browning's kind letter, as an illustration of *his* character, was modest, proper, and in radiant good taste.—In Witness whereof, etc., etc., 1891 ÆT. 41

ROBERT LOUIS STEVENSON.

TO MISS RAWLINSON

The next is written to a young friend and visitor of Bournemouth days on the news of her engagement.

VAILIMA, APIA, SAMOA, *April, 1891.*

MY DEAR MAY,—I never think of you by any more ceremonial name, so I will not pretend. There is not much chance that I shall forget you until the time comes for me to forget all this little turmoil in a corner (though indeed I have been in several corners) of an inconsiderable planet. You remain in my mind for a good reason, having given me (in so short a time) the most delightful pleasure. I shall remember, and you must still be beautiful. The truth is, you must grow more so, or you will soon be less. It is not so easy to be a flower, even when you bear a flower's name. And if I admired you so much, and still remember you, it is not because of your face, but because you were then worthy of it, as you must still continue.

Will you give my heartiest congratulations to Mr. S.? He has my admiration; he is a brave man; when I was young, I should have run away from the sight of you, pierced with the sense of my unfitness. He is more wise and manly. What a good husband he will have to be! And you—what a good wife! Carry your love tenderly. I will never forgive him—or you—it

1891 ÆT. 41 is in both your hands — if the face that once gladdened my heart should be changed into one sour or sorrowful.

What a person you are to give flowers! It was so I first heard of you; and now you are giving the May flower!

Yes, Skerryvore has passed; it was, for us. But I wish you could see us in our new home on the mountain, in the middle of great woods, and looking far out over the Pacific. When Mr. S. is very rich, he must bring you round the world and let you see it, and see the old gentleman and the old lady. I mean to live quite a long while yet, and my wife must do the same, or else I could n't manage it; so, you see, you will have plenty of time; and it 's a pity not to see the most beautiful places, and the most beautiful people moving there, and the real stars and moon overhead, instead of the tin imitations that preside over London. I do not think my wife very well; but I am in hopes she will now have a little rest. It has been a hard business, above all for her; we lived four months in the hurricane season in a miserable house, overborne with work, ill-fed, continually worried, drowned in perpetual rain, beaten upon by wind, so that we must sit in the dark in the evenings; and then I ran away, and she had a month of it alone. Things go better now; the back of the work is broken; and we are still foolish enough to look forward to a little peace. I am a very different person from the prisoner of Skerryvore. The other day I was three-and-twenty hours in an open boat; it made me pretty ill; but fancy it 's not killing me half-way! It is like a fairy story that I should have recovered liberty and strength, and should go round again among

my fellow men, boating, riding, bathing, toiling hard 1891 ÆT. 41
with a wood-knife in the forest. I can wish you nothing more delightful than my fortune in life; I wish it you; and better, if the thing be possible.

Lloyd is tinkling below me on the typewriter; my wife has just left the room; she asks me to say she would have written had she been well enough, and hopes to do it still.—Accept the best wishes of your admirer,
ROBERT LOUIS STEVENSON.

To MISS ADELAIDE BOODLE

The reference in the first paragraph is to a previous letter concerning private matters, in which Stevenson had remonstrated with his correspondent on what seemed to him her mistaken reasons for a certain course of conduct.

[VAILIMA, *May, 1891.*]

MY DEAR ADELAIDE,—I will own you just did manage to tread on my gouty toe; and I beg to assure you with most people I should simply have turned away and said no more. My cudgelling was therefore in the nature of a caress or testimonial.

God forbid, I should seem to judge for you on such a point; it was what you seemed to set forth as your reasons that fluttered my old Presbyterian spirit—for, mind you, I am a child of the Covenanters—whom I do not love, but they are mine after all, my father's and my mother's—and they had their merits too, and their ugly beauties, and grotesque heroisms, that I love them for, the while I laugh at them; but in their name and mine do what you think right, and let the world fall. That is the privilege and the duty of private persons; and I shall think the more of you at the greater distance,

1891 ÆT. 41 because you keep a promise to your fellow man, your helper and creditor in life, by just so much as I was tempted to think the less of you (O not much, or I would never have been angry) when I thought you were the swallower of a (tinfoil) formula.

I must say I was uneasy about my letter, not because it was too strong as an expression of my unregenerate sentiments, but because I knew full well it should be followed by something kinder. And the mischief has been in my health. I fell sharply sick in Sydney, was put aboard the *Lübeck* pretty bad, got to Vailima, hung on a month there, and did n't pick up as well as my work needed; set off on a journey, gained a great deal, lost it again; and am back at Vailima, still no good at my necessary work. I tell you this for my imperfect excuse that I should not have written you again sooner to remove the bad taste of my last.

A road has been called Adelaide Road; it leads from the back of our house to the bridge, and thence to the garden, and by a bifurcation to the pig pen. It is thus much traversed, particularly by Fanny. An oleander, the only one of your seeds that prospered in this climate, grows there; and the name is now some week or ten days applied and published. ADELAIDE ROAD leads also into the bush, to the banana patch, and by a second bifurcation over the left branch of the stream to the plateau and the right hand of the gorges. In short, it leads to all sorts of good, and is besides, in itself, a pretty winding path, bound downhill among big woods to the margin of the stream.

What a strange idea, to think me a Jew-hater! Isaiah and David and Heine are good enough for me; and I leave more unsaid. Were I of Jew blood, I do not think I could ever forgive the Christians; the ghettos would get in my nostrils like mustard or lit gunpowder. Just so you as being a child of the Presbytery, I retain—I need not dwell on that. The ascendant hand is what I feel most strongly; I am bound in and in with my forebears; were he one of mine, I should not be struck at all by Mr. Moss of Bevis Marks, I should still see behind him Moses of the Mount and the Tables and the shining face. We are all nobly born; fortunate those who know it; blessed those who remember. 1891 ÆT. 41

I am, my dear Adelaide, most genuinely yours,

ROBERT LOUIS STEVENSON.

Write by return to say you are better, and I will try to do the same.

TO CHARLES BAXTER

The following refers to a literary project which had occupied the writer's mind for years, but which never got executed, beyond, that is, a few unrevised opening chapters composed at Bournemouth.

[VAILIMA], *Tuesday, 19th May, '91.*

MY DEAR CHARLES,—I don't know what you think of me, not having written to you at all during your illness. I find two sheets begun with your name, but that is no excuse. . . . I am keeping bravely; getting about better every day, and hope soon to be in my usual fettle. My books begin to come; and I fell once more on the Old Bailey session papers. I have 1778, 1784, and 1786. Should you be able to lay hands on any other volumes, above all a little later, I should be

1891 ÆT. 41 very glad you should buy them for me. I particularly want *one* or *two* during the course of the Peninsular War. Come to think, I ought rather to have communicated this want to Bain. Would it bore you to communicate to that effect with the great man? The sooner I have them, the better for me. 'T is for Henry Shovel. But Henry Shovel has now turned into a work called "The Shovels of Newton French: Including Memoirs of Henry Shovel, a Private in the Peninsular War," which work is to begin in 1664 with the marriage of Skipper, afterwards Alderman Shovel of Bristol, Henry's great-great-grandfather, and end about 1832 with his own second marriage to the daughter of his runaway aunt. Will the public ever stand such an opus? Gude kens, but it tickles me. Two or three historical personages will just appear: Judge Jeffreys, Wellington, Colquhoun, Grant, and I think Townsend the runner. I know the public won't like it; let 'em lump it then; I mean to make it good; it will be more like a saga.—Adieu, yours ever affectionately, R. L. STEVENSON.

TO E. L. BURLINGAME

For the result of the suggestion made in the following, see *Scribner's Magazine* for October, 1893, p. 494.

VAILIMA [*Summer, 1891*].

MY DEAR BURLINGAME,—I find among my grandfather's papers his own reminiscences of his voyage round the north with Sir Walter, eighty years ago, *labuntur anni!* They are not remarkably good, but he was not a bad observer, and several touches seem to me speaking. It has occurred to me you might like them to appear in the Magazine. If you would, kindly let me know, and tell me how you would like it handled. My granddad's MS. runs to between six and seven thousand words, which I could abbreviate of anecdotes that scarce touch Sir W. Would you like this done? Would you like me to introduce the old gentleman? I had something of the sort in my mind, and could fill a few columns rather *apropos*. I give you the first offer of this, according to your request; for though it may forestall one of the interests of my biography, the thing seems to me particularly suited for prior appearance in a magazine.

I see the first number of *The Wrecker;* I thought it went lively enough; and by a singular accident, the picture is not unlike Tai-o-hae!

Thus we see the age of miracles, etc.—Yours very sincerely,

R. L. S.

Proofs for next mail.

To W. Craibe Angus

[*Summer, 1891.*]

DEAR MR. ANGUS,—You can use my letter as you will. The parcel has not come; pray Heaven the next post bring it safe. Is it possible for me to write a preface here? I will try if you like, if you think I must: though surely there are Rivers in Assyria. Of course you will send me sheets of the catalogue; I suppose it (the preface) need not be long; perhaps it should be rather very short? Be sure you give me your views

1891 ÆT. 41 upon these points. Also tell me what names to mention among those of your helpers, and do remember to register everything, else it is not safe.

The true place (in my view) for a monument to Fergusson were the churchyard of Haddington. But as that would perhaps not carry many votes, I should say one of the two following sites:—First, either as near the site of the old Bedlam as we could get, or, second, beside the Cross, the heart of his city. Upon this I would have a fluttering butterfly, and, I suggest, the citation,

Poor butterfly, thy case I mourn.

For the case of Fergusson is not one to pretend about. A more miserable tragedy the sun never shone upon, or (in consideration of our climate) I should rather say refused to brighten.—Yours truly,

ROBERT LOUIS STEVENSON.

Where Burns goes will not matter. He is no local poet, like your Robin the First; he is general as the casing air. Glasgow, as the chief city of Scottish men, would do well; but for God's sake, don't let it be like the Glasgow memorial to Knox: I remember, when I first saw this, laughing for an hour by Shrewsbury clock. R. L. S.

To H. C. Ide

The following is written to the American Land Commissioner (later Chief Justice for a term) in Samoa, whose younger daughter, then at home in the States, had been born on a Christmas Day, and consequently regarded herself as defrauded of her natural rights to a private anniversary of her own.

[VAILIMA, *June 19, 1891.*] 1891 ÆT. 41

DEAR MR. IDE,—Herewith please find the DOCUMENT, which I trust will prove sufficient in law. It seems to me very attractive in its eclecticism; Scots, English, and Roman law phrases are all indifferently introduced, and a quotation from the works of Haynes Bailey can hardly fail to attract the indulgence of the Bench.—Yours very truly, ROBERT LOUIS STEVENSON.

I, Robert Louis Stevenson, Advocate of the Scots Bar, author of *The Master of Ballantrae* and *Moral Emblems*, stuck civil engineer, sole owner and patentee of the Palace and Plantation known as Vailima in the island of Upolu, Samoa, a British Subject, being in sound mind, and pretty well, I thank you, in body:

In consideration that Miss Annie H. Ide, daughter of H. C. Ide, in the town of Saint Johnsbury, in the county of Caledonia, in the state of Vermont, United States of America, was born, out of all reason, upon Christmas Day, and is therefore out of all justice denied the consolation and profit of a proper birthday;

And considering that I, the said Robert Louis Stevenson, have attained an age when O, we never mention it, and that I have now no further use for a birthday of any description;

And in consideration that I have met H. C. Ide, the father of the said Annie H. Ide, and found him about as white a land commissioner as I require:

Have transferred, and *do hereby transfer*, to the said Annie H. Ide, *all and whole* my rights and privileges in the thirteenth day of November, formerly my birthday, now, hereby, and henceforth, the birthday of the

1891 ÆT. 41 said Annie H. Ide, to have, hold, exercise, and enjoy the same in the customary manner, by the sporting of fine raiment, eating of rich meats, and receipt of gifts, compliments, and copies of verse, according to the manner of our ancestors;

And I direct the said Annie H. Ide to add to the said name of Annie H. Ide the name Louisa—at least in private; and I charge her to use my said birthday with moderation and humanity, *et tamquam bona filia familia,* the said birthday not being so young as it once was, and having carried me in a very satisfactory manner since I can remember;

And in case the said Annie H. Ide shall neglect or contravene either of the above conditions, I hereby revoke the donation and transfer my rights in the said birthday to the President of the United States of America for the time being:

In witness whereof I have hereto set my hand and seal this nineteenth day of June in the year of grace eighteen hundred and ninety-one.

ROBERT LOUIS STEVENSON.

Witness, LLOYD OSBOURNE,
Witness, HAROLD WATTS.

TO HENRY JAMES

Stevenson had been reading Mr. James's *Lesson of the Master;* Adela Chart is the heroine of the second story in that collection, called "The Marriage."

[VAILIMA, *October, 1891.*] 1891 ÆT. 41

MY DEAR HENRY JAMES,—From this perturbed and hunted being, expect but a line, and that line shall be but a whoop for Adela. O she 's delicious, delicious; I could live and die with Adela — die, rather the better of the two; you never did a straighter thing, and never will.

David Balfour, second part of *Kidnapped,* is on the stocks at last; and is not bad, I think. As for *The Wrecker,* it 's a machine, you know — don't expect aught else — a machine, and a police machine; but I believe the end is one of the most genuine butcheries in literature; and we point to our machine with a modest pride, as the only police machine without a villain. Our criminals are a most pleasing crew, and leave the dock with scarce a stain upon their character.

What a different line of country to be trying to draw Adela, and trying to write the last four chapters of *The Wrecker!* Heavens, it 's like two centuries; and ours is such rude, transpontine business, aiming only at a certain fervour of conviction and sense of energy and violence in the men; and yours is so neat and bright and of so exquisite a surface! Seems dreadful to send such a book to such an author; but your name is on the list. And we do modestly ask you to consider the chapters on the *Norah Creina* with the study of Captain Nares, and the forementioned last four, with their brutality of substance and the curious (and perhaps unsound) technical manœuvre of running the story together to a point as we go along, the narrative becoming more succinct and the details fining off with every page.— Sworn affidavit of R. L. S.

1891 ÆT. 41 *No person now alive has beaten Adela: I adore Adela and her Maker. Sic subscrib.*

ROBERT LOUIS STEVENSON.

A Sublime Poem to follow.

Adela, Adela, Adela Chart,
What have you done to my elderly heart?
Of all the ladies of paper and ink
I count you the paragon, call you the pink.
The word of your brother depicts you in part:
"You raving maniac!" Adela Chart;
But in all the asylums that cumber the ground,
So delightful a maniac was ne'er to be found.

I pore on you, dote on you, clasp you to heart,
I laud, love, and laugh at you, Adela Chart,
And thank my dear maker the while I admire
That I can be neither your husband nor sire.

Your husband's, your sire's were a difficult part;
You 're a byway to suicide, Adela Chart;
But to read of, depicted by exquisite James,
O, sure you're the flower and quintessence of dames.

R. L. S.

Eructavit cor meum.

My heart was inditing a goodly matter about Adela Chart.

Though oft I 've been touched by the volatile dart,
To none have I grovelled but Adela Chart.
There are passable ladies, no question, in art—

But where is the marrow of Adela Chart?
I dreamed that to Tyburn I passed in the cart—
I dreamed I was married to Adela Chart:
From the first I awoke with a palpable start,
The second dumfoundered me, Adela Chart!

Another verse bursts from me, you see; no end to the violence of the Muse.

To E. L. Burlingame

October 8th, 1891.

MY DEAR BURLINGAME,—All right, you shall have the *Tales of my Grandfather* soon, but I guess we'll try and finish off *The Wrecker* first. *Apropos* of whom, please send some advanced sheets to Cassell's—away ahead of you—so that they may get a dummy out.

Do you wish to illustrate *My Grandfather?* He mentions as excellent a portrait of Scott by Basil Hall's brother. I don't think I ever saw this engraved; would it not, if you could get track of it, prove a taking embellishment? I suggest this for your consideration and inquiry. A new portrait of Scott strikes me as good. There is a hard, tough, constipated old portrait of my grandfather hanging in my aunt's house, Mrs. Alan Stevenson, 16 St. Leonard's Terrace, Chelsea, which has never been engraved—the better portrait, Joseph's bust, has been reproduced, I believe, twice—and which, I am sure, my aunt would let you have a copy of. The plate could be of use for the book when we get so far, and thus to place it in the Magazine might be an actual saving.

1891 ÆT. 41 I am swallowed up in politics for the first, I hope for the last, time in my sublunary career. It is a painful, thankless trade; but one thing that came up I could not pass in silence. Much drafting, addressing, deputationising has eaten up all my time, and again (to my contrition) I leave you Wreckerless. As soon as the mail leaves I tackle it straight.—Yours very sincerely,

ROBERT LOUIS STEVENSON.

To E. L. Burlingame

VAILIMA [*Autumn, 1891*].

MY DEAR BURLINGAME,—The time draws nigh, the mail is near due, and I snatch a moment of collapse so that you may have at least some sort of a scratch of note along with the \ end
of
The
Wrecker. Hurray!

which I mean to go herewith. It has taken me a devil of a pull, but I think it 's going to be ready. If I did not know you were on the stretch waiting for it and trembling for your illustrations, I would keep it for another finish; but things being as they are, I will let it go the best way I can get it. I am now within two pages of the end of Chapter XXV., which is the last chapter, the end, with its gathering up of loose threads, being the dedication to Low, and addressed to him: this is my last and best expedient for the knotting up of these loose cards. 'T is possible I may not get that finished in time, in which case you 'll receive only

Chapters XXII. to XXV. by this mail, which is all that can be required for illustration. 1891 ÆT. 41

I wish you would send me *Memoirs of Baron Marbot* (French); *Introduction to the Study of the History of Language*, Strong, Logeman & Wheeler; *Principles of Psychology*, William James; Morris & Magnusson's *Saga Library*, any volumes that are out; George Meredith's *One of our Conquerors; Là Bas*, by Huysmans (French); O'Connor Morris's *Great Commanders of Modern Times; Life's Handicap*, by Kipling; of Taine's *Origines de la France Contemporaine*, I have only as far as *la Révolution*, vol. iii.; if another volume is out, please add that. There is for a book-box.

I hope you will like the end; I think it is rather strong meat. I have got into such a deliberate, dilatory, expansive turn, that the effort to compress this last yarn was unwelcome; but the longest yarn has to come to an end sometime. Please look it over for carelessnesses, and tell me if it had any effect upon your jaded editorial mind. I 'll see if ever I have time to add more.

I add to my book-box list Adams' *Historical Essays;* the Plays of A. W. Pinero — all that have appeared, and send me the rest in course as they do appear; *Noughts and Crosses* by Q.; Robertson's *Scotland under her Early Kings.*

Sunday.

The deed is done, didst thou not hear a noise? "The end" has been written to this endless yarn, and I am once more a free man. What will he do with it?

1891
ÆT. 41

To W. Craibe Angus

Vailima, Samoa, *November, 1891.*

MY DEAR MR. ANGUS,— Herewith the invaluable sheets. They came months after your letter, and I trembled; but here they are, and I have scrawled my vile name on them, and "thocht shame" as I did it. I am expecting the sheets of your catalogue, so that I may attack the preface. Please give me all the time you can. The sooner the better; you might even send me early proofs as they are sent out, to give me more incubation. I used to write as slow as judgment; now I write rather fast; but I am still "a slow study," and sit a long while silent on my eggs. Unconscious thought, there is the only method: macerate your subject, let it boil slow, then take the lid off and look in — and there your stuff is, good or bad. But the journalist's method is the way to manufacture lies; it is will-worship — if you know the luminous Quaker phrase; and the will is only to be brought in the field for study, and again for revision. The essential part of work is not an act, it is a state.

I do not know why I write you this trash.

Many thanks for your handsome dedication. I have not yet had time to do more than glance at Mrs. Begg; it looks interesting.— Yours very truly,

Robert Louis Stevenson.

To Miss Annie H. Ide

Vailima, Samoa [*November, 1891*].

My dear Louisa,—Your picture of the church, the photograph of yourself and your sister, and your very witty and pleasing letter, came all in a bundle, and made me feel I had my money's worth for that birthday. I am now, I must be, one of your nearest relatives; exactly what we are to each other, I do not know, I doubt if the case has ever happened before—your papa ought to know, and I don't believe he does; but I think I ought to call you in the meanwhile, and until we get the advice of counsel learned in the law, my name-daughter. Well, I was extremely pleased to see by the church that my name-daughter could draw; by the letter, that she was no fool; and by the photograph, that she was a pretty girl, which hurts nothing. See how virtues are rewarded! My first idea of adopting you was entirely charitable; and here I find that I am quite proud of it, and of you, and that I chose just the kind of name-daughter I wanted. For I can draw too, or rather I mean to say I could before I forgot how; and I am very far from being a fool myself, however much I may look it; and I am as beautiful as the day, or at least I once hoped that perhaps I might be going to be. And so I might. So that you see we are well met, and peers on these important points. I am very glad also that you are older than your sister. So should I have been, if I had had one. So that the number of points and virtues which you have inherited from your name-father is already quite surprising.

1891 ÆT. 41 I wish you would tell your father—not that I like to encourage my rival—that we have had a wonderful time here of late, and that they are having a cold day on Mulinuu, and the consuls are writing reports, and I am writing to the *Times*, and if we don't get rid of our friends this time I shall begin to despair of everything but my name-daughter.

You are quite wrong as to the effect of the birthday on your age. From the moment the deed was registered (as it was in the public press with every solemnity), the 13th of November became your own *and only* birthday, and you ceased to have been born on Christmas Day. Ask your father: I am sure he will tell you this is sound law. You are thus become a month and twelve days younger than you were, but will go on growing older for the future in the regular and human manner from one 13th November to the next. The effect on me is more doubtful; I may, as you suggest, live for ever; I might, on the other hand, come to pieces like the one-horse shay at a moment's notice; doubtless the step was risky, but I do not the least regret that which enables me to sign myself your revered and delighted name-father, ROBERT LOUIS STEVENSON.

TO NED ORR

The following is in answer to an application for an autograph from a young gentleman in the United States.

VAILIMA, UPOLU, SAMOA, *November 28th, 1891.*

DEAR SIR,—Your obliging communication is to hand. I am glad to find that you have read some of my books, and to see that you spell my name right. This is a point (for some reason) of great difficulty; and I believe that a gentleman who can spell Stevenson with a *v* at sixteen should have a show for the Presidency before fifty. By that time 1891 ÆT. 41

"I, nearer to the wayside inn,"

predict that you will have outgrown your taste for autographs, but perhaps your son may have inherited the collection, and on the morning of the great day will recall my prophecy to your mind. And in the papers of 1921 (say) this letter may arouse a smile.

Whatever you do, read something else besides novels and newspapers; the first are good enough when they are good; the second, at their best, are worth nothing. Read great books of literature and history; try to understand the Roman Empire and the Middle Ages; be sure you do not understand when you dislike them; condemnation is non-comprehension. And if you know something of these two periods, you will know a little more about to-day, and may be a good President.

I send you my best wishes, and am yours,

ROBERT LOUIS STEVENSON,
Author of a vast quantity of little books.

TO E. L. BURLINGAME

The next letter announces to his New York publishers the beginning of his volume on the troubles of Samoa, *A Foot-note to History*.

[VAILIMA, *December, 1891.*]

MY DEAR BURLINGAME,—The end of *The Wrecker* having but just come in, you will, I dare say, be appalled to receive three (possibly four) chapters of a new book of the least attractive sort: a history of nowhere in a corner, for no time to mention, running to a volume! Well, it may very likely be an illusion; it is very likely no one could possibly wish to read it, but I wish to publish it. If you don't cotton to the idea, kindly set it up at my expense, and let me know your terms for publishing. The great affair to me is to have per return (if it might be) four or five — better say half a dozen — sets of the roughest proofs that can be drawn. There are a good many men here whom I want to read the blessed thing, and not one would have the energy to read MS. At the same time, if you care to glance at it, and have the time, I should be very glad of your opinion as to whether I have made any step at all towards possibly inducing folk at home to read matter so extraneous and outlandish. I become heavy and owlish; years sit upon me; it begins to seem to me to be a man's business to leave off his damnable faces and say his say. Else I could have made it pungent and light and lively. In considering, kindly forget that I am R. L. S.; think of the four chapters as a book you are reading, by an inhabitant of our "lovely but fatil" islands; and see if it could possibly amuse the hebetated public. I have to publish anyway, you understand; I have a purpose beyond; I am concerned for some of the parties to this quarrel. What I want to hear is from curiosity; what I want you to judge of is what we are to do with the book in a business sense. To me it is not business at all; I had meant originally to lay all the profits to the credit of Samoa; when it comes to the pinch of writing, I judge this unfair — I give too much — and I

A bit of a sketch map appears to me necessary for my *History;* perhaps two. If I do not have any, 't is impossible any one should follow; and I, even when not at all interested, demand that I shall be able to follow; even a tourist book without a map is a cross to me; and there must be others of my way of thinking. I enclose the very artless one that I think needful. Vailima, in case you are curious, is about as far again behind Tanugamanono as that is from the sea. 1892 ÆT. 42

M'Clure is publishing a short story of mine, some 50,000 words, I think, *The Beach of Falesá;* when he 's done with it, I want you and Cassell to bring it out in a little volume; I shall send you a dedication for it; I believe it good; indeed, to be honest, very good. Good gear that pleases the merchant.

The other map that I half threaten is a chart for the hurricane. Get me Kimberley's report of the hurricane: not to be found here. It is of most importance; I *must* have it with my proofs of that part, if I cannot have it earlier, which now seems impossible.—Yours in hot haste, R. L. STEVENSON.

To J. M. BARRIE

The following is the first of several letters to Mr. J. M. Barrie, for whose work Stevenson had a warm admiration, and with whom he soon established by correspondence a cordial friendship.

VAILIMA, SAMOA, *February, 1892.*

DEAR MR. BARRIE,—This is at least the third letter I have written you, but my correspondence has a bad habit of not getting so far as the post. That which I possess of manhood turns pale before the business of the address and envelope. But I hope to be more fortunate with this: for, besides the usual and often recurrent desire to thank you for your work—you are one of four that have come to the front since I was watching and had a corner of my own to watch, and there is no reason, unless it be in these mysterious tides that ebb and flow, and make and mar and murder the works of poor scribblers, why you should not do work of the best order. The tides have borne away my sentence, of which I was weary at any rate, and between authors I may allow myself so much freedom as to leave it pending. We are both Scots besides, and I suspect both rather Scotty Scots; my own Scotchness tends to intermittency, but is at times erisypelitous—if that be rightly spelt. Lastly, I have gathered we had both made our stages in the metropolis of the winds, our Virgil's "grey metropolis," and I count that a lasting bond. No place so brands a man.

Finally, I feel it a sort of duty to you to report progress. This may be an error, but I believed I detected your hand in an article—it may be an illusion, it may have been by one of those industrious insects who catch up and reproduce the handling of each emergent man—but I 'll still hope it was yours—and hope it may please you to hear that the continuation of *Kidnapped* is under way. I have not yet got to Alan, so I do not know if he is still alive, but David seems to have a kick or two in his shanks. I was pleased to see how the Anglo-Saxon theory fell into the trap: I gave my Lowlander a Gaelic name, and even commented on the fact in the text; yet almost all critics recognised in Alan and David a Saxon and a Celt. I know not about England; in Scotland at least, where Gaelic was spoken in Fife little over the century ago, and in Galloway not much earlier, I deny that there exists such a thing as a pure Saxon, and I think it more than questionable if there be such a thing as a pure Celt. 1892 ÆT. 42

But what have you to do with this? and what have I? Let us continue to inscribe our little bits of tales, and let the heathen rage! — Yours, with sincere interest in your career, ROBERT LOUIS STEVENSON.

TO WILLIAM MORRIS

The following draft letter addressed to Mr. William Morris was found among Stevenson's papers after his death. It has touches of affectation and constraint not usual with him, and it is no doubt on that account that he did not send it; but though not in his best manner, it seems worth printing as illustrating the variety of his interests and admirations in literature.

VAILIMA, SAMOA, *Feb.*, *1892*.

MASTER, — A plea from a place so distant should have some weight, and from a heart so grateful should have some address. I have been long in your debt, Master, and I did not think it could be so much increased as you have now increased it. I was long in your debt and deep in your debt for many poems that I shall never forget, and for *Sigurd* before all, and now you have plunged me beyond payment by the *Saga Library*. And so now, true to human nature, being plunged beyond payment, I come and bark at your heels.

For surely, Master, that tongue that we write, and

1892 that you have illustrated so nobly, is yet alive. She
ÆT. 42 has her rights and laws, and is our mother, our queen, and our instrument. Now in that living tongue *where* has one sense, *whereas* another. In the *Heathslayings Story*, p. 241, line 13, it bears one of its ordinary senses. Elsewhere and usually through the two volumes, which is all that has yet reached me of this entrancing publication, *whereas* is made to figure for *where*.

For the love of God, my dear and honoured Morris, use *where*, and let us know *whereas* we are, wherefore our gratitude shall grow, whereby you shall be the more honoured wherever men love clear language, whereas now, although we honour, we are troubled.

Whereunder, please find inscribed to this very impudent but yet very anxious document, the name of one of the most distant but not the youngest or the coldest of those who honour you.

ROBERT LOUIS STEVENSON.

TO MRS. CHARLES FAIRCHILD

The projected visit of Mr. Kipling, with his wife and brother-in-law, to Samoa, which is mentioned towards the close of this letter, never took place, much to the regret of both authors.

[VAILIMA, *March, 1892.*]

MY DEAR MRS. FAIRCHILD,—I am guilty in your sight, but my affairs besiege me. The chief-justiceship of a family of nineteen persons is in itself no sinecure, and sometimes occupies me for days: two weeks ago for four days almost entirely, and for two days entirely. Besides which, I have in the last few months written all but one chapter of a *History of Samoa* for the last eight or nine years; and while I was unavoidably delayed in the writing of this, awaiting material, put in one-half of *David Balfour*, the sequel to *Kidnapped*. Add the ordinary impediments of life, and admire my busyness. I am now an old, but healthy skeleton, and degenerate much towards the machine. By six at work: stopped at half-past ten to give a history lesson to a step-grandson; eleven, lunch; after lunch we have a musical performance till two; then to work again; bath, 4.40; dinner, five; cards in the evening till eight; and then to bed — only I have no bed, only a chest with a mat and blankets — and read myself to sleep. This is the routine, but often sadly interrupted. Then you may see me sitting on the floor of my verandah haranguing and being harangued by squatting chiefs on a question of a road; or more privately holding an inquiry into some dispute among our familiars, myself on my bed, the boys on the floor — for when it comes to the judicial I play dignity — or else going down to Apia on some more or less unsatisfactory errand. Altogether it is a life that suits me, but it absorbs me like an ocean. That is what I have always envied and admired in Scott; with all that immensity of work and study, his mind kept flexible, glancing to all points of natural interest. But the lean hot spirits, such as mine, become hypnotised with their bit occupations — if I may use Scotch to you — it is so far more scornful than any English idiom. Well, I can't help being a skeleton, and you are to take this devious passage for an apology.

1892
ÆT. 42

I thought *Aladdin* capital fun; but why, in fortune,

1892 ÆT. 42 did he pretend it was moral at the end? The so-called nineteenth century, *où va-t-il se nicher?* 'T is a trifle, but Pyle would do well to knock the passage out, and leave his bogey tale a bogey tale, and a good one at that.

The arrival of your box was altogether a great success to the castaways. You have no idea where we live. Do you know, in all these islands there are not five hundred whites, and no postal delivery, and only one village — it is no more — and would be a mean enough village in Europe? We were asked the other day if Vailima were the name of our post town, and we laughed. Do you know, though we are but three miles from the village metropolis, we have no road to it, and our goods are brought on the pack-saddle? And do you know — or I should rather say, can you believe — or (in the famous old Tichborne trial phrase) would you be surprised to learn, that all you have read of Vailima — or Subpriorsford, as I call it — is entirely false, and we have no ice-machine, and no electric light, and no water supply but the cistern of the heavens, and but one public room, and scarce a bedroom apiece? But, of course, it is well known that I have made enormous sums by my evanescent literature, and you will smile at my false humility. The point, however, is much on our minds just now. We are expecting an invasion of Kiplings; very glad we shall be to see them; but two of the party are ladies, and I tell you we had to hold a council of war to stow them. You European ladies are so particular; with all of mine, sleeping has long become a public function, as with natives and those who go down much into the sea in ships.

Dear Mrs. Fairchild, I must go to my work. I have but two words to say in conclusion. 1892 ÆT. 42

First, civilisation is rot.

Second, console a savage with more of the milk of that over-civilised being, your adorable schoolboy.

As I wrote these remarkable words, I was called down to eight o'clock prayers, and have just worked through a chapter of Joshua and five verses, with five treble choruses, of a Samoan hymn; but the music was good, our boys and precentress ('t is always a woman that leads) did better than I ever heard them, and to my great pleasure I understood it all except one verse. This gave me the more time to try and identify what the parts were doing, and further convict my dull ear. Beyond the fact that the soprano rose to the tonic above on one occasion, I could recognise nothing. This is sickening, but I mean to teach my ear better before I am done with it or this vile carcase.

I think it will amuse you (for a last word) to hear that our precentress — she is the washerwoman — is our shame. She is a good, healthy, comely, strapping young wench, full of energy and seriousness, a splendid workwoman, delighting to train our chorus, delighting in the poetry of the hymns, which she reads aloud (on the least provocation) with a great sentiment of rhythm. Well, then, what is curious? Ah, we did not know! but it was told us in a whisper from the cook-house — she is not of good family. Don't let it get out, please; everybody knows it, of course, here; there is no reason why Europe and the States should have the advantage of me also. And the rest of my housefolk are all chief-people, I assure you. And my late overseer (far the

1892 ÆT. 42 best of his race) is a really serious chief with a good "name." Tina is the name; it is not in the Almanach de Gotha, it must have got dropped at press. The odd thing is, we rather share the prejudice. I have almost always—though not quite always—found the higher the chief the better the man through all the islands; or, at least, that the best man came always from a highish rank. I hope Helen will continue to prove a bright exception.

With love to Fairchild and the Huge Schoolboy, I am, my dear Mrs. Fairchild, yours very sincerely,

ROBERT LOUIS STEVENSON.

To E. L. Burlingame

The first sentences of the following refer to the *Foot-note to History*, Chapter x. of which, relating to the hurricane of 1889, was first published in the *Scots Observer*, edited by Mr. Henley.

[VAILIMA, *March, 1892.*]

MY DEAR BURLINGAME,—Herewith Chapters IX. and X., and I am left face to face with the horrors and dilemmas of the present regimen: pray for those that go down to the sea in ships. I have promised Henley shall have a chance to publish the hurricane chapter if he like, so please let the slips be sent *quam primum* to C. Baxter, W. S., 11 S. Charlotte Street, Edinburgh. I got on mighty quick with that chapter—about five days of the toughest kind of work. God forbid I should ever have such another pirn to wind. When I invent a language, there shall be a direct and an indirect pronoun differently declined—then writing would be some fun.

DIRECT	INDIRECT
He	Tu
Him	Tum
His	Tus

Ex.: *He* seized *tum* by *tus* throat; but *tu* at the same moment caught *him* by *his* hair. A fellow could write hurricanes with an inflection like that! Yet there would be difficulties too.

Do what you please about *The Beach;* and I give you *carte blanche* to write in the matter to Baxter—or telegraph if the time press—to delay the English contingent. Herewith the two last slips of *The Wrecker.* I cannot go beyond. By the way, pray compliment the printers on the proofs of the Samoa racket, but hint to them that it is most unbusiness-like and unscholarly to clip the edges of the galleys; these proofs should really have been sent me on large paper; and I and my friends here are all put to a great deal of trouble and confusion by the mistake. For, as you must conceive, in a matter so contested and complicated, the number of corrections and the length of explanations is considerable.

Please add to my former orders—

Le Chevalier des Touches
Les Diaboliques . . } by Barbey d'Aurévilly.

Correspondance de Henri Beyle (Stendhal).

Yours sincerely, R. L. STEVENSON.

To T. W. DOVER

Stevenson's correspondent in this case is an artizan, who had been struck by the truth of a remark in his essay on "Beggars," that it is

1892 only or mainly the poor who habitually give to the poor; and who
ÆT. 42 wrote to ask whether it was from experience that Stevenson knew this.

VAILIMA PLANTATION, UPOLU, SAMOA,
June 20th, 1892.

SIR,—In reply to your very interesting letter, I cannot fairly say that I have ever been poor, or known what it was to want a meal. I have been reduced, however, to a very small sum of money, with no apparent prospect of increasing it; and at that time I reduced myself to practically one meal a day, with the most disgusting consequences to my health. At this time I lodged in the house of a working-man, and associated much with others. At the same time, from my youth up, I have always been a good deal and rather intimately thrown among the working-classes, partly as a civil engineer in out-of-the-way places, partly from a strong and, I hope, not ill-favoured sentiment of curiosity. But the place where, perhaps, I was most struck with the fact upon which you comment was the house of a friend, who was exceedingly poor, in fact, I may say destitute, and who lived in the attic of a very tall house entirely inhabited by persons in varying stages of poverty. As he was also in ill-health, I made a habit of passing my afternoon with him, and when there it was my part to answer the door. The steady procession of people begging, and the expectant and confident manner in which they presented themselves, struck me more and more daily; and I could not but remember with surprise that though my father lived but a few streets away in a fine house, beggars scarce came to the door once a fortnight or a month. From that time forward I made it my business to inquire, and in the stories which I am very fond of hearing from all sorts and conditions of men, learned that in the time of their distress it was always from the poor they sought assistance, and almost always from the poor they got it. 1892 ÆT. 42

Trusting I have now satisfactorily answered your question, which I thank you for asking, I remain, with sincere compliments, ROBERT LOUIS STEVENSON.

TO E. L. BURLINGAME

VAILIMA, *Summer, 1892.*

MY DEAR BURLINGAME,—First of all, *you have all the corrections on "The Wrecker."* I found I had made what I meant and forgotten it, and was so careless as not to tell you.

Second, of course, and by all means, charge corrections on the Samoa book to me; but there are not near so many as I feared. The Lord hath dealt bountifully with me, and I believe all my advisers were amazed to see how nearly correct I had got the truck, at least I was. With this you will receive the whole revise and a typewritten copy of the last chapter. And the thing now is Speed, to catch a possible revision of the treaty. I believe Cassells are to bring it out, but Baxter knows, and the thing has to be crammed through *prestissimo, à la chasseur.*

You mention the belated Barbeys; what about the equally belated Pineros? And I hope you will keep your bookshop alive to supplying me continuously with the *Saga Library.* I cannot get enough of *Sagas;* I wish there were nine thousand; talk about realism!

1892 ÆT. 42 All seems to flourish with you; I also prosper; none the less for being quit of that abhorred task, Samoa. I could give a supper party here were there any one to sup. Never was such a disagreeable task, but the thing had to be told. . . .

There, I trust I am done with this cursed chapter of my career, bar the rotten eggs and broken bottles that may follow, of course. Pray remember, speed is now all that can be asked, hoped, or wished. I give up all hope of proofs, revises, proof of the map, or sic like; and you on your side will try to get it out as reasonably seemly as may be.

Whole Samoa book herewith. Glory be to God.—Yours very sincerely, ROBERT LOUIS STEVENSON.

TO CHARLES BAXTER

VAILIMA PLANTATION, UPOLU, SAMOAN ISLANDS,
18th July, 1892.

MY DEAR CHARLES,—. . . I have been now for some time contending with powers and principalities, and I have never once seen one of my own letters to the *Times*. So when you see something in the papers that you think might interest the exiles of Upolu, do not think twice, out with your saxpence, and send it flying to Vailima. Of what you say of the past, eh, man, it was a queer time, and awful miserable, but there 's no sense in denying it was awful fun. Do you mind the youth in Highland garb and the tableful of coppers? Do you mind the SIGNAL of Waterloo Place?—Hey, how the blood stands to the heart at such a memory!—Hae ye the notes o't? Gie 's them.—Gude's sake, man, gie 's the notes o't; I mind ye made a tüne o't an' played it on your pinanny; gie 's the notes. Dear Lord, that past. 1892 ÆT. 42

Glad to hear Henley's prospects are fair: his new volume is the work of a real poet. He is one of those who can make a noise of his own with words, and in whom experience strikes an individual note. There is perhaps no more genuine poet living, bar the Big Guns. In case I cannot overtake an acknowledgment to himself by this mail, please let him hear of my pleasure and admiration. How poorly —— compares! He is all smart journalism and cleverness: it is all bright and shallow and limpid, like a business paper—a good one, *s'entend;* but there is no blot of heart's blood and the Old Night: there are no harmonics, there is scarce harmony to his music; and in Henley—all of these; a touch, a sense within sense, a sound outside the sound, the shadow of the inscrutable, eloquent beyond all definition. The First London Voluntary knocked me wholly.—Ever yours affectionately, my dear Charles,

ROBERT LOUIS STEVENSON.

Kind memories to your father and all friends.

TO W. E. HENLEY

VAILIMA PLANTATION, UPOLU, SAMOA,
August 1st, 1892.

MY DEAR HENLEY,—It is impossible to let your new volume pass in silence. I have not received the same thrill of poetry since G. M.'s *Joy of Earth* volume and

1892 ÆT. 42 *Love in a Valley;* and I do not know that even that was so intimate and deep. Again and again I take the book down, and read, and my blood is fired as it used to be in youth. *Andante con moto* in the *Voluntaries*, and the thing about the trees at night (No. XXIV. I think) are up to date my favourites. I did not guess you were so great a magician; these are new tunes, this is an undertone of the true Apollo; these are not verse, they are poetry—inventions, creations, in language. I thank you for the joy you have given me, and remain your old friend and present huge admirer,

ROBERT LOUIS STEVENSON.

The hand is really the hand of Esau, but under a course of threatened scrivener's cramp.

For the next edition of the Book of Verses, pray accept an emendation. Last three lines of Echoes No. XLIV. read—

"But life in act? How should the grave
Be victor over these,
Mother, a mother of men?"

The two vocatives scatter the effect of this inimitable close. If you insist on the longer line, equip "grave" with an epithet. R. L. S.

To E. L. BURLINGAME

VAILIMA, UPOLU, *August 1st, '92.*

MY DEAR BURLINGAME,—Herewith *My Grandfather.* I have had rather a bad time suppressing the old gentleman, who was really in a very garrulous stage; as for getting him *in order*, I could do but little towards that; however, there are one or two points of interest which may justify us in printing. The swinging of his stick and not knowing the sailor of Coruiskin, in particular and the account of how he wrote the lives in the Bell Book particularly please me. I hope my own little introduction is not egoistic; or rather I do not care if it is. It was that old gentleman's blood that brought me to Samoa. 1892 ÆT. 42

By the by, vols. vii., viii., and ix. of Adams's *History* have never come to hand; no more have the dictionaries.

Please send me *Stonehenge on the Horse*, *Stories and Interludes* by Barry Pain, and *Edinburgh Sketches and Memoirs* by David Masson. *The Wrecker* has turned up. So far as I have seen it is very satisfactory, but on pp. 548, 549, there has been a devil of a miscarriage, the two Latin quotations instead of following each other being separated (doubtless for printing considerations) by a line of prose. My compliments to the printers; there is doubtless such a thing as good printing, but there is such a thing as good sense.

The sequel to *Kidnapped*, *David Balfour* by name, is about three-quarters done and gone to press for serial publication. By what I can find out it ought to be through hand with that and ready for volume form early next spring.—Yours very sincerely, R. L. S.

To Andrew Lang

Mr. Andrew Lang had been supplying Stevenson with some books and historical references for his proposed novel of *The Young Chevalier*.

1892
ÆT. 42

[VAILIMA, *August, 1892.*]

MY DEAR LANG,—I knew you would prove a trusty purveyor. The books you have sent are admirable. I got the name of my hero out of Brown—Blair of Balmyle—Francie Blair. But whether to call the story *Blair of Balmyle*, or whether to call it *The Young Chevalier* I have not yet decided. The admirable Cameronian tract—perhaps you will think this a cheat—is to be boned into *David Balfour*, where it will fit better, and really furnishes me with a desired foothold over a boggy place.

Later: no, it won't go in, and I fear I must give up "the idolatrous occupant upon the throne," a phrase that overjoyed me beyond expression. I am in a deuce of a flutter with politics, which I hate, and in which I certainly do not shine; but a fellow cannot stand aside and look on at such an exhibition as our government. 'T ain't decent; no gent can hold a candle to it. But it 's a grind to be interrupted by midnight messengers and pass your days writing proclamations (which are never proclaimed), and petitions (which ain't petited), and letters to the *Times*, which it makes my jaws yawn to re-read, and all your time have your heart with David Balfour: he has just left Glasgow this morning for Edinburgh, James More has escaped from the castle; it is far more real to me than the Behring Sea or the Baring brothers either—he got the news of James More's escape from the Lord Advocate, and started off straight to comfort Catriona. You don't know her; she 's James More's daughter, and a respectable young wumman; the Miss Grants think so—the Lord Advocate's daughters—so there can't be anything really wrong.

Pretty soon we all go to Holland, and be hanged; 1892 ÆT. 42
thence to Dunkirk, and be damned; and the tale concludes in Paris, and be Poll-parroted. This is the last authentic news. You are not a real hard-working novelist; not a practical novelist; so you don't know the temptation to let your characters maunder. Dumas did it, and lived. But it is not war; it ain't sportsmanlike, and I have to be stopping their chatter all the time. Brown's appendix is great reading.

My only grief is that I can't
Use the idolatrous occupant.

Yours ever, R. L. S.

Blessing and praising you for a useful (though idolatrous) occupant of Kensington.

To the Countess of Jersey

In the month of August this year, Stevenson derived much pleasure and entertainment from a visit paid to Apia by the Countess of Jersey, who came over from Sydney with her brother Captain Leigh and her young daughter Lady Margaret Villers. "A warm friendship," writes Lady Jersey, "was the immediate result; we constantly met, either in the hospitable abode of our host Mr. Bazett Haggard, or in Mr. Stevenson's delightful mountain home, and passed many happy hours in riding, walking, and conversation." Among other things, it was arranged that the party should pay a visit of curiosity to the "rebel King," or more properly the rival claimant to the kingly power, Mataafa, in his camp at Malie. Stevenson at once treated the adventure as a chapter out of a Waverley novel (see *Vailima Letters*, p. 205). "The wife of the new Governor of New South Wales," continues Lady Jersey, "could not pay such a visit in her own name, so Mr. Stevenson adopted me as his cousin, 'Amelia Balfour.' This transparent disguise was congenial to his romantic instincts, and he writes concerning the arrangements made for the expedition, carefully dating his letter, 'August 14, 1745.'"

1892
ÆT. 42

August 14, 1745.

TO MISS AMELIA BALFOUR—MY DEAR COUSIN,—We are going an expedition to leeward on Tuesday morning. If a lady were perhaps to be encountered on horseback—say, towards the Gasi-gasi river—about six A. M., I think we should have an episode somewhat after the style of the '45. What a misfortune, my dear cousin, that you should have arrived while your cousin Graham was occupying my only guest-chamber—for Osterley Park is not so large in Samoa as it was at home—but happily our friend Haggard has found a corner for you!

The King over the Water—the Gasi-gasi water—will be pleased to see the clan of Balfour mustering so thick around his standard.

I have (one serious word) been so lucky as to get a really secret interpreter, so all is for the best in our little adventure into the *Waverley Novels.*—I am your affectionate cousin, ROBERT LOUIS STEVENSON.

Observe the stealth with which I have blotted my signature, but we must be political *à outrance.*

TO THE COUNTESS OF JERSEY

MY DEAR COUSIN,—I send for your information a copy of my last letter to the gentleman in question. 'T is thought more wise, in consideration of the difficulty and peril of the enterprise, that we should leave the town in the afternoon, and by several detachments. If you would start for a ride with the Master of Haggard and Captain Lockhart of Lee, say at three o'clock of the afternoon, you would make some rencounters by the wayside which might be agreeable to your political opinions. All present will be staunch. 1892 ÆT. 42

The Master of Haggard might extend his ride a little, and return through the marsh and by the nuns' house (I trust that has the proper flavour), so as a little to diminish the effect of separation.—I remain, your affectionate cousin to command, O TUSITALA.

P. S.—It is to be thought this present year of grace will be historical.

TO MRS. CHARLES FAIRCHILD

[VAILIMA, *August, 1892.*]

MY DEAR MRS. FAIRCHILD,—Thank you a thousand times for your letter. You are the Angel of (the sort of) Information (that I care about); I appoint you successor to the newspaper press; and I beg of you, whenever you wish to gird at the age, or think the bugs out of proportion to the roses, or despair, or enjoy any cosmic or epochal emotion, to sit down again and write to the Hermit of Samoa. What do I think of it all? Well, I love the romantic solemnity of youth; and even in this form, although not without laughter, I have to love it still. They are such ducks! But what are they made of? We were just as solemn as that about atheism and the stars and humanity; but we were all for belief anyway—we held atheism and sociology (of which none of us, nor indeed anybody, knew anything) for a gospel and an iron rule of life; and it

1892 ÆT. 42 was lucky enough, or there would have been more windows broken. What is apt to puzzle one at first sight in the New Youth is that, with such rickety and risky problems always at heart, they should not plunge down a Niagara of Dissolution. But let us remember the high practical timidity of youth. I was a particularly brave boy — it is, I think, of myself, looking back — and plunged into adventures and experiments, and ran risks that it still surprises me to recall. But, dear me, what a fear I was in of that strange blind machinery in the midst of which I stood; and with what a compressed heart and what empty lungs I would touch a new crank and await developments! I do not mean to say I do not fear life still; I do; and that terror (for an adventurer like myself) is still one of the chief joys of living.

But it was different indeed while I was yet girt with the priceless robes of inexperience; then the fear was exquisite and infinite. And so, when you see all these little Ibsens, who seem at once so dry and so excitable, and faint in swathes over a play (I suppose — for a wager) that would seem to me merely tedious, smile behind your hand, and remember the little dears are all in a blue funk. It must be very funny, and to a spectator like yourself I almost envy it. But never get desperate; human nature is human nature; and the Roman Empire, since the Romans founded it and made our European human nature what it is, bids fair to go on and to be true to itself. These little bodies will all grow up and become men and women, and have heaps of fun; nay, and are having it now; and whatever happens to the fashion of the age, it makes no difference

—there are always high and brave and amusing lives to be lived; and a change of key, however exotic, does not exclude melody. Even Chinamen, hard as we find it to believe, enjoy being Chinese. And the Chinaman stands alone to be unthinkable; natural enough, as the representative of the only other great civilisation. Take my people here at my doors; their life is a very good one; it is quite thinkable, quite acceptable to us. And the little dears will be soon skating on the other foot; sooner or later, in each generation, the one-half of them at least begin to remember all the material they had rejected when first they made and nailed up their little theory of life; and these become reactionaries or conservatives, and the ship of man begins to fill upon the other tack.

Here is a sermon, by your leave! It is your own fault, you have amused and interested me so much by your breath of the New Youth, which comes to me from so far away, where I live up here in my mountain, and secret messengers bring me letters from rebels, and the government sometimes seizes them, and generally grumbles in its beard that Stevenson should really be deported. O, my life is the more lively, never fear!

It has recently been most amusingly varied by a visit from Lady Jersey. I took her over mysteriously (under the pseudonym of my cousin, Miss Amelia Balfour) to visit Mataafa, our rebel; and we had great fun, and wrote a Ouida novel on our life here, in which every author had to describe himself in the Ouida glamour, and of which—for the Jerseys intend printing it—I must let you have a copy. My wife's chapter, and my description of myself, should, I think, amuse you. But

1892 ÆT. 42 there were finer touches still; as when Belle and Lady Jersey came out to brush their teeth in front of the rebel King's palace, and the night guard squatted opposite on the grass and watched the process; or when I and my interpreter, and the King with his secretary, mysteriously disappeared to conspire.—Ever yours sincerely,

R. L. STEVENSON.

TO GORDON BROWNE

VAILIMA, SAMOA, *Autumn, 1892.*

To the Artist who did the illustrations to "Uma."

DEAR SIR,—I only know you under the initials G. B., but you have done some exceedingly spirited and satisfactory illustrations to my story *The Beach of Falesá*, and I wish to write and thank you expressly for the care and talent shown. Such numbers of people can do good black and whites! So few can illustrate a story, or apparently read it. You have shown that you can do both, and your creation of Wiltshire is a real illumination of the text. It was exactly so that Wiltshire dressed and looked, and you have the line of his nose to a nicety. His nose is an inspiration. Nor should I forget to thank you for Case, particularly in his last appearance. It is a singular fact—which seems to point still more directly to inspiration in your case—that your missionary actually resembles the flesh-and-blood person from whom Mr. Tarleton was drawn. The general effect of the islands is all that could be wished; indeed, I have but one criticism to make, that in the background of Case taking the dollar from Mr. Tarleton's head — head — not hand, as the fools have printed it — the natives have a little too much the look of Africans. 1892 ÆT. 42

But the great affair is that you have been to the pains to illustrate my story instead of making conscientious black and whites of people sitting talking. I doubt if you have left unrepresented a single pictorial incident. I am writing by this mail to the editor in the hopes that I may buy from him the originals, and I am, dear sir, your very much obliged

ROBERT LOUIS STEVENSON.

TO MISS MORSE

The next is an answer to an acknowledgment from a lady in the United States, one of many similar which he from time to time received, of help and encouragement derived from his writings.

VAILIMA, SAMOAN ISLANDS, *October 7th, 1892.*

DEAR MADAM,— I have a great diffidence in answering your valued letter. It would be difficult for me to express the feelings with which I read it—and am now trying to re-read it as I dictate this.

You ask me to forgive what you say "must seem a liberty," and I find that I cannot thank you sufficiently or even find a word with which to qualify your letter. Dear Madam, such a communication even the vainest man would think a sufficient reward for a lifetime of labour. That I should have been able to give so much help and pleasure to your sister is the subject of my grateful wonder.

1892 ÆT. 42 That she, being dead, and speaking with your pen, should be able to repay the debt with such a liberal interest, is one of those things that reconcile us with the world and make us take hope again. I do not know what I have done to deserve so beautiful and touching a compliment; and I feel there is but one thing fit for me to say here, that I will try with renewed courage to go on in the same path, and to deserve, if not to receive, a similar return from others.

You apologise for speaking so much about yourselves. Dear Madam, I thought you did so too little. I should have wished to have known more of those who were so sympathetic as to find a consolation in my work, and so graceful and so tactful as to acknowledge it in such a letter as was yours.

Will you offer to your mother the expression of a sympathy which (coming from a stranger) must seem very airy, but which yet is genuine; and accept for yourself my gratitude for the thought which inspired you to write to me and the words which you found to express it. ROBERT LOUIS STEVENSON.

TO E. L. BURLINGAME

VAILIMA PLANTATION, SAMOAN ISLANDS,
Oct. 10th, 1892.

MY DEAR BURLINGAME,—It is now, as you see, the 10th of October, and there has not reached the Island of Upolu one single copy, or rag of a copy, of the Samoa book. I lie; there has come one, and that in the pocket of a missionary man who is at daggers drawn with me, who lends it to all my enemies, conceals it from all my friends, and is bringing a lawsuit against me on the strength of expressions in the same which I have forgotten, and now cannot see. This is pretty tragic, I think you will allow; and I was inclined to fancy it was the fault of the Post-Office. But I hear from my sister-in-law Mrs. Sanchez that she is in the same case, and has received no "Foot-note." I have also to consider that I had no letter from you last mail, although you ought to have received by that time "My Grandfather and Scott," and "Me and my Grandfather." Taking one consideration with another, therefore, I prefer to conceive that No. 743 Broadway has fallen upon gentle and continuous slumber, and is become an enchanted palace among publishing houses. If it be not so, if the "Foot-notes" were really sent, I hope you will fall upon the Post-Office with all the vigour you possess. How does *The Wrecker* go in the States? It seems to be doing exceptionally well in England.—Yours sincerely,

ROBERT LOUIS STEVENSON.

To J. M. BARRIE

VAILIMA PLANTATION, SAMOAN ISLANDS,
November 1st, 1892.

DEAR MR. BARRIE,—I can scarce thank you sufficiently for your extremely amusing letter. No, the *Auld Licht Idylls* never reached me—I wish it had, and I wonder extremely whether it would not be good for me to have a pennyworth of the Auld Licht pulpit. It is a singular thing that I should live here in the South

1892 ÆT. 42 Seas under conditions so new and so striking, and yet my imagination so continually inhabit that cold old huddle of grey hills from which we come. I have just finished *David Balfour;* I have another book on the stocks, *The Young Chevalier*, which is to be part in France and part in Scotland, and to deal with Prince Charlie about the year 1749; and now what have I done but begun a third which is to be all moorland together, and is to have for a centrepiece a figure that I think you will appreciate—that of the immortal Braxfield—Braxfield himself is my *grand premier*, or since you are so much involved in the British drama, let me say my heavy lead. . . .

Your descriptions of your dealings with Lord Rintoul are frightfully unconscientious. You should never write about anybody until you persuade yourself at least for the moment that you love him, above all anybody on whom your plot revolves. It will always make a hole in the book; and if he has anything to do with the mechanism, prove a stick in your machinery. But you know all this better than I do, and it is one of your most promising traits that you do not take your powers too seriously. *The Little Minister* ought to have ended badly; we all know it did; and we are infinitely grateful to you for the grace and good feeling with which you lied about it. If you had told the truth, I for one could never have forgiven you. As you had conceived and written the earlier parts, the truth about the end, though indisputably true to fact, would have been a lie, or what is worse, a discord in art. If you are going to make a book end badly, it must end badly from the beginning. Now your book began to end well. You let yourself fall in love with, and fondle, and smile at your puppets. Once you had done that your honour was committed—at the cost of truth to life you were bound to save them. It is the blot on *Richard Feverel*, for instance, that it begins to end well; and then tricks you and ends ill. But in that case there is worse behind, for the ill-ending does not inherently issue from the plot—the story *had*, in fact, *ended well* after the great last interview between Richard and Lucy—and the blind, illogical bullet which smashes all has no more to do between the boards than a fly has to do with the room into whose open window it comes buzzing. It *might* have so happened; it needed not; and unless needs must, we have no right to pain our readers. I have had a heavy case of conscience of the same kind about my Braxfield story. Braxfield—only his name is Hermiston—has a son who is condemned to death; plainly, there is a fine tempting fitness about this; and I meant he was to hang. But now on considering my minor characters, I saw there were five people who would—in a sense who must—break prison and attempt his rescue. They were capable, hardy folks, too, who might very well succeed. Why should they not then? Why should not young Hermiston escape clear out of the country? and be happy, if he could, with his—— But soft! I will not betray my secret or my heroine. Suffice it to breathe in your ear that she was what Hardy calls (and others in their plain way don't) a Pure Woman. Much virtue in a capital letter, such as yours was.

1892
ÆT. 42

Write to me again in my infinite distance. Tell me about your new book. No harm in telling *me*; I am

1892 ÆT. 42 too far off to be indiscreet; there are too few near me who would care to hear. I am rushes by the riverside, and the stream is in Babylon: breathe your secrets to me fearlessly; and if the Trade Wind caught and carried them away, there are none to catch them nearer than Australia, unless it were the Tropic Birds. In the unavoidable absence of my amanuensis, who is buying eels for dinner, I have thus concluded my despatch, like St. Paul, with my own hand.

And in the inimitable words of Lord Kames, Faur ye weel, ye bitch.—Yours very truly,

ROBERT LOUIS STEVENSON.

To E. L. Burlingame

VAILIMA PLANTATION, *Nov. 2nd, 1892.*

MY DEAR BURLINGAME,—In the first place, I have to acknowledge receipt of your munificent cheque for three hundred and fifty dollars. Glad you liked the Scott voyage; rather more than I did upon the whole. As the proofs have not turned up at all there can be no question of returning them, and I am therefore very much pleased to think you have arranged not to wait. The volumes of Adams arrived along with yours of October 6th. One of the dictionaries has also blundered home, apparently from the Colonies, the other is still to seek. I note and sympathise with your bewilderment as to *Falesá*. My own direct correspondence with Mr. Baxter is now about three months in abeyance. Altogether you see how well it would be if you could do anything to wake up the Post-Office. Not a single copy of the "Foot-note" has yet reached Samoa, but I hear of one having come to its address in Hawaii. Glad to hear good news of Stoddard.— Yours sincerely, 1892 ÆT. 42

R. L. STEVENSON.

P. S.— Since the above was written an aftermath of post matter came in, among which were the proofs of *My Grandfather*. I shall correct and return them, but as I have lost all confidence in the Post-Office, I shall mention here: first galley, 4th line from the bottom, for "AS" read "OR."

Should you ever again have to use my work without waiting for proofs, bear in mind this golden principle. From a congenital defect, I must suppose, I am unable to write the word OR—wherever I write it the printer unerringly puts AS—and those who read for me had better, wherever it is possible, substitute OR for AS. This the more so since many writers have a habit of using AS, which is death to my temper and confusion to my face.

R. L. S.

TO LIEUTENANT EELES

The following is addressed to one of Stevenson's best friends among the officers of H. M. S. the *Curaçoa*, which had been for some time on the South Pacific station.

VAILIMA PLANTATION, UPOLU, SAMOAN ISLANDS,
November 15th, 1892.

DEAR EELES,—In the first place, excuse me writing to you by another hand, as that is the way in which alone all my correspondence gets effected. Before I took to

1892 ÆT. 42 this method, or rather before I found a victim, it simply did n't get effected.

Thank you again and again, first for your kind thought of writing to me, and second for your extremely amusing and interesting letter. You can have no guess how immediately interesting it was to our family. First of all, the poor soul at Nukufetau is an old friend of ours, and we have actually treated him ourselves on a former visit to the island. I don't know if Hoskin would approve of our treatment; it consisted, I believe, mostly in a present of stout and a recommendation to put nails in his water-tank. We also (as you seem to have done) recommended him to leave the island; and I remember very well how wise and kind we thought his answer. He had half-caste children (he said) who would suffer and perhaps be despised if he carried them elsewhere; if he left them there alone, they would almost certainly miscarry; and the best thing was that he should stay and die with them. But the cream of the fun was your meeting with Buckland. We not only know him, but (as the French say) we don't know anybody else; he is our intimate and adored original; and — prepare your mind — he was, is, and ever will be, TOMMY HADDON![1] As I don't believe you to be inspired, I suspect you to have suspected this. At least it was a mighty happy suspicion. You are quite right: Tommy is really "a good chap," though about as comic as they make them.

I was extremely interested in your Fiji legend, and perhaps even more so in your capital account of the *Curaçoa's* misadventure. Alas, we have nothing

[1] A character in *The Wrecker*.

so thrilling to relate. All hangs and fools on in this isle of misgovernment, without change, though not without novelty, but wholly without hope, unless perhaps you should consider it hopeful that I am still more immediately threatened with arrest. The confounded thing is, that if it comes off, I shall be sent away in the *Ringarooma* instead of the *Curaçoa*. The former ship burst upon by the run — she had been sent off by despatch and without orders — and to make me a little more easy in my mind she brought newspapers clamouring for my incarceration. Since then I have had a conversation with the German Consul. He said he had read a review of my Samoa book, and if the review were fair, must regard it as an insult, and one that would have to be resented. At the same time, I learn that letters addressed to the German squadron lie for them here in the Post-Office. Reports are current of other English ships being on the way — I hope to goodness yours will be among the number. And I gather from one thing and another that there must be a holy row going on between the powers at home, and that the issue (like all else connected with Samoa) is on the knees of the gods. One thing, however, is pretty sure — if that issue prove to be a German Protectorate, I shall have to tramp. Can you give us any advice as to a fresh field of energy? We have been searching the atlas, and it seems difficult to fill the bill. How would Raratonga do? I forget if you have been there. The best of it is that my new house is going up like winking, and I am dictating this letter to the accompaniment of saws and hammers. A hundred black boys and about a score draught-oxen perished, or at least barely

1892 ÆT. 42

escaped with their lives, from the mud-holes on our road bringing up the materials. It will be a fine legacy to H. I. G. M.'s Protectorate, and doubtless the Governor will take it for his country-house. The *Ringarooma* people, by the way, seem very nice. I liked Stansfield particularly.

Our middy[1] has gone up to San Francisco in pursuit of the phantom Education. We have good word of him, and I hope he will not be in disgrace again, as he was when the hope of the British Navy — need I say that I refer to Admiral Burney? — honoured us last. The next time you come, as the new house will be finished, we shall be able to offer you a bed. Nares and Meiklejohn may like to hear that our new room is to be big enough to dance in. It will be a very pleasant day for me to see the *Curaçoa* in port again and at least a proper contingent of her officers "skipping in my 'all."

We have just had a feast on my birthday at which we had three of the Ringaroomas, and I wish they had been three Curaçoas — say yourself, Hoskin, and Burney the ever Great. (Consider this an invitation.) Our boys had got the thing up regardless. There were two huge sows — oh, brutes of animals that would have broken down a hansom cab — four smaller pigs, two barrels of beef, and a horror of vegetables and fowls. We sat down between forty and fifty in a big new native house behind the kitchen that you have never seen, and ate and public spoke till all was blue. Then we had about half an hour's holiday, with some beer and sherry and brandy and soda to restrengthen the

[1] The lad Austin Strong.

European heart, and then out to the old native house to see a siva. Finally, all the guests were packed off in a trackless black night and down a road that was rather fitted for the *Curaçoa* than any human pedestrian, though to be sure I do not know the draught of the *Curaçoa*. My ladies one and all desire to be particularly remembered to our friends on board, and all look forward, as I do myself, in the hope of your return.—Yours sincerely, ROBERT LOUIS STEVENSON. 1892 ÆT. 42

And let me hear from you again!

TO CHARLES BAXTER

The following extract gives a hint of Stevenson's intended management of one of the most difficult points in the plot of *Weir of Hermiston*.

1st Dec., '92.

. . . I have a novel on the stocks to be called *The Justice-Clerk*. It is pretty Scotch, the Grand Premier is taken from Braxfield—(Oh, by the by, send me Cockburn's *Memorials*)—and some of the story is—well—queer. The heroine is seduced by one man, and finally disappears with the other man who shot him. . . . Mind you, I expect *The Justice-Clerk* to be my masterpiece. My Braxfield is already a thing of beauty and a joy for ever, and so far as he has gone *far* my best character.

[*Later.*]

Second thought. I wish Pitcairn's *Criminal Trials quam primum*. Also, an absolutely correct text of the Scots judiciary oath.

1892 ÆT. 42 Also, in case Pitcairn does not come down late enough, I wish as full a report as possible of a Scotch murder trial between 1790–1820. Understand, *the fullest possible.*

Is there any book which would guide me as to the following facts?

The Justice-Clerk tries some people capitally on circuit. Certain evidence cropping up, the charge is transferred to the J.-C.'s own son. Of course, in the next trial the J.-C. is excluded, and the case is called before the Lord-Justice General.

Where would this trial have to be? I fear in Edinburgh, which would not suit my view. Could it be again at the circuit town?

ROBERT LOUIS STEVENSON.

TO MRS. FLEEMING JENKIN

December 5th, 1892.

MY DEAR MRS. JENKIN,—. . . So much said, I come with guilty speed to what more immediately concerns myself. Spare us a month or two for old sake's sake, and make my wife and me happy and proud. We are only fourteen days from San Francisco, just about a month from Liverpool; we have our new house almost finished. The thing *can* be done; I believe we can make you almost comfortable. It is the loveliest climate in the world, our political troubles seem near an end. It can be done, *it must!* Do, please, make a virtuous effort, come and take a glimpse of a new world I am sure you do not dream of, and some old friends who do often dream of your arrival. 1892 ÆT. 42

Alas, I was just beginning to get eloquent, and there goes the lunch bell, and after lunch I must make up the mail.

Do come. You must not come in February or March — bad months. From April on it is delightful.—Your sincere friend, ROBERT LOUIS STEVENSON.

TO HENRY JAMES

December 5th, 1892.

MY DEAR JAMES,—How comes it so great a silence has fallen? The still small voice of self-approval whispers me it is not from me. I have looked up my register, and find I have neither written to you nor heard from you since June 22nd, on which day of grace that invaluable work began. This is not as it should be. How to get back? I remember acknowledging with rapture *The Lesson of the Master*, and I remember receiving *Marbot*: was that our last relation?

Hey, well! anyway, as you may have probably gathered from the papers, I have been in devilish hot water, and (what may be new to you) devilish hard at work. In twelve calendar months I finished *The Wrecker*, wrote all of *Falesá* but the first chapter (well, much of), the *History of Samoa*, did something here and there to my *Life of my Grandfather*, and began And Finished *David Balfour*. What do you think of it for a year? Since then I may say I have done nothing beyond draft three chapters of another novel, *The Justice-Clerk*, which

1892 ÆT. 42 ought to be a snorter and a blower — at least if it don't make a spoon, it will spoil the horn of an Aurochs (if that 's how it should be spelt).

On the hot water side it may entertain you to know that I have been actually sentenced to deportation by my friends on Mulinuu, C. J. Cedercrantz and Baron Senfft von Pilsach. The awful doom, however, declined to fall, owing to Circumstances over Which. I only heard of it (so to speak) last night. I mean officially, but I had walked among rumours. The whole tale will be some day put into my hand, and I shall share it with humorous friends.

It is likely, however, by my judgment, that this epoch of gaiety in Samoa will soon cease; and the fierce white light of history will beat no longer on Yours Sincerely and his fellows here on the beach. We ask ourselves whether the reason will more rejoice over the end of a disgraceful business, or the unregenerate man more sorrow over the stoppage of the fun. For, say what you please, it has been a deeply interesting time. You don't know what news is, nor what politics, nor what the life of man, till you see it on so small a scale and with your own liberty on the board for stake. I would not have missed it for much. And anxious friends beg me to stay at home and study human nature in Brompton drawing-rooms! *Farceurs!* And anyway you know that such is not my talent. I could never be induced to take the faintest interest in Brompton *qua* Brompton or a drawing-room *qua* a drawing-room. I am an Epick Writer with a *k* to it, but without the necessary genius.

Hurry up with another book of stories. I am now

reduced to two of my contemporaries, you and Barrie—O, and Kipling—you and Barrie and Kipling are now my Muses Three. And with Kipling, as you know, there are reservations to be made. And you and Barrie don't write enough. I should say I also read Anstey when he is serious, and can almost always get a happy day out of Marion Crawford—*ce n'est pas toujours la guerre*, but it 's got life to it and guts, and it moves. Did you read *The Witch of Prague?* Nobody could read it twice, of course; and the first time even it was necessary to skip. *E pur si muove.* But Barrie is a beauty, *The Little Minister* and the *Window in Thrums*, eh? Stuff in that young man; but he must see and not be too funny. Genius in him, but there 's a journalist at his elbow—there 's the risk. Look, what a page is the glove business in the *Window!* knocks a man flat; that 's guts, if you please. 1892 ÆT. 42

Why have I wasted the little time that is left with a sort of naked review article? I don't know, I 'm sure. I suppose a mere ebullition of congested literary talk. I am beginning to think a visit from friends would be due. Wish you could come!

Let us have your news anyway, and forgive this silly stale effusion.—Yours ever,

ROBERT LOUIS STEVENSON.

To J. M. Barrie

[VAILIMA, *December, 1892.*]

DEAR J. M. BARRIE,—You will be sick of me soon; I cannot help it. I have been off my work for some time,

1892 ÆT. 42 and re-read the Edinburgh Eleven, and had a great mind to write a parody and give you all your sauce back again, and see how you would like it yourself. And then I read (for the first time—I know not how) the *Window in Thrums;* I don't say that it is better than *The Minister;* it 's less of a tale—and there is a beauty, a material beauty, of the tale *ipse,* which clever critics nowadays long and love to forget; it has more real flaws; but somehow it is—well, I read it last anyway, and it 's by Barrie. And he 's the man for my money. The glove is a great page; it is startlingly original, and as true as death and judgment. Tibbie Birse in the Bur'al is great, but I think it was a journalist that got in the word "official." The same character plainly had a word to say to Thomas Haggard. Thomas affects me as a lie—I beg your pardon; doubtless he was somebody you knew, that leads people so far astray. The actual is not the true.

I am proud to think you are a Scotchman—though to be sure I know nothing of that country, being only an English tourist, quo' Gavin Ogilvy. I commend the hard case of Mr. Gavin Ogilvy to J. M. Barrie, whose work is to me a source of living pleasure and heartfelt national pride. There are two of us now that the Shirra might have patted on the head. And please do not think when I thus seem to bracket myself with you, that I am wholly blinded with vanity. Jess is beyond my frontier line; I could not touch her skirt; I have no such glamour of twilight on my pen. I am a capable artist; but it begins to look to me as if you were a man of genius. Take care of yourself for my sake. It 's a devilish hard thing for a man who writes so many novels as I do, that I should get so few to read. And I can read yours, and I love them. 1892 ÆT. 42

A pity for you that my amanuensis is not on stock to-day, and my own hand perceptibly worse than usual.—Yours, ROBERT LOUIS STEVENSON.

December 5th, 1892.

P. S.—We have, for a wonder of wonders, visitors here. They tell me your health is not strong. Man, come out here and try the Prophet's chamber. There 's only one bad point to us—we do rise early. The Amanuensis states that you are a lover of silence—and that ours is a noisy house—and she is a chatterbox. I am not answerable for these statements, though I do think there is a touch of garrulity about my premises. We have so little to talk about, you see. The house is three miles from town, in the midst of great silent forests. There is a burn close by, and when we are not talking you can hear the burn, and the birds, and the sea breaking on the coast three miles away and six hundred feet below us, and about three times a month a bell—I don't know where the bell is, nor who rings it; it may be the bell in Hans Andersen's story for all I know. It is never hot here—86 in the shade is about our hottest—and it is never cold except just in the early mornings. Take it for all in all, I suppose this island climate to be by far the healthiest in the world—even the influenza entirely lost its sting. Only two patients died, and one was a man nearly eighty, and the other a child below four months. I won't tell you if it is beautiful, for I want you to come here and see for yourself. Everybody on the premises except my wife has some Scotch blood in

1892 ÆT. 42 their veins — I beg your pardon — except the natives — and then my wife is a Dutchwoman — and the natives are the next thing conceivable to Highlanders before the forty-five. We would have some grand cracks!

R. L. S.

Come, it will broaden your mind, and be the making of me.

XII

LIFE IN SAMOA

Continued

(January, 1893 – December, 1894)

XII

LIFE IN SAMOA

Continued

(JANUARY, 1893–DECEMBER, 1894)

FROM about the date of the last letter, that is, from the end of 1892, things began to go less fortunately for the exile of Vailima. The influenza did not pass away without leaving its usual weakening and depressing consequences. From a trip which the family took for the sake of change to Sydney, in February, 1893, they returned with health unimproved; and in April of the same year the illness of Mrs. Stevenson caused her husband some weeks of the gravest anxiety. In August he had the chagrin of witnessing the outbreak of war in the island, which he had vainly striven to prevent, and the defeat and banishment of Mataafa, in whom he believed as the one man of governing capacity among the native chiefs, and whom, in the interest alike of whites and natives, he had desired to see the Powers not crush, but conciliate. Later in the autumn of the same year he took a trip to Honolulu, where he had a renewed attack of influenza, and again underwent some weeks of fever and prostration. The only work he was able to finish during the year was *The Ebb Tide*, and that on a plan much abridged from his original intention; it remains an episode of ocean adventure and villainy, set forth indeed with extraordinary vividness and force, but lapsing, as its author was painfully aware, into that sin of ugliness which he himself most of all condemned in the art of his age. For the rest, he felt his power of work to be flagging. With *St. Ives* and his own family history he made indeed fair progress, but both of these he regarded as in a manner holiday tasks, not calling for any very serious exercise of his powers. He fell into arrears in regard to one or two magazine stories for which he had contracted, and with none of his more ambitious schemes of historical romance, *Sophia Scarlet*, *The Young Chevalier*, *Heather-cat*, and *Weir of Hermiston*, did he feel himself well able to cope.

This state of things lasted through the spring and summer of 1894, and brought with it a considerable degree of inward strain and anxiety. He had not yet put by any provision for his wife and step-family (the income from the moderate fortune left by his father naturally going to his mother during her life). His gains from literature had since 1887 been considerable, at the rate of between £4000 and £5000 a year; but his hospitable, though in no sense extravagant, mode of life at Vailima, together with his habitual generosity, which scarce knew check or limit, towards the less fortunate among his friends and acquaintances in various parts of the world, made his expenditure about equal to his income. What if his power of earning were now to cease? The thought haunted him much during the last two years of his life, and its importunity was no doubt increased by some physical premonition that his vital powers, so frail from the cradle, and always with so cheerful a courage overtaxed, were near exhaustion. In the end, as all his readers know, they revived for one crowning effort upon *Weir of Hermiston;* and in that effort he fell. Some of the letters which follow give glimpses of the fits of depression and life-weariness which now at times assailed him. But it was only in writing, and then but rarely, that he let such signs appear. At the end of this book, as at the beginning, the reader must be warned, if he would form a faithful picture of the man, that at the touch of direct human intercourse the cast of gravity, nay, sadness, which was part of his character, and which will be found overshadowing his spirits in some of these letters, was at once and almost invariably dispersed. To those about him, whether visitors or inmates, he remained the impersonation of life and spirit, maintaining to the last the same charming gaiety as ever, the same happy eagerness in all pursuits and interests; and fulfilling without failure the words of his own prayer, "Give us to awake with smiles, give us to labour smiling. . . . As the sun lightens the world, so let our loving-kindness make bright this house of our habitation."

To Charles Baxter

Of the books mentioned below, *Dr. Syntax's Tour* and Rowlandson's *Dance of Death* had been for use in furnishing customs and manners in the English part of *St. Ives;* "Pitcairn" is *Pitcairn's Criminal* 1893 ÆT. 43

1893 *Trials of Scotland from 1488 to 1624.* As to the name of Stevenson
ÆT. 43 and its adoption by some members of the proscribed clan of Macgregor, Stevenson had been greatly interested by the facts laid before him by his correspondent here mentioned, Mr. Macgregor Stevenson of New York, and had at first delightedly welcomed the idea that his own ancestors might have been fellow clansmen of Rob Roy. But further correspondence on the subject of his own descent held with a trained genealogist, his namesake Mr. J. Horne Stevenson of Edinburgh, convinced him that the notion must be abandoned.

[*April, 1893.*]

. . . About *The Justice-Clerk*, I long to go at it, but will first try to get a short story done. Since January I have had two severe illnesses, my boy, and some heartbreaking anxiety over Fanny; and am only now convalescing. I came down to dinner last night for the first time, and that only because the service had broken down, and to relieve an inexperienced servant. Nearly four months now I have rested my brains; and if it be true that rest is good for brains, I ought to be able to pitch in like a giant refreshed. Before the autumn, I hope to send you some *Justice-Clerk*, or *Weir of Hermiston*, as Colvin seems to prefer; I own to indecision. Received *Syntax*, *Dance of Death*, and *Pitcairn*, which last I have read from end to end since its arrival, with vast improvement. What a pity it stops so soon! I wonder is there nothing that seems to prolong the series? Why does n't some young man take it up? How about my old friend Fountainhall's *Decisions?* I remember as a boy that there was some good reading there. Perhaps you could borrow me that, and send it on loan; and perhaps Laing's *Memorials* therewith; and a work I 'm ashamed to say I have never read, *Balfour's Letters*. . . . I have come by accident, through a correspondent, on one very curious and interesting fact—namely, that Stevenson was one of the names adopted by the Macgregors at the proscription. The details supplied by my correspondent are both convincing and amusing; but it would be highly interesting to find out more of this. R. L. S. 1893 ÆT. 43

To A. Conan Doyle

The reference in the postscript here is, I believe, to the Journals of the Society for Psychical Research.

Vailima, Apia, Samoa, *April 5th, 1893.*

DEAR SIR,—You have taken many occasions to make yourself very agreeable to me, for which I might in decency have thanked you earlier. It is now my turn; and I hope you will allow me to offer you my compliments on your very ingenious and very interesting adventures of Sherlock Holmes. That is the class of literature that I like when I have the toothache. As a matter of fact, it was a pleurisy I was enjoying when I took the volume up; and it will interest you as a medical man to know that the cure was for the moment effectual. Only the one thing troubles me: can this be my old friend Joe Bell?—I am, yours very truly,

Robert Louis Stevenson.

P. S.—And lo, here is your address supplied me here in Samoa! But do not take mine, O frolic fellow Spookist, from the same source; mine is wrong.

R. L. S.

1893
ÆT. 43

To S. R. Crockett

Glencorse Church in the Pentlands, mentioned by Stevenson with so much emotion in the course of this letter, served him for the scene of Chapter VI. in *Weir of Hermiston*, where his old associations and feelings in connection with the place have so admirably inspired him.

Vailima, Samoa, *May 17th, 1893.*

DEAR MR. CROCKETT,—I do not owe you two letters, nor yet nearly one, sir! The last time I heard of you, you wrote about an accident, and I sent you a letter to my lawyer, Charles Baxter, which does not seem to have been presented, as I see nothing of it in his accounts. Query, was that lost? I should not like you to think I had been so unmannerly and so inhuman. If you have written since, your letter also has miscarried, as is much the rule in this part of the world, unless you register.

Your book is not yet to hand, but will probably follow next month. I detected you early in the *Bookman*, which I usually see, and noted you in particular as displaying a monstrous ingratitude about the foot-note. Well, mankind is ungrateful; "Man's ingratitude to man makes countless thousands mourn," quo' Rab—or words to that effect. By the way, an anecdote of a cautious sailor: "Bill, Bill," says I to him, "*or words to that effect.*"

I shall never take that walk by the Fisher's Tryst and Glencorse. I shall never see Auld Reekie. I shall never set my foot again upon the heather. Here I am until I die, and here will I be buried. The word is out and the doom written. Or, if I do come, it will be a voyage to a further goal, and in fact a suicide; which, however, if I could get my family all fixed up in the money way, I might, perhaps, perform, or attempt. But there is a plaguey risk of breaking down by the way; and I believe I shall stay here until the end comes like a good boy, as I am. If I did it, I should put upon my trunks: "Passenger to — Hades." 1893 ÆT. 43

How strangely wrong your information is! In the first place, I should never carry a novel to Sydney; I should post it from here. In the second place, *Weir of Hermiston* is as yet scarce begun. It 's going to be excellent, no doubt; but it consists of about twenty pages. I have a tale, a shortish tale in length, but it has proved long to do, *The Ebb Tide*, some part of which goes home this mail. It is by me and Mr. Osbourne, and is really a singular work. There are only four characters, and three of them are bandits — well, two of them are, and the third is their comrade and accomplice. It sounds cheering, does n't it? Barratry, and drunkenness, and vitriol, and I cannot tell you all what, are the beams of the roof. And yet — I don't know — I sort of think there 's something in it. You 'll see (which is more than I ever can) whether Davis and Attwater come off or not.

Weir of Hermiston is a much greater undertaking, and the plot is not good, I fear; but Lord Justice Clerk Hermiston ought to be a plum. Of other schemes, more or less executed, it skills not to speak.

I am glad to hear so good an account of your activity and interests, and shall always hear from you with pleasure; though I am, and must continue, a mere sprite of the inkbottle, unseen in the flesh. Please

1893 remember me to your wife and to the four-year-old
ÆT. 43 sweetheart, if she be not too engrossed with higher matters. Do you know where the road crosses the burn under Glencorse Church? Go there, and say a prayer for me: *moriturus salutat.* See that it 's a sunny day; I would like it to be a Sunday, but that 's not possible in the premises; and stand on the right-hand bank just where the road goes down into the water, and shut your eyes, and if I don't appear to you! well, it can't be helped, and will be extremely funny.

I have no concern here but to work and to keep an eye on this distracted people. I live just now wholly alone in an upper room of my house, because the whole family are down with influenza, bar my wife and myself. I get my horse up sometimes in the afternoon and have a ride in the woods; and I sit here and smoke and write, and rewrite, and destroy, and rage at my own impotence, from six in the morning till eight at night, with trifling and not always agreeable intervals for meals.

I am sure you chose wisely to keep your country charge. There a minister can be something, not in a town. In a town, the most of them are empty houses—and public speakers. Why should you suppose your book will be slated because you have no friends? A new writer, if he is any good, will be acclaimed generally with more noise than he deserves. But by this time you will know for certain.—I am, yours sincerely,

ROBERT LOUIS STEVENSON.

P. S.—Be it known to this fluent generation that I,

R. L. S., in the forty-third of my age and the twentieth of my professional life, wrote twenty-four pages in twenty-one days, working from six to eleven, and again in the afternoon from two to four or so, without fail or interruption. Such are the gifts the gods have endowed us withal: such was the facility of this prolific writer! R. L. S.

To Augustus St. Gaudens

Vailima, Samoa, *May 29th, 1893.*

MY DEAR GOD-LIKE SCULPTOR,—I wish in the most delicate manner in the world to insinuate a few commissions:—

No. 1. Is for a couple of copies of my medallion, as gilt-edged and high-toned as it is possible to make them. One is for our house here, and should be addressed as above. The other is for my friend Sidney Colvin, and should be addressed—Sidney Colvin, Esq., Keeper of the Print Room, British Museum, London.

No. 2. This is a rather large order, and demands some explanation. Our house is lined with varnished wood of a dark ruddy colour, very beautiful to see; at the same time, it calls very much for gold; there is a limit to picture frames, and really you know there has to be a limit to the pictures you put inside of them. Accordingly, we have had an idea of a certain kind of decoration, which, I think, you might help us to make practical. What we want is an alphabet of gilt letters (very much such as people play with), and all mounted

1893
ÆT. 43
on spikes like drawing-pins; say two spikes to each letter, one at top, and one at bottom. Say that they were this height, I and that you chose a model of some really exquisitely fine, clear type from some Roman monument, and that they were made either of metal or some composition gilt—the point is, could not you, in your land of wooden houses, get a manufacturer to take the idea and manufacture them at a venture, so that I could get two or three hundred pieces or so at a moderate figure? You see, suppose you entertain an honoured guest, when he goes he leaves his name in gilt letters on your walls; an infinity of fun and decoration can be got out of hospitable and festive mottoes; and the doors of every room can be beautified by the legend of their names. I really think there is something in the idea, and you might be able to push it with the brutal and licentious manufacturer, using my name if necessary, though I should think the name of the godlike sculptor would be more germane. In case you should get it started, I should tell you that we should require commas in order to write the Samoan language, which is full of words written thus: la'u, ti'e ti'e. As the Samoan language uses but a very small proportion of the consonants, we should require a double or treble stock of all vowels and of F, G, L, U, N, P, S, T, and V.

The other day in Sydney, I think you might be interested to hear, I was sculpt a second time by a man called ——, as well as I can remember and read. I must n't criticise a present, and he had very little time to do it in. It is thought by my family to be an excellent likeness of Mark Twain. This poor fellow, by the by, met with the devil of an accident. A model of a statue which he had just finished with a desperate effort was smashed to smithereens on its way to exhibition. 1893 ÆT. 43

Please be sure and let me know if anything is likely to come of this letter business, and the exact cost of each letter, so that I may count the cost before ordering.—Yours sincerely,

ROBERT LOUIS STEVENSON.

To EDMUND GOSSE

"My Grandfather" in the following means not the *Scribner* paper already several times referred to, but the chapters on Robert Stevenson in the projected book of family memoirs, variously called *Northern Lights*, *History of the Stevensons*, and finally *History of a Family of Engineers*.

June 10th, 1893.

MY DEAR GOSSE,—My mother tells me you never received the very long and careful letter that I sent you more than a year ago; or is it two years?

I was indeed so much surprised at your silence that I wrote to Henry James and begged him to inquire if you had received it; his reply was an (if possible) higher power of the same silence; whereupon I bowed my head and acquiesced. But there is no doubt the letter was written and sent; and I am sorry it was lost, for it contained, among other things, an irrecoverable criticism of your father's *Life*, with a number of suggestions for another edition, which struck me at the time as excellent.

1893 ÆT. 43 Well, suppose we call that cried off, and begin as before? It is fortunate indeed that we can do so, being both for a while longer in the day. But, alas! when I see "works of the late J. A. S.,"[1] I can see no help and no reconciliation possible. I wrote him a letter, I think, three years ago, heard in some roundabout way that he had received it, waited in vain for an answer (which had probably miscarried), and in a humour between frowns and smiles wrote to him no more. And now the strange, poignant, pathetic, brilliant creature is gone into the night, and the voice is silent that uttered so much excellent discourse; and I am sorry that I did not write to him again. Yet I am glad for him; light lie the turf! The *Saturday* is the only obituary I have seen, and I thought it very good upon the whole. I should be half tempted to write an *In Memoriam*, but I am submerged with other work. Are you going to do it? I very much admire your efforts that way; you are our only academician.

So you have tried fiction? I will tell you the truth: when I saw it announced, I was so sure you would send it to me, that I did not order it! But the order goes this mail, and I will give you news of it. Yes, honestly, fiction is very difficult; it is a terrible strain to *carry* your characters all that time. And the difficulty of according the narrative and the dialogue (in a work in the third person) is extreme. That is one reason out of half a dozen why I so often prefer the first. It is much in my mind just now, because of my last work, just off the stocks three days ago, *The Ebb Tide:* a dreadful, grimy business in the third person, where

[1] John Addington Symonds.

the strain between a vilely realistic dialogue and a narrative style pitched about (in phrase) "four notes higher" than it should have been has sown my head with grey hairs; or I believe so — if my head escaped, my heart has them. 1893 ÆT. 43

The truth is, I have a little lost my way, and stand bemused at the cross-roads. A subject? Ay, I have dozens; I have at least four novels begun, they are none good enough; and the mill waits, and I 'll have to take second best. *The Ebb Tide* I make the world a present of; I expect, and, I suppose, deserve to be torn to pieces; but there was all that good work lying useless, and I had to finish it!

All your news of your family is pleasant to hear. My wife has been very ill, but is now better; I may say I am ditto, *The Ebb Tide* having left me high and dry, which is a good example of the mixed metaphor. Our home and estate, and our boys, and the politics of the island, keep us perpetually amused and busy; and I grind away with an odd, dogged, down sensation — and an idea *in petto* that the game is about played out. I have got too realistic, and I must break the trammels — I mean I would if I could; but the yoke is heavy. I saw with amusement that Zola says the same thing; and truly the *Débâcle* was a mighty big book, I have no need for a bigger, though the last part is a mere mistake in my opinion. But the Emperor, and Sedan, and the doctor at the ambulance, and the horses in the field of battle, Lord, how gripped it is! What an epical performance! According to my usual opinion, I believe I could go over that book and leave a masterpiece by blotting and no ulterior art.

1893 ÆT. 43 But that is an old story, ever new with me. Taine gone, and Renan, and Symonds, and Tennyson, and Browning; the suns go swiftly out, and I see no suns to follow, nothing but a universal twilight of the demi-divinities, with parties like you and me and Lang beating on toy drums and playing on penny whistles about glow-worms. But Zola is big anyway; he has plenty in his belly; too much, that is all; he wrote the *Débâcle* and he wrote *La Bête Humaine*, perhaps the most excruciatingly silly book that I ever read to an end. And why did I read it to an end, W. E. G.? Because the animal in me was interested in the lewdness. Not sincerely, of course, my mind refusing to partake in it; but the flesh was slightly pleased. And when it was done, I cast it from me with a peal of laughter, and forgot it, as I would forget a Montépin. Taine is to me perhaps the chief of these losses; I did luxuriate in his *Origines;* it was something beyond literature, not quite so good, if you please, but so much more systematic, and the pages that had to be "written" always so adequate. Robespierre, Napoleon, were both excellent good.

June 18th, '93.

Well, I have left fiction wholly, and gone to my *Grandfather*, and on the whole found peace. By next month my *Grandfather* will begin to be quite grown up. I have already three chapters about as good as done; by which, of course, as you know, I mean till further notice or the next discovery. I like biography far better than fiction myself: fiction is too free. In biography you have your little handful of facts, little bits of a puzzle, and you sit and think, and fit 'em together this way and that, and get up and throw 'em down, and say damn, and go out for a walk. And it 's real soothing; and when done, gives an idea of finish to the writer that is very peaceful. Of course, it 's not really so finished as quite a rotten novel; it always has and always must have the incurable illogicalities of life about it, the fathoms of slack and the miles of tedium. Still, that 's where the fun comes in; and when you have at last managed to shut up the castle spectre (dulness), the very outside of his door looks beautiful by contrast. There are pages in these books that may seem nothing to the reader; but you *remember what they were, you know what they might have been*, and they seem to you witty beyond comparison. In my *Grandfather* I 've had (for instance) to give up the temporal order almost entirely; doubtless the temporal order is the great foe of the biographer; it is so tempting, so easy, and lo! there you are in the bog!—Ever yours,

1893
ÆT. 43

R. L. STEVENSON.

With all kind messages from self and wife to you and yours. My wife is very much better, having been the early part of this year alarmingly ill. She is now all right, only complaining of trifles, annoying to her, but happily not interesting to her friends. I am in a hideous state, having stopped drink and smoking; yes, both. No wine, no tobacco; and the dreadful part of it is that—looking forward—I have—what shall I say?—nauseating intimations that it ought to be for ever.

1893
ÆT. 43

To Henry James

Vailima Plantation, Samoan Islands,
June 17th, 1893.

MY DEAR HENRY JAMES,—I believe I have neglected a mail in answering yours. You will be very sorry to hear that my wife was exceedingly ill, and very glad to hear that she is better. I cannot say that I feel any more anxiety about her. We shall send you a photograph of her taken in Sydney in her customary island habit as she walks and gardens and shrilly drills her brown assistants. She was very ill when she sat for it, which may a little explain the appearance of the photograph. It reminds me of a friend of my grandmother's who used to say when talking to younger women, "Aweel, when I was young, I wasnae just exactly what ye wad call *bonny*, but I was pale, penetratin', and interestin'." I would not venture to hint that Fanny is "no bonny," but there is no doubt but that in this presentment she is "pale, penetratin', and interestin'."

As you are aware, I have been wading deep waters and contending with the great ones of the earth, not wholly without success. It is, you may be interested to hear, a dreary and infuriating business. If you can get the fools to admit one thing, they will always save their face by denying another. If you can induce them to take a step to the right hand, they generally indemnify themselves by cutting a caper to the left. I always held (upon no evidence whatever, from a mere sentiment or intuition) that politics was the dirtiest, the most foolish, and the most random of human employments. I always held, but now I know it! Fortunately, you have nothing to do with anything of the kind, and I may spare you the horror of further details. 1893 ÆT. 43

I received from you a book by a man by the name of Anatole France. Why should I disguise it? I have no use for Anatole. He writes very prettily, and then afterwards? Baron Marbot was a different pair of shoes. So likewise is the Baron de Vitrolles, whom I am now perusing with delight. His escape in 1814 is one of the best pages I remember anywhere to have read. But Marbot and Vitrolles are dead, and what has become of the living? It seems as if literature were coming to a stand. I am sure it is with me; and I am sure everybody will say so when they have the privilege of reading *The Ebb Tide.* My dear man, the grimness of that story is not to be depicted in words. There are only four characters, to be sure, but they are such a troop of swine! And their behaviour is really so deeply beneath any possible standard, that on a retrospect I wonder I have been able to endure them myself until the yarn was finished. Well, there is always one thing; it will serve as a touchstone. If the admirers of Zola admire him for his pertinent ugliness and pessimism, I think they should admire this; but if, as I have long suspected, they neither admire nor understand the man's art, and only wallow in his rancidness like a hound in offal, then they will certainly be disappointed in *The Ebb Tide.* Alas! poor little tale, it is not *even* rancid.

By way of an antidote or febrifuge, I am going on at

1893 ÆT. 43 a great rate with my *History of the Stevensons*, which I hope may prove rather amusing in some parts at least. The excess of materials weighs upon me. My grandfather is a delightful comedy part; and I have to treat him besides as a serious and (in his way) a heroic figure, and at times I lose my way, and I fear in the end will blur the effect. However, *à la grâce de Dieu!* I 'll make a spoon or spoil a horn. You see, I have to do the Building of the Bell Rock by cutting down and packing my grandsire's book, which I rather hope I have done, but do not know. And it makes a huge chunk of a very different style and quality between Chapters II. and IV. And it can't be helped! It is just a delightful and exasperating necessity. You know, the stuff is really excellent narrative: only, perhaps there 's too much of it! There is the rub. Well, well, it will be plain to you that my mind is affected; it might be with less. *The Ebb Tide* and *Northern Lights* are a full meal for any plain man.

I have written and ordered your last book, *The Real Thing*, so be sure and don't send it. What else are you doing or thinking of doing? News I have none, and don't want any. I have had to stop all strong drink and all tobacco, and am now in a transition state between the two, which seems to be near madness. You never smoked, I think, so you can never taste the joys of stopping it. But at least you have drunk, and you can enter perhaps into my annoyance when I suddenly find a glass of claret or a brandy-and-water give me a splitting headache the next morning. No mistake about it; drink anything, and there 's your headache. Tobacco just as bad for me. If I live through this breach of habit, I shall be a white-livered puppy indeed. Actually I am so made, or so twisted, that I do not like to think of a life without the red wine on the table and the tobacco with its lovely little coal of fire. It does n't amuse me from a distance. I may find it the Garden of Eden when I go in, but I don't like the colour of the gate-posts. Suppose somebody said to you, you are to leave your home, and your books, and your clubs, and go out and camp in mid-Africa, and command an expedition, you would howl, and kick, and flee. I think the same of a life without wine and tobacco; and if this goes on, I 've got to go and do it, sir, in the living flesh! 1893 ÆT. 43

I thought Bourget was a friend of yours? And I thought the French were a polite race? He has taken my dedication with a stately silence that has surprised me into apoplexy. Did I go and dedicate my book[1] to the nasty alien, and the 'norrid Frenchman, and the Bloody Furrineer? Well, I would n't do it again; and unless his case is susceptible of explanation, you might perhaps tell him so over the walnuts and the wine, by way of speeding the gay hours. Sincerely, I thought my dedication worth a letter.

If anything be worth anything here below! Do you know the story of the man who found a button in his hash, and called the waiter? "What do you call that?" says he. "Well," said the waiter, "what d' you expect? Expect to find a gold watch and chain?" Heavenly apologue, is it not? I expected (rather) to find a gold watch and chain; I expected to be able to smoke to excess and drink to comfort all the

[1] *Across the Plains.*

1893 ÆT. 43 days of my life; and I am still indignantly staring on this button! It 's not even a button; it 's a teetotal badge!—Ever yours, ROBERT LOUIS STEVENSON.

To Henry James

APIA, *July, 1893.*

MY DEAR HENRY JAMES,—Yes. *Les Trophées*[1] is, on the whole, a book. It is excellent; but is it a life's work? I always suspect *you* of a volume of sonnets up your sleeve; when is it coming down? I am in one of my moods of wholesale impatience with all fiction and all verging on it, reading instead, with rapture, *Fountainhall's Decisions.* You never read it: well, it has n't much form, and is inexpressibly dreary, I should suppose, to others—and even to me for pages. It 's like walking in a mine underground, and with a damned bad lantern, and picking out pieces of ore. This, and war, will be my excuse for not having read your (doubtless) charming work of fiction. The revolving year will bring me round to it; and I know, when fiction shall begin to feel a little *solid* to me again, that I shall love it, because it 's James. Do you know, when I am in this mood, I would rather try to read a bad book? It 's not so disappointing, anyway. And *Fountainhall* is prime, two big folio volumes, and all dreary, and all true, and all as terse as an obituary; and about one interesting fact on an average in twenty pages, and ten of them unintelligible for technicalities. There 's literature, if you like! It feeds; it falls about you genuine

[1] Volume of sonnets by Joseph-Marie de Hérédia.

like rain. Rain: nobody has done justice to rain in literature yet: surely a subject for a Scot. But then you can't do rain in that ledger-book style that I am trying for—or between a ledger-book and an old ballad. How to get over, how to escape from, the besotting *particularity* of fiction. "Roland approached the house; it had green doors and window blinds; and there was a scraper on the upper step." To hell with Roland and the scraper!—Yours ever, R. L. S.

To A. Conan Doyle

Vailima, *July 12, 1893.*

My dear Dr. Conan Doyle,—*The White Company* has not yet turned up; but when it does—which I suppose will be next mail—you shall hear news of me. I have a great talent for compliment, accompanied by a hateful, even a diabolic frankness.

Delighted to hear I have a chance of seeing you and Mrs. Doyle; Mrs. Stevenson bids me say (what is too true) that our rations are often spare. Are you Great Eaters? Please reply.

As to ways and means, here is what you will have to do. Leave San Francisco by the down mail, get off at Samoa, and twelve days or a fortnight later you can continue your journey to Auckland per Upolu, which will give you a look at Tonga and possibly Fiji by the way. Make this a *first part of your plans.*

We are in the midst of war here; rather a nasty business, with the head-taking; and there seem signs of other trouble. But I believe you need make no

1893 ÆT. 43 change in your design to visit us. All should be well over; and if it were not, why! you need not leave the steamer.—Yours very truly,

ROBERT LOUIS STEVENSON.

TO CHARLES BAXTER

19th July, '93.

. . . We are in the thick of war—see *Illustrated London News*—we have only two outside boys left to us. Nothing is doing, and *per contra* little paying. . . . My life here is dear; but I can live within my income for a time at least—so long as my prices keep up—and it seems a clear duty to waste none of it on gadding about. . . . My life of my family fills up intervals, and should be an excellent book when it is done, but big, damnably big.

My dear old man, I perceive by a thousand signs that we grow old, and are soon to pass away; I hope with dignity; if not, with courage at least. I am myself very ready; or would be—will be—when I have made a little money for my folks. The blows that have fallen upon you are truly terrifying; I wish you strength to bear them. It is strange, I must seem to you to blaze in a Birmingham prosperity and happiness; and to myself I seem a failure. The truth is, I have never got over the last influenza yet, and am miserably out of heart and out of kilter. Lungs pretty right, stomach nowhere, spirits a good deal overshadowed; but we 'll come through it yet, and cock our bonnets. (I confess with sorrow that I am not yet quite sure about the *in-*

tellects; but I hope it is only one of my usual periods of non-work. They are more unbearable now, because I cannot rest. *No rest but the grave for Sir Walter!* O, the words ring in a man's head.) R. L. S. 1893 ÆT. 43

To A. Conan Doyle

Vailima, *August 23rd, 1893.*

My dear Dr. Conan Doyle,—I am reposing after a somewhat severe experience upon which I think it my duty to report to you. Immediately after dinner this evening it occurred to me to re-narrate to my native overseer Simalè your story of *The Engineer's Thumb.* And, sir, I have done it. It was necessary, I need hardly say, to go somewhat farther afield than you have done. To explain (for instance) what a railway is, what a steam hammer, what a coach and horse, what coining, what a criminal, and what the police. I pass over other and no less necessary explanations. But I did actually succeed; and if you could have seen the drawn, anxious features and the bright, feverish eyes of Simalè, you would have (for the moment at least) tasted glory. You might perhaps think that, were you to come to Samoa, you might be introduced as the Author of *The Engineer's Thumb.* Disabuse yourself. They do not know what it is to make up a story. *The Engineer's Thumb* (God forgive me) was narrated as a piece of actual and factual history. Nay, and more, I who write to you have had the indiscretion to perpetuate a trifling piece of fiction entitled *The Bottle Imp.* Parties who

1893 ÆT. 43 come up to visit my unpretentious mansion, after having admired the ceilings by Vanderputty and the tapestry by Gobbling, manifest towards the end a certain uneasiness which proves them to be fellows of an infinite delicacy. They may be seen to shrug a brown shoulder, to roll up a speaking eye, and at last the secret bursts from them: "Where is the bottle?" Alas, my friends (I feel tempted to say), you will find it by the Engineer's Thumb! Talofa-soifuia.

Oaie, O lau no moni, O Tusitala.
More commonly known as R. L. STEVENSON.

Have read *The Refugees;* Condé and old P. Murat very good; Louis XIV. and Louvois with the letter-bag very rich. You have reached a trifle wide perhaps; too *many* celebrities? Though I was delighted to re-encounter my old friend Du Chaylu. Old Murat is perhaps your high-water mark; 't is excellently human, cheerful, and real. Do it again. Madame de Maintenon struck me as quite good. Have you any document for the decapitation? It sounds steepish. The devil of all that first part is that you see old Dumas; yet your Louis XIV. is *distinctly good.* I am much interested with this book, which fulfils a good deal, and promises more. Question: how far a Historical Novel should be wholly episodic? I incline to that view, with trembling. I shake hands with you on old Murat. R. L. S.

1893
ÆT. 43

To George Meredith

September 5th, 1893,
Vailima Plantation, Upolu, Samoa.

MY DEAR MEREDITH,—I have again and again taken up the pen to write to you, and many beginnings have gone into the waste paper basket (I have one now—for the second time in my life—and feel a big man on the strength of it). And no doubt it requires some decision to break so long a silence. My health is vastly restored, and I am now living patriarchally in this place six hundred feet above the sea on the shoulder of a mountain of 1500. Behind me, the unbroken bush slopes up to the backbone of the island (3 to 4000) without a house, with no inhabitants save a few runaway black boys, wild pigs and cattle, and wild doves and flying foxes, and many parti-coloured birds, and many black, and many white: a very eerie, dim, strange place and hard to travel. I am the head of a household of five whites, and of twelve Samoans, to all of whom I am the chief and father: my cook comes to me and asks leave to marry—and his mother, a fine old chief woman, who has never lived here, does the same. You may be sure I granted the petition. It is a life of great interest, complicated by the Tower of Babel, that old enemy. And I have all the time on my hands for literary work. My house is a great place; we have a hall fifty feet long with a great red-wood stair ascending from it, where we dine in state—myself usually dressed in a singlet and a pair of trousers—and attended on by servants in

1893 a single garment, a kind of kilt—also flowers and
ÆT. 43 leaves—and their hair often powdered with lime. The European who came upon it suddenly would think it was a dream. We have prayers on Sunday night—I am a perfect pariah in the island not to have them oftener, but the spirit is unwilling and the flesh proud, and I cannot go it more. It is strange to see the long line of the brown folk crouched along the wall with lanterns at intervals before them in the big shadowy hall, with an oak cabinet at one end of it and a group of Rodin's (which native taste regards as *prodigieusement leste*) presiding over all from the top—and to hear the long rambling Samoan hymn rolling up (God bless me, what style! But I am off business to-day, and this is not meant to be literature).

I have asked Colvin to send you a copy of *Catriona*, which I am sometimes tempted to think is about my best work. I hear word occasionally of the *Amazing Marriage*. It will be a brave day for me when I get hold of it. Gower Woodsere is now an ancient, lean, grim, exiled Scot, living and labouring as for a wager in the tropics; still active, still with lots of fire in him, but the youth—ah, the youth, where is it? For years after I came here, the critics (those genial gentlemen) used to deplore the relaxation of my fibre and the idleness to which I had succumbed. I hear less of this now; the next thing is they will tell me I am writing myself out! and that my unconscientious conduct is bringing their grey hairs with sorrow to the dust. I do not know—I mean I do know one thing. For fourteen years I have not had a day's real health; I have wakened sick and gone to bed weary; and I have done my work unflinchingly. I have written in bed, and written out of it, written in hemorrhages, written in sickness, written torn by coughing, written when my head swam for weakness; and for so long, it seems to me I have won my wager and recovered my glove. I am better now; have been, rightly speaking, since first I came to the Pacific; and still, few are the days when I am not in some physical distress. And the battle goes on — ill or well, is a trifle; so as it goes. I was made for a contest, and the Powers have so willed that my battle-field should be this dingy, inglorious one of the bed and the physic bottle. At least I have not failed, but I would have preferred a place of trumpetings, and the open air over my head.

1893
ÆT. 43

This is a devilish egotistical yarn. Will you try to imitate me in that if the spirit ever moves you to reply? And meantime be sure that way in the midst of the Pacific there is a house on a wooded island where the name of George Meredith is very dear, and his memory (since it must be no more) is continually honoured.—Ever your friend,

ROBERT LOUIS STEVENSON.

Remember me to Mariette, if you please; and my wife sends her most kind remembrances to yourself.

R. L. S.

1893
ÆT. 43

To Augustus St. Gaudens

Mr. St. Gaudens's large medallion portrait in bronze, executed from sittings given in 1887, had at last found its way to Apia, but not yet to Vailima.

Vailima, *September, 1893.*

My dear St. Gaudens,— I had determined not to write to you till I had seen the medallion, but it looks as if that might mean the Greek Kalends or the day after to-morrow. Reassure yourself, your part is done, it is ours that halts — the consideration of conveyance over our sweet little road on boys' backs, for we cannot very well apply the horses to this work; there is only one; you cannot put it in a panier; to put it on the horse's back we have not the heart. Beneath the beauty of R. L. S., to say nothing of his verses, which the publishers find heavy enough, and the genius of the god-like sculptor, the spine would snap and the well-knit limbs of the (ahem) cart-horse would be loosed by death. So you are to conceive me, sitting in my house, dubitative, and the medallion chuckling in the warehouse of the German firm, for some days longer; and hear me meanwhile on the golden letters.

Alas, they are all my fancy painted, but the price is prohibitive. I cannot do it. It is another day-dream burst. Another gable of Abbotsford has gone down, fortunately before it was builded, so there 's nobody injured—except me. I had a strong conviction that I was a great hand at writing inscriptions, and meant to exhibit and test my genius on the walls of my house; and now I see I can't. It is generally thus. The Battle of the Golden Letters will never be delivered. On making preparation to open the campaign, the King found himself face to face with invincible difficulties, in which the rapacity of a mercenary soldiery and the complaints of an impoverished treasury played an equal part.—Ever yours, 1893 ÆT. 43

ROBERT LOUIS STEVENSON.

I enclose a bill for the medallion; have been trying to find your letter, quite in vain, and therefore must request you to pay for the bronze letters yourself and let me know the damage. R. L. S.

TO J. HORNE STEVENSON

The following refers to the introduction to the history of his own family which Stevenson was then preparing under the title "A Family of Engineers," and which remained in a fragmentary condition at his death. I give this letter as a sample of many which passed between the two namesakes on this subject; omitting the remainder as too technical to be of general interest.

VAILIMA, SAMOA, *November 5th, 1893.*

MY DEAR STEVENSON,—A thousand thanks for your voluminous and delightful collections. Baxter—so soon as it is ready—will let you see a proof of my introduction, which is only sent out as a sprat to catch whales. And you will find I have a good deal

1893 ÆT. 43 of what you have, only mine in a perfectly desultory manner, as is necessary to an exile. My uncle's pedigree is wrong; there was never a Stevenson of Caldwell, of course, but they were tenants of the Muirs; the farm held by them is in my introduction; and I have already written to Charles Baxter to have a search made in the Register House. I hope he will have had the inspiration to put it under your surveillance. Your information as to your own family is intensely interesting, and I should not wonder but what you and we and old John Stevenson, "land labourer in the parish of Dailly," came all of the same stock. Ayrshire — and probably Cunningham — seems to be the home of the race — our part of it. From the distribution of the name — which your collections have so much extended without essentially changing my knowledge of — we seem rather pointed to a British origin. What you say of the Engineers is fresh to me, and must be well thrashed out. This introduction of it will take a long while to walk about! — as perhaps I may be tempted to let it become long; after all, I am writing *this* for my own pleasure solely. Greetings to you and other Speculatives of our date, long bygone, alas! — Yours very sincerely,

ROBERT LOUIS STEVENSON.

P. S.— I have a different version of my grandfather's arms — or my father had if I could find it. R. L. S.

To John P——n

The next two numbers are in answer to letters of appreciation received from two small boys in England, whose mother desires that they should remain nameless.

VAILIMA, SAMOA, *December 3rd, 1893.*

DEAR JOHNNIE,—Well, I must say you seem to be a tremendous fellow! Before I was eight I used to write stories—or dictate them at least—and I had produced an excellent history of Moses, for which I got £1 from an uncle; but I had never gone the length of a play, so you have beaten me fairly on my own ground. I hope you may continue to do so, and thanking you heartily for your nice letter, I shall beg you to believe me yours truly,

ROBERT LOUIS STEVENSON.

To Russell P——n

VAILIMA, SAMOA, *December 3rd, 1893.*

DEAR RUSSELL,—I have to thank you very much for your capital letter, which came to hand here in Samoa along with your mother's. When you "grow up and write stories like me," you will be able to understand that there is scarce anything more painful than for an author to hold a pen; he has to do it so

1893 much that his heart sickens and his fingers ache at the
ÆT. 43 sight or touch of it; so that you will excuse me if I do not write much, but remain (with compliments and greetings from one Scot to another—though I was not born in Ceylon—you 're ahead of me there), yours very truly, ROBERT LOUIS STEVENSON.

TO ALISON CUNNINGHAM

VAILIMA, *December 5, 1893.*

MY DEAREST CUMMY,—This goes to you with a Merry Christmas and a Happy New Year. The Happy New Year anyway, for I think it should reach you about *Noor's Day*. I dare say it may be cold and frosty. Do you remember when you used to take me out of bed in the early morning, carry me to the back windows, show me the hills of Fife, and quote to me

"A' the hills are covered wi' snaw,
An' winter 's noo come fairly"?

There is not much chance of that here! I wonder how my mother is going to stand the winter. If she can, it will be a very good thing for her. We are in that part of the year which I like the best—the Rainy or Hurricane Season. "When it is good, it is very, very good; and when it is bad, it is horrid," and our fine days are certainly fine like heaven; such a blue of the sea, such green of the trees, and such crimson of the hibiscus flowers, you never saw; and the air as mild and gentle as a baby's breath, and yet not hot! 1893 ÆT. 43

The mail is on the move, and I must let up.—With much love, I am, your laddie, R. L. S.

To Charles Baxter

The following quotes the extract from *Fountainhall's Decisions of the Lords of Council*, etc., which suggested to Stevenson the romances of Cameronian days and the Darien adventure of which, under the title of *Heathercat*, he only lived to write the first few introductory chapters.

6th December, 1893.

"*October 25, 1685.*—At Privy Council, George Murray, Lieutenant of the King's Guard, and others, did, on the 21st of September last, obtain a clandestine order of Privy Council to apprehend the person of Janet Pringle, daughter to the late Clifton, and she having retired out of the way upon information, he got an order against Andrew Pringle, her uncle, to produce her. . . . But she having married Andrew Pringle, her uncle's son (to disappoint all their designs of selling her), a boy of thirteen years old." But my boy is to be fourteen, so I extract no further.—Fountainhall, i. 320.

"*May 6, 1685.*—Wappus Pringle of Clifton was still alive after all, and in prison for debt, and transacts with Lieutenant Murray, giving security for 7000 marks."—i. 372.

No, it seems to have been *her* brother who had succeeded.

1893 ÆT. 43 MY DEAR CHARLES,—The above is my story, and I wonder if any light can be thrown on it. I prefer the girl's father dead; and the question is, How in that case could Lieutenant George Murray get his order to "apprehend" and his power to "sell" her in marriage?

Or—might Lieutenant G. be her tutor, and she fugitive to the Pringles, and on the discovery of her whereabouts hastily married?

A good legal note on these points is very ardently desired by me; it will be the corner-stone of my novel.

This is for—I am quite wrong to tell you—for you will tell others—and nothing will teach you that all my schemes are in the air, and vanish and reappear again like shapes in the clouds—it is for *Heathercat:* whereof the first volume will be called *The Killing Time,* and I believe I have authorities ample for that. But the second volume is to be called (I believe) *Darien,* and for that I want, I fear, a good deal of truck:—

Darien Papers,
Carstairs Papers,
Marchmont Papers,
Jerviswoode Correspondence,

I hope may do me. Some sort of general history of the Darien affair (if there is a decent one, which I misdoubt), it would also be well to have—the one with most details, if possible. It is singular how obscure to me this decade of Scots history remains, 1690–1700—a deuce of a want of light and grouping to it! However, I believe I shall be mostly out of Scotland in my tale; first in Carolina, next in Darien. I want also—I am the daughter of the horse-leech truly — "Black's new large map of Scotland," sheets 3, 4, and 5, a 7*s.* 6*d.* touch. I believe, if you can get the 1893 ÆT. 43

Caldwell Papers,

they had better come also; and if there be any reasonable work — but no, I must call a halt. . . .

I fear the song looks doubtful, but I 'll consider of it, and I can promise you some reminiscences which it will amuse me to write, whether or not it will amuse the public to read of them. But it 's an unco business to supply deid-heid coapy.

To J. M. Barrie

VAILIMA, SAMOA, *December 7th, 1893.*

MY DEAR BARRIE, — I have received duly the *magnum opus*, and it really is a *magnum opus.*[1] It is a beautiful specimen of Clark's printing, paper sufficient, and the illustrations all my fancy painted. But the particular flower of the flock to whom I have hopelessly lost my heart is Tibby Birse. I must have known Tibby Birse when she was a servant's mantua-maker in Edinburgh and answered to the name of Miss *Broddie.* She used to come and sew with my nurse, sitting with her legs crossed in a masculine manner; and swinging her foot emphatically, she used to pour forth a perfectly un-

1 *A Window in Thrums*, with illustrations by W. Hole, R. S. A. (Hodder & Stoughton, 1892).

1893 ÆT. 43 broken stream of gossip. I did n't hear it, I was immersed in far more important business with a box of bricks, but the recollection of that thin, perpetual, shrill sound of a voice has echoed in my ears sinsyne. I am bound to say she was younger than Tibbie, but there is no mistaking that and the indescribable and eminently Scottish expression.

I have been very much prevented of late, having carried out thoroughly to my own satisfaction two considerable illnesses, had a birthday, and visited Honolulu, where politics are (if possible) a shade more exasperating than they are with us. I am told that it was just when I was on the point of leaving that I received your superlative epistle about the cricket eleven. In that case it is impossible I should have answered it, which is inconsistent with my own recollection of the fact. What *I* remember is that I sat down under your immediate inspiration and wrote an answer in every way worthy. If I did n't, as it seems proved that I could n't, it will never be done now. However, I did the next best thing, I equipped my cousin Graham Balfour with a letter of introduction, and from him, if you know how — for he is rather of the Scottish character — you may elicit all the information you can possibly wish to have as to us and ours. Do not be bluffed off by the somewhat stern and monumental first impression that he may make upon you. He is one of the best fellows in the world, and the same sort of fool that we are, only better-looking, with all the faults of Vailimans and some of his own — I say nothing about virtues.

I have lately been returning to my wallowing in the mire. When I was a child, and indeed until I was nearly a man, I consistently read Covenanting books. Now that I am a greybeard — or would be, if I could raise the beard — I have returned, and for weeks back have read little else but Wodrow, Walker, Shields, etc. Of course this is with an idea of a novel, but in the course of it I made a very curious discovery. I have been accustomed to hear refined and intelligent critics — those who know so much better what we are than we do ourselves, those who tell us it is time to stop working in I and to work it B.C. — trace down my literary descent from all sorts of people, including Addison, of whom I could never read a word. Well, laigh i' your lug, sir — the clue was found. My style is from the Covenanting writers. Take a particular case — the fondness for rhymes. I don't know of any English prose-writer who rhymes except by accident, and then a stone had better be tied around his neck and himself cast into the sea. But my Covenanting buckies rhyme all the time — a beautiful example of the unconscious rhyme above referred to.

Do you know, and have you really tasted, these delightful works? If not, it should be remedied; there is enough of the Auld Licht in you to be ravished.

I suppose you know that success has so far attended my banners — my political banners I mean, and not my literary. In conjunction with the Three Great Powers I have succeeded in getting rid of My President and My Chief-Justice. They 've gone home, the one to Germany, the other to Souwegia. I hear little echoes of footfalls of their departing footsteps through the medium of the newspapers. . . .

Whereupon I make you my salute with the firm re-

1893 ÆT. 43 mark that it is time to be done with trifling and give us a great book, and my ladies fall into line with me to pay you a most respectful courtesy, and we all join in the cry, "Come to Vailima!"

My dear sir, your soul's health is in it—you will never do the great book, you will never cease to work in L., etc., till you come to Vailima.

ROBERT LOUIS STEVENSON.

TO RICHARD LE GALLIENNE

VAILIMA, SAMOA, *December 28th, 1893.*

DEAR MR. LE GALLIENNE,—I have received some time ago, through our friend Miss Taylor, a book of yours. But that was by no means my first introduction to your name. The same book had stood already on my shelves; I had read articles of yours in the *Academy;* and by a piece of constructive criticism (which I trust was sound) had arrived at the conclusion that you were Log-roller. Since then I have seen your beautiful verses to your wife. You are to conceive me, then, as only too ready to make the acquaintance of a man who loved good literature and could make it. I had to thank you, besides, for a triumphant exposure of a paradox of my own: the literary-prostitute disappeared from view at a phrase of yours—"The essence is not in the pleasure but the sale." True: you are right, I was wrong; the author is not the whore, but the libertine; and yet I shall let the passage stand. It is an error, but it illustrated the truth for which I was contending, that literature — painting — all art, are no other than pleasures, which we turn into trades. 1893 ÆT. 43

And more than all this, I had and I have to thank you for the intimate loyalty you have shown to myself; for the eager welcome you give to what is good — for the courtly tenderness with which you touch on my defects. I begin to grow old; I have given my top note, I fancy;— and I have written too many books. The world begins to be weary of the old booth; and if not weary, familiar with the familiarity that breeds contempt. I do not know that I am sensitive to criticism, if it be hostile; I am sensitive indeed, when it is friendly; and when I read such criticism as yours, I am emboldened to go on and praise God.

You are still young, and you may live to do much. The little, artificial popularity of style in England tends, I think, to die out; the British pig returns to his true love, the love of the styleless, of the shapeless, of the slapdash and the disorderly. There is trouble coming, I think; and you may have to hold the fort for us in evil days.

Lastly, let me apologise for the crucifixion that I am inflicting on you (*bien à contrecœur*) by my bad writing. I was once the best of writers; landladies, puzzled as to my "trade," used to have their honest bosoms set at rest by a sight of a page of manuscript. — "Ah," they would say, "no wonder they pay you for that"; — and when I sent it in to the printers, it was given to the boys! I was about thirty-nine, I think, when I had a turn of scrivener's palsy; my hand got worse; and for the first time, I received clean proofs. But it has gone beyond that now, I know I

1893 ÆT. 43 am like my old friend James Payn, a terror to correspondents; and you would not believe the care with which this has been written.—Believe me to be, very sincerely yours, ROBERT LOUIS STEVENSON.

TO MRS. A. BAKER

The next is in answer to a request for permission to print some of the writings of R. L. S. in Braille type for the use of the blind.

December, 1893.

DEAR MADAM,—There is no trouble, and I wish I could help instead. As it is, I fear I am only going to put you to trouble and vexation. This Braille writing is a kind of consecration, and I would like if I could to have your copy perfect. The two volumes are to be published as Vols. I. and II. of *The Adventures of David Balfour*. 1st, *Kidnapped;* 2nd, *Catriona*. I am just sending home a corrected *Kidnapped* for this purpose to Messrs. Cassell, and in order that I may if possible be in time, I send it to you first of all. Please, as soon as you have noted the changes, forward the same to Cassell and Co., La Belle Sauvage Yard, Ludgate Hill.

I am writing to them by this mail to send you *Catriona*.

You say, dear madam, you are good enough to say, it is "a keen pleasure" to you to bring my book within the reach of the blind.

Conceive then what it is to me! and believe me, sincerely yours, ROBERT LOUIS STEVENSON.

I was a barren tree before, 1893 ÆT. 43
  I blew a quenchèd coal,
I could not, on their midnight shore,
  The lonely blind console.

A moment, lend your hand, I bring
  My sheaf for you to bind,
And you can teach my words to sing
  In the darkness of the blind.

R. L. S.

To Henry James

Apia, *December, 1893.*

MY DEAR HENRY JAMES,—The mail has come upon me like an armed man three days earlier than was expected; and the Lord help me! It is impossible I should answer anybody the way they should be. Your jubilation over *Catriona* did me good, and still more the subtlety and truth of your remark on the starving of the visual sense in that book. 'T is true, and unless I make the greater effort—and am, as a step to that, convinced of its necessity—it will be more true, I fear, in the future. I *hear* people talking, and I *feel* them acting, and that seems to me to be fiction. My two aims may be described as—

1st. War to the adjective.
2nd. Death to the optic nerve.

Admitted we live in an age of the optic nerve in literature. For how many centuries did literature get along without a sign of it? However, I'll consider your letter.

1894
ÆT. 44
How exquisite is your character of the critic in *Essays in London!* I doubt if you have done any single thing so satisfying as a piece of style and of insight.—Yours ever, R. L. S.

To Charles Baxter

Mr. Baxter, after much preliminary consideration and inquiry, had matured and submitted to Stevenson the scheme of the Edinburgh edition, to which this letter is his reply. The paper on *Treasure Island* appeared in the *Idler* for August, 1889, and was afterwards reprinted in the miscellany, *My First Book* (Chatto and Windus, 1894). (See Edinburgh edition, *Miscellanies*, vol. iv., p. 285.)

1st January, '94.

MY DEAR CHARLES,—I am delighted with your idea, and first, I will here give an amended plan and afterwards give you a note of some of the difficulties.

[Plan of the Edinburgh edition — 14 vols.]

. . . It may be a question whether my *Times* letters might not be appended to the *Foot-note* with a note of the dates of discharge of Cedercrantz and Pilsach.

I am particularly pleased with this idea of yours, because I am come to a dead stop. I never can remember how bad I have been before, but at any rate I am bad enough just now, I mean as to literature; in health I am well and strong. I take it I shall be six months before I 'm heard of again, and this time I could put in to some advantage in revising the text and (if it were thought desirable) writing prefaces. I do not know how many of them might be thought desirable. I have written a paper on *Treasure Island*, which is to appear shortly. *Master of Ballantrae*—I have one drafted. *The Wrecker* is quite sufficiently done already with the last chapter, but I suppose an historic introduction to *David Balfour* is quite unavoidable. *Prince Otto* I don't think I could say anything about, and *Black Arrow* don't want to. But it is probable I could say something to the volume of *Travels*. In the verse business I can do just what I like better than anything else, and extend *Underwoods* with a lot of unpublished stuff. *Apropos*, if I were to get printed off a very few poems which are somewhat too intimate for the public, could you get them run up in some luxurious manner, so that fools might be induced to buy them in just a sufficient quantity to pay expenses and the thing remain still in a manner private? We could supply photographs of the illustrations—and the poems are of Vailima and the family—I should much like to get this done as a surprise for Fanny. R. L. S.

To H. B. Baildon

Vailima, *January 15th, 1894*.

My dear Baildon,—Last mail brought your book and its Dedication. "Frederick Street and the gardens, and the short-lived Jack o' Lantern," are again with me—and the note of the east wind, and Freebel's voice, and the smell of soup in Thomson's stair. Truly, you had no need to put yourself under the protection of any other saint, were that saint our Tamate himself! Yourself were enough, and yourself coming with so rich a sheaf.

1894 ÆT. 44 For what is this that you say about the Muses? They have certainly never better inspired you than in *'ael and Sisera*, and *Herodias and John the Baptist*, good stout poems, fiery and sound. "'T is but a mask and behind it chuckles the God of the Garden," I shall never forget. By the by, an error of the press, page 49, line 4, "No infant's lesson are the ways of God." *The* is dropped.

And this reminds me you have a bad habit which is to be comminated in my theory of letters. Same page, two lines lower: "But the vulture's track" is surely as fine to the ear as "But vulture's track," and this latter version has a dreadful baldness. The reader goes on with a sense of impoverishment, of unnecessary sacrifice; he has been robbed by footpads, and goes scouting for his lost article! Again, in the second refade, these fine verses would surely sound much finer if they began, "As a hardy climber who has set his heart," than with the jejune "As hardy climber." I do not know why you permit yourself this license with grammar; you show, in so many pages, that you are superior to the paltry sense of rhythm which usually dictates it—as though some poetaster had been suffered to correct the poet's text. By the way, I confess to a heartfelt weakness for *Auriculas.*—Believe me the very grateful and characterising buik-thank, but still sincere and affectionate, ROBERT LOUIS STEVENSON.

To W. H. Low

VAILIMA, *January 15th, 1894.*

MY DEAR LOW,— . . . Pray you, stoop your proud head, and sell yourself to some Jew magazine, and make the visit out. I assure you, this is the spot for a sculptor or painter. This, and no other — I don't say to stay there, but to come once and get the living colour into them. I am used to it; I do not notice it; rather prefer my grey, freezing recollections of Scotland; but there it is, and every morning is a thing to give thanks for, and every night another — bar when it rains, of course.

About *The Wrecker* — rather late days, and I still suspect I had somehow offended you; however, all 's well that ends well, and I am glad I am forgiven — did you not fail to appreciate the attitude of Dodd? He was a fizzle and a stick, he knew it, he knew nothing else, and there is an undercurrent of bitterness in him. And then the problem that Pinkerton laid down: why the artist can *do nothing else* — is one that continually exercises myself. He cannot: granted. But Scott could. And Montaigne. And Julius Cæsar. And many more. And why can't R. L. S.? Does it not amaze you? It does me. I think of the Renaissance fellows, and their all-round human sufficiency, and compare it with the ineffable smallness of the field in which we labour and in which we do so little. I think *David Balfour* a nice little book, and very artistic, and just the thing to occupy the leisure of a busy man; but for the top flower of a man's life it seems to me inadequate. Small is the

1894 ÆT. 44 word; it is a small age, and I am of it. I could have wished to be otherwise busy in this world. I ought to have been able to build lighthouses and write *David Balfours* too. *Hinc illæ lacrymæ.* I take my own case as most handy, but it is as illustrative of my quarrel with the age. We take all these pains, and we don't do as well as Michael Angelo or Leonardo, or even Fielding, who was an active magistrate, or Richardson, who was a busy bookseller. *J'ai honte pour nous;* my ears burn.

I am amazed at the effect which this Chicago exhibition has produced upon you and others. It set Mrs. Fairchild literally mad—to judge by her letters. And I wish I had seen anything so influential. I suppose there was an aura, a halo, some sort of effulgency about the place; for here I find you louder than the rest. Well, it may be there is a time coming; and I wonder, when it comes, whether it will be a time of little, exclusive, one-eyed rascals like you and me, or parties of the old stamp who can paint and fight, and write and keep books of double entry, and sculp, and scalp. It might be. You have a lot of stuff in the kettle, and a great deal of it Celtic. I have changed my mind progressively about England: practically the whole of Scotland is Celtic, and the western half of England, and all Ireland, and the Celtic blood makes a rare blend for art. If it is stiffened up with Latin blood, you get the French. We were less lucky: we had only Scandinavians, themselves decidedly artistic, and the low German lot. However, that is a good starting-point, and with all the other elements in your crucible, it may come to something great very easily. I wish you would hurry up and let me see it. Here is a long while I have been waiting for something *good* in art; and what have I seen? Zola's *Débâcle* and a few of Kipling's tales. Are you a reader of Barbey d'Aurévilly? He is a never-failing source of pleasure to me, for my sins, I suppose. What a work is the *Rideau Cramoisi!* and *L'Ensorcelée!* and *Le Chevalier des Touches!* 1894 ÆT. 44

This is degenerating into mere twaddle. So please remember us all most kindly to Mrs. Low, and believe me ever yours, ROBERT LOUIS STEVENSON.

P. S.—Were all your privateers voiceless in the war of 1812? Did *no one* of them write memoirs? I shall have to do my privateer from chic, if you can't help me.[1] My application to Scribner has been quite in vain. See if you can get hold of some historic sharp in the club, and tap him; they must some of them have written memoirs or notes of some sort; perhaps still unprinted; if that be so, get them copied for me.

R. L. S.

To H. B. BAILDON

VAILIMA, *January 30th, 1894*.

MY DEAR BAILDON,—"Call not blessed."—Yes, if I could die just now, or say in half a year, I should have had a splendid time of it on the whole. But it gets a little stale, and my work will begin to senesce; and

1 This question is with a view to the adventures of the hero in *St. Ives*, who, according to Stevenson's original plan, was to have been picked up from his foundered balloon by an American privateer.

1894 Æt. 44 parties to shy bricks at me; and now it begins to look as if I should survive to see myself impotent and forgotten. It 's a pity suicide is not thought the ticket in the best circles.

But your letter goes on to congratulate me on having done the one thing I am a little sorry for; a little — not much — for my father himself lived to think that I had been wiser than he. But the cream of the jest is that I have lived to change my mind; and think that he was wiser than I. Had I been an engineer, and literature my amusement, it would have been better perhaps. I pulled it off, of course, I won the wager, and it is pleasant while it lasts; but how long will it last? I don't know, say the Bells of Old Bow.

All of which goes to show that nobody is quite sane in judging himself. Truly, had I given way and gone in for engineering, I should be dead by now. Well, the gods know best.

. . . I hope you got my letter about the rescue.—
Adieu, R. L. S.

True for you about the benefit: except by kisses, jests, song, *et hoc genus omne,* man *cannot* convey benefit to another. The universal benefactor has been there before him.

To J. H. Bates

The next is to a correspondent in Cincinnati, who had been the founder of an R. L. S. Society in that city, "originally," he writes me, under date April 7, 1895, "the outcome of a boyish fancy, but it has now grown into something more substantial."

VAILIMA, SAMOA, *March 25th, 1894.* 1894 ÆT. 44

MY DEAR MR. JOE H. BATES,—I shall have the greatest pleasure in acceding to your complimentary request. I shall think it an honour to be associated with your chapter, and I need not remind you (for you have said it yourself) how much depends upon your own exertions, whether to make it to me a real honour or only a derision. This is to let you know that I accept the position that you have seriously offered to me in a quite serious spirit. I need scarce tell you that I shall always be pleased to receive reports of your proceedings; and if I do not always acknowledge them, you are to remember that I am a man very much occupied otherwise, and not at all to suppose that I have lost interest in my chapter.

In this world, which (as you justly say) is so full of sorrow and suffering, it will always please me to remember that my name is connected with some efforts after alleviation, nor less so with purposes of innocent recreation which, after all, are the only certain means at our disposal for bettering human life.

With kind regards, to yourself, to Mr. L. C. Congdon, to E. M. G. Bates, and to Mr. Edward Hugh Higlee Bates, and the heartiest wishes for the future success of the chapter, believe me, yours cordially,

ROBERT LOUIS STEVENSON.

TO WILLIAM ARCHER

VAILIMA, SAMOA, *March 27th, 1894.*

MY DEAR ARCHER,—Many thanks for your *Theatrical World.* Do you know, it strikes me as being really

1894 very good? I have not yet read much of it, but so far
ÆT. 44 as I have looked, there is not a dull and not an empty page in it. Hazlitt, whom you must often have thought of, would have been pleased. Come to think of it, I shall put this book upon the Hazlitt shelf. You have acquired a manner that I can only call august; otherwise, I should have to call it such amazing impudence. The *Bauble Shop* and *Becket* are examples of what I mean. But it "sets you weel."

Marjorie Fleming I have known, as you surmise, for long. She was possibly—no, I take back possibly—she was one of the greatest works of God. Your note about the resemblance of her verses to mine gave me great joy, though it only proved me a plagiarist. By the by, was it not over the *Child's Garden of Verses* that we first scraped acquaintance? I am sorry indeed to hear that my esteemed correspondent Tomarcher has such poor taste in literature.[1] I fear he cannot have inherited this trait from his dear papa. Indeed, I may say I know it, for I remember the energy of papa's disapproval when the work passed through his hands on its way to a second birth, which none regrets more than myself. It is an odd fact, or perhaps a very natural one: I find few greater pleasures than reading my own works, but I never, O I never read *The Black Arrow*. In that country Tomarcher reigns supreme. Well, and after all, if Tomarcher likes it, it has not been written in vain.

We have just now a curious breath from Europe. A young fellow just beginning letters, and no fool, turned up here with a letter of introduction in the well-known

[1] As to admire *The Black Arrow*.

myself telling myself, "O, I must tell this to Lysaght," or, "This will interest him," in a manner very unusual after so brief an acquaintance. The whole of my family shared in this favourable impression, and my halls have re-echoed ever since, I am sure he will be amused to know, with *Widdicombe Fair*. 1894 ÆT. 44

He will have told you doubtless more of my news than I could tell you myself; he has your European perspective, a thing long lost to me. I heard with a great deal of interest the news of Box Hill. And so I understand it is to be enclosed! Allow me to remark, that seems a far more barbaric trait of manners than the most barbarous of ours. We content ourselves with cutting off an occasional head.

I hear we may soon expect the *Amazing Marriage*. You know how long, and with how much curiosity, I have looked forward to the book. Now, in so far as you have adhered to your intention, Gower Woodsere will be a family portrait, age twenty-five, of the highly respectable and slightly influential and fairly aged *Tusitala*. You have not known that gentleman; console yourself, he is not worth knowing. At the same time, my dear Meredith, he is very sincerely yours—for what he is worth, for the memories of old times, and in the expectation of many pleasures still to come. I suppose we shall never see each other again; flitting youths of the Lysaght species may occasionally cover these unconscionable leagues and bear greetings to and fro. But we ourselves must be content to converse on an occasional sheet of notepaper, and I shall never see whether you have grown older, and you shall never deplore that Gower Woodsere should have declined

1894 ÆT. 44 into the pantaloon *Tusitala.* It is perhaps better so. Let us continue to see each other as we were, and accept, my dear Meredith, my love and respect.

ROBERT LOUIS STEVENSON.

P. S.—My wife joins me in the kindest messages to yourself and Mariette.

TO CHARLES BAXTER

[VAILIMA], *April 17, '94.*

MY DEAR CHARLES,—*St. Ives* is now well on its way into the second volume. There remains no mortal doubt that it will reach the three volume standard.

I am very anxious that you should send me—

1st. *Tom and Jerry*, a cheap edition.

2nd. The book by Ashton—the *Dawn of the Century*, I think it was called—which Colvin sent me, and which has miscarried, and

3rd. If it is possible, a file of the *Edinburgh Courant* for the years 1811, 1812, 1813, or 1814. I should not care for a whole year. If it were possible to find me three months, winter months by preference, it would do my business not only for *St. Ives*, but for *The Justice-Clerk* as well. Suppose this to be impossible, perhaps I could get the loan of it from somebody; or perhaps it would be possible to have some one read a file for me and make notes. This would be extremely bad, as unhappily one man's food is another man's poison, and the reader would probably leave out everything I should choose. But if you are reduced to that, you might mention to the man who is to read for me that balloon ascensions are in the order of the day. 1894 ÆT. 44

4th. It might be as well to get a book on balloon ascension, particularly in the early part of the century.

. . . .

III. At last this book has come from Scribner, and, alas! I have the first six or seven chapters of *St. Ives* to recast entirely. Who could foresee that they clothed the French prisoners in yellow? But that one fatal fact—and also that they shaved them twice a week—damns the whole beginning. If it had been sent in time, it would have saved me a deal of trouble. . . .

I have had a long letter from Dr. Scott Dalgleish, 25 Mayfield Terrace, asking me to put my name down to the Ballantine Memorial Committee. I have sent him a pretty sharp answer in favour of cutting down the memorial and giving more to the widow and children. If there is to be any foolery in the way of statues or other trash, please send them a guinea; but if they are going to take my advice and put up a simple tablet with a few heartfelt words, and really devote the bulk of the subscriptions to the wife and family, I will go to the length of twenty pounds, if you will allow me (and if the case of the family be at all urgent), and at least I direct you to send ten pounds. I suppose you had better see Scott Dalgleish himself on the matter. I take the opportunity here to warn you that my head is simply spinning with a multitude of affairs, and I shall probably forget a half of my business at last.

R. L. S.

1894
ÆT. 44

To Mrs. Sitwell

Vailima, *April, 1894.*

MY DEAR FRIEND,—I have at last got some photographs, and hasten to send you, as you asked, a portrait of Tusitala. He is a strange person; not so lean, say experts, but infinitely battered; mighty active again on the whole; going up and down our break-neck road at all hours of the day and night on horseback; holding meetings with all manner of chiefs; quite a political personage—God save the mark!—in a small way, but at heart very conscious of the inevitable flat failure that awaits every one. I shall never do a better book than *Catriona*, that is my high-water mark, and the trouble of production increases on me at a great rate—and mighty anxious about how I am to leave my family: an elderly man, with elderly preoccupations, whom I should be ashamed to show you for your old friend; but not a hope of my dying soon and cleanly, and "winning off the stage." Rather I am daily better in physical health. I shall have to see this business out, after all; and I think, in that case, they should have—they might have—spared me all my ill-health this decade past, if it were not to unbar the doors. I have no taste for old age, and my nose is to be rubbed in it in spite of my face. I was meant to die young, and the gods do not love me.

This is very like an epitaph, bar the handwriting, which is anything but monumental, and I dare say I had better stop. Fanny is down at her own cottage planting or deplanting or replanting, I know not which, and she will not be home till dinner, by which time the mail will be all closed, else she would join me in all good messages and remembrances of love. I hope you will congratulate Burne-Jones from me on his baronetcy. I cannot make out to be anything but raspingly, harrowingly sad; so I will close, and not affect levity which I cannot feel. Do not altogether forget me; keep a corner of your memory for the exile LOUIS.

TO CHARLES BAXTER

[VAILIMA, *May, 1894.*]

MY DEAR CHARLES,—My dear fellow, I wish to assure you of the greatness of the pleasure that this Edinburgh Edition gives me. I suppose it was your idea to give it that name. No other would have affected me in the same manner. Do you remember, how many years ago—I would be afraid to hazard a guess—one night when I communicated to you certain intimations of early death and aspirations after fame? I was particularly maudlin; and my remorse the next morning on a review of my folly has written the matter very deeply in my mind; from yours it may easily have fled. If any one at that moment could have shown me the Edinburgh Edition, I suppose I should have died. It is with gratitude and wonder that I consider "the way in which I have been led." Could a more preposterous idea have occurred to us in those days when we used to search our pockets for coppers, too often in vain,

1894 Æt. 44 and combine forces to produce the threepence necessary for two glasses of beer, or wander down the Lothian Road without any, than that I should be strong and well at the age of forty-three in the island of Upolu, and that you should be at home bringing out the Edinburgh Edition? If it had been possible, I should almost have preferred the Lothian Road Edition, say, with a picture of the old Dutch smuggler on the covers. I have now something heavy on my mind. I had always a great sense of kinship with poor Robert Fergusson—so clever a boy, so wild, of such a mixed strain, so unfortunate, born in the same town with me, and, as I always felt, rather by express intimation than from evidence, so like myself. Now the injustice with which the one Robert is rewarded and the other left out in the cold sits heavy on me, and I wish you could think of some way in which I could do honour to my unfortunate namesake. Do you think it would look like affectation to dedicate the whole edition to his memory? I think it would. The sentiment which would dictate it to me is too abstruse; and besides, I think my wife is the proper person to receive the dedication of my life's work. At the same time, it is very odd—it really looks like the transmigration of souls—I feel that I must do something for Fergusson; Burns has been before me with the gravestone. It occurs to me you might take a walk down the Canongate and see in what condition the stone is. If it be at all uncared for, we might repair it, and perhaps add a few words of inscription.

I must tell you, what I just remembered in a flash as I was walking about dictating this letter—there was in the original plan of *The Master of Ballantrae* a sort of introduction describing my arrival in Edinburgh on a visit to yourself and your placing in my hands the papers of the story. I actually wrote it, and then condemned the idea as being a little too like Scott, I suppose. Now I must really find the MS. and try to finish it for the E. E. It will give you, what I should so much like you to have, another corner of your own in that lofty monument. 1894 ÆT. 44

Suppose we do what I have proposed about Fergusson's monument, I wonder if an inscription like this would look arrogant—

> This stone originally erected
> by Robert Burns has been
> repaired at the
> charges of Robert Louis Stevenson,
> and is by him rededicated to
> the memory of Robert Fergusson,
> as the gift of one Edinburgh
> lad to another.

In spacing this inscription I would detach the names of Fergusson and Burns, but leave mine in the text.

Or would that look like sham modesty, and is it better to bring out the three Roberts?

1894
ÆT. 44

To R. A. M. Stevenson

Vailima, *June, 1894.*

MY DEAR BOB,—I must make out a letter this mail or perish in the attempt. All the same, I am deeply stupid, in bed with a cold, deprived of my amanuensis, and conscious of the wish but not the furnished will. You may be interested to hear how the family inquiries go. It is now quite certain that we are a second-rate lot, and came out of Cunningham or Clydesdale, therefore *British* folk; so that you are Cymry on both sides, and I Cymry and Pict. We may have fought with King Arthur and known Merlin. The first of the family, Stevenson of Stevenson, was quite a great party, and dates back to the wars of Edward First. The last male heir of Stevenson of Stevenson died 1670, £220 10*s.* to the bad, from drink. About the same time the Stevensons, who were mostly in Cunningham before, crop up suddenly in the parish of Neilston, over the border in Renfrewshire. Of course, they may have been there before, but there is no word of them in that parish till 1675 in any extracts I have. Our first traceable ancestor was a tenant-farmer of Muir of Cauldwells—James in Nether-Carsewell. Presently two families of maltmen are found in Glasgow, both, by reduplicated proofs, related to James (the son of James) in Nether-Carsewell. We descend by his second marriage from Robert; one of these died 1733. It is not very romantic up to now, but has interested me surprisingly to fish out, always hoping for more — and occasionally getting at least a little clearness and confirmation. But the earliest date, 1655, apparently the marriage of James in Nether-Carsewell, cannot as yet be pushed back. From which of any number of dozen little families in Cunningham we should derive, God knows! Of course, it does n't matter a hundred years hence, an argument fatal to all human enterprise, industry, or pleasure. And to me it will be a deadly disappointment if I cannot roll this stone away! One generation further might be nothing, but it is my present object of desire, and we are so near it! There is a man in the same parish called Constantine; if I could only trace to him, I could take you far afield by that one talisman of the strange Christian name of Constantine. But no such luck! And I kind of fear we shall stick at James. 1894 ÆT. 44

So much, though all inchoate, I trouble you with, knowing that you, at least, must take an interest in it. So much is certain of that strange Celtic descent, that the past has an interest for it apparently gratuitous, but fiercely strong. I wish to trace my ancestors a thousand years, if I trace them by gallowses. It is not love, not pride, not admiration; it is an expansion of the identity, intimately pleasing, and wholly uncritical; I can expend myself in the person of an inglorious ancestor with perfect comfort; or a disgraced, if I could find one. I suppose, perhaps, it is more to me who am childless, and refrain with a certain shock from looking forwards. But, I am sure, in the solid grounds of race, that you have it also in some degree.

1894
ÆT. 44

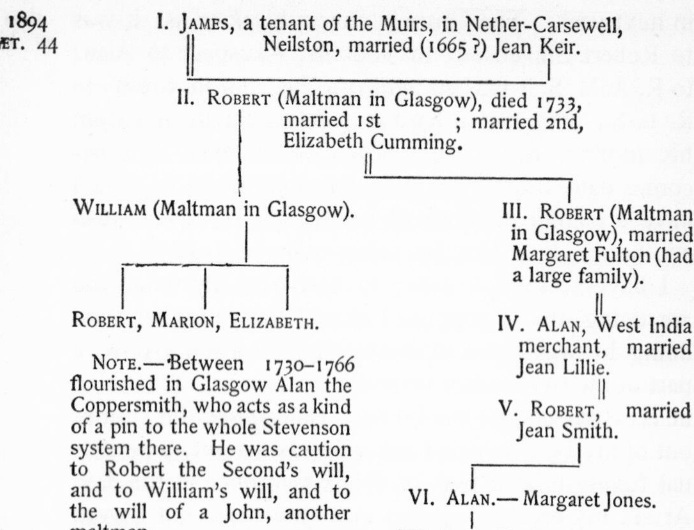
I. James, a tenant of the Muirs, in Nether-Carsewell, Neilston, married (1665 ?) Jean Keir.
II. Robert (Maltman in Glasgow), died 1733, married 1st ; married 2nd, Elizabeth Cumming.
William (Maltman in Glasgow).
Robert, Marion, Elizabeth.
Note.—Between 1730–1766 flourished in Glasgow Alan the Coppersmith, who acts as a kind of a pin to the whole Stevenson system there. He was caution to Robert the Second's will, and to William's will, and to the will of a John, another maltman.
III. Robert (Maltman in Glasgow), married Margaret Fulton (had a large family).
IV. Alan, West India merchant, married Jean Lillie.
V. Robert, married Jean Smith.
VI. Alan.—Margaret Jones.
VII. R. A. M. S.

Enough genealogy. I do not know if you will be able to read my hand. Unhappily, Belle, who is my amanuensis, is out of the way on other affairs, and I have to make the unwelcome effort. (O, this is beautiful, I am quite pleased with myself.) Graham has just arrived last night (my mother is coming by the other steamer in three days), and has told me of your meeting, and he said you looked a little older than I did; so that I suppose we keep step fairly on the downward side of the hill. He thought you looked harassed, and I could imagine that too. I sometimes feel harassed. I have a great family here about me, a great anxiety. The loss (to use my grandfather's expression), the "loss" of our family is that we are disbelievers in the morrow—perhaps I should say, rather, in next year. The future is *always* black to us; it was to Robert Stevenson; to Thomas; I suspect to Alan; to R. A. M. S. it was so almost to his ruin in youth; to R. L. S., who had a hard hopeful strain in him from his mother, it was not so much so once, but becomes daily more so. Daily so much more so, that I have a painful difficulty in believing I can ever finish another book, or that the public will ever read it. 1894 ÆT. 44

I have so huge a desire to know exactly what you are doing, that I suppose I should tell you what I am doing by way of an example. I have a room now, a part of the twelve-foot verandah sparred in, at the most inaccessible end of the house. Daily I see the sunrise out of my bed, which I still value as a tonic, a perpetual tuning-fork, a look of God's face once in the day. At six my breakfast comes up to me here, and I work till eleven. If I am quite well, I sometimes go out and bathe in the river before lunch, twelve. In the afternoon I generally work again, now alone drafting, now with Belle dictating. Dinner is at six, and I am often in bed by eight. This is supposing me to stay at home. But I must often be away, sometimes all day long, sometimes till twelve, one, or two at night, when you might see me coming home to the sleeping house, sometimes in a trackless darkness, sometimes with a glorious tropic moon, everything drenched with dew—unsaddling and creeping to bed; and you would no longer be surprised that I live out in this country, and not in Bournemouth—in bed.

My great recent interruptions have (as you know) come from politics; not much in my line, you will say. But it is impossible to live here and not feel very sorely

1894 the consequences of the horrid white mismanagement.
ÆT. 44 I tried standing by and looking on, and it became too much for me. They are such illogical fools; a logical fool in an office, with a lot of red tape, is conceivable. Furthermore, he is as much as we have any reason to expect of officials — a thoroughly commonplace, unintellectual lot. But these people are wholly on wires; laying their ears down, skimming away, pausing as though shot, and presto! full spread on the other tack. I observe in the official class mostly an insane jealousy of the smallest kind, as compared to which the artist's is of a grave, modest character — the actor's, even; a desire to extend his little authority, and to relish it like a glass of wine, that is *impayable*. Sometimes, when I see one of these little kings strutting over one of his victories — wholly illegal, perhaps, and certain to be reversed to his shame if his superiors ever heard of it — I could weep. The strange thing is that they *have nothing else*. I auscultate them in vain; no real sense of duty, no real comprehension, no real attempt to comprehend, no wish for information — you cannot offend one of them more bitterly than by offering information, though it is certain that you have *more*, and obvious that you have *other*, information than they have; and talking of policy, they could not play a better stroke than by listening to you, and it need by no means influence their action. *Tenez*, you know what a French post-office or railway official is? That is the diplomatic card to the life. Dickens is not in it; caricature fails.

All this keeps me from my work, and gives me the unpleasant side of the world. When your letters are disbelieved it makes you angry, and that is rot; and I wish I could keep out of it with all my soul. But I have just got into it again, and farewell peace! 1894 ÆT. 44

My work goes along but slowly. I have got to a crossing-place, I suppose; the present book, *Saint Ives*, is nothing; it is in no style in particular, a tissue of adventures, the central character not very well done, no philosophic pith under the yarn; and, in short, if people will read it, that 's all I ask; and if they won't, damn them! I like doing it, though; and if you ask me, why!—After that I am on *Weir of Hermiston* and *Heathercat*, two Scotch stories, which will either be something different, or I shall have failed. The first is generally designed, and is a private story of two or three characters in a very grim vein. The second—alas! the thought—is an attempt at a real historical novel, to present a whole field of time; the race—our own race—the west land and Clydesdale bluebonnets, under the influence of their last trial, when they got to a pitch of organisation in madness that no other peasantry has ever made an offer at. I was going to call it *The Killing Time*, but this man Crockett has forestalled me in that. Well, it 'll be a big smash if I fail in it; but a gallant attempt. All my weary reading as a boy, which you remember well enough, will come to bear on it; and if my mind will keep up to the point it was in a while back, perhaps I can pull it through.

For two months past, Fanny, Belle, Austin (her child), and I have been alone; but yesterday, as I mentioned, Graham Balfour arrived, and on Wednesday my mother and Lloyd will make up the party to its full strength. I wish you could drop in for a month or a week, or two

1894 ÆT. 44 hours. That is my chief want. On the whole, it is an unexpectedly pleasant corner I have dropped into for an end of it, which I could scarcely have foreseen from Wilson's shop, or the Princes Street Gardens, or the Portobello Road. Still, I would like to hear what my *alter ego* thought of it; and I would sometimes like to have my old *maître ès arts* express an opinion on what I do. I put this very tamely, being on the whole a quiet elderly man; but it is a strong passion with me, though intermittent. Now, try to follow my example and tell me something about yourself, Louisa, the Bab, and your work; and kindly send me some specimens of what you 're about. I have only seen one thing by you, about Notre Dame in the *Westminster* on St. James, since I left England, now I suppose six years ago.

I have looked this trash over, and it is not at all the letter I wanted to write—not truck about officials, ancestors, and the like rancidness—but you have to let your pen go in its own broken-down gait, like an old butcher's pony, stop when it pleases, and go on again as it will.—Ever, my dear Bob, your affectionate cousin, R. L. STEVENSON.

TO HENRY JAMES

VAILIMA, *July 7, 1894*.

DEAR HENRY JAMES,—I am going to try and dictate to you a letter or a note, and begin the same without any spark of hope, my mind being entirely in abeyance. This malady is very bitter on the literary man. I have had it now coming on for a month, and it seems to get worse instead of better. If it should prove to be softening of the brain, a melancholy interest will attach to the present document. I heard a great deal about you from my mother and Graham Balfour; the latter declares that you could take a First in any Samoan subject. If that be so, I should like to hear you on the theory of the constitution. Also to consult you on the force of the particles *o lo' o* and *ua*, which are the subject of a dispute among local pundits. You might, if you ever answer this, give me your opinion on the origin of the Samoan race, just to complete the favour. 1894 ÆT. 44

They both say that you are looking well, and I suppose I may conclude from that that you are feeling passably. I wish I was. Do not suppose from this that I am ill in body; it is the numskull that I complain of. And when that is wrong, as you must be very keenly aware, you begin every day with a smarting disappointment, which is not good for the temper. I am in one of the humours when a man wonders how any one can be such an ass as to embrace the profession of letters, and not get apprenticed to a barber or keep a baked-potato stall. But I have no doubt in the course of a week, or perhaps to-morrow, things will look better.

We have at present in port the model warship of Great Britain. She is called the *Curaçoa*, and has the nicest set of officers and men conceivable. They, the officers, are all very intimate with us, and the front verandah is known as the Curaçoa Club, and the road up to Vailima is known as the Curaçoa Track. It was rather a surprise to me; many naval officers have I known, and somehow had not learned to think entirely well of them, and perhaps sometimes ask myself a little uneasily how that kind of men could do great actions?

1894 and behold! the answer comes to me, and I see a ship
ÆT. 44 that I would guarantee to go anywhere it was possible for men to go, and accomplish anything it was permitted man to attempt. I had a cruise on board of her not long ago to Manu'a, and was delighted. The goodwill of all on board; the grim playfulness of [1] quarters, with the wounded falling down at the word; the ambulances hastening up and carrying them away; the captain suddenly crying, "Fire in the ward-room!" and the squad hastening forward with the hose; and last and most curious spectacle of all, all the men in their dust-coloured fatigue clothes, at a note of the bugle, falling simultaneously flat on deck, and the ship proceeding with its prostrate crew—*quasi* to ram an enemy; our dinner at night in a wild open anchorage, the ship rolling almost to her gunwales, and showing us alternately her bulwarks up in the sky, and then the wild broken cliffy palm-crested shores of the island with the surf thundering and leaping close aboard. We had the ward-room mess on deck, lit by pink wax tapers, everybody, of course, in uniform but myself, and the first lieutenant (who is a rheumaticky body) wrapped in a boat cloak. Gradually the sunset faded out, the island disappeared from the eye, though it remained menacingly present to the ear with the voice of the surf; and then the captain turned on the search-light and gave us the coast, the beach, the trees, the native houses, and the cliffs by glimpses of daylight, a kind of deliberate lightning. About which time, I suppose, we must have come as far as the dessert, and were probably drinking our first glass of port to Her

[1] Word omitted in MS.

Majesty. We stayed two days at the island, and had, in addition, a very picturesque snapshot at the native life. The three islands of Manu'a are independent, and are ruled over by a little slip of a half-caste girl about twenty, who sits all day in a pink gown, in a little white European house with about a quarter of an acre of roses in front of it, looking at the palm-trees on the village street, and listening to the surf. This, so far as I could discover, was all she had to do. "This is a very dull place," she said. It appears she could go to no other village for fear of raising the jealousy of her own people in the capital. And as for going about "tapatafaoing," as we say here, its cost was too enormous. A strong able-bodied native must walk in front of her and blow the conch shell continuously from the moment she leaves one house until the moment she enters another. Did you ever blow the conch shell? I presume not; but the sweat literally hailed off that man, and I expected every moment to see him burst a blood-vessel. We were entertained to kava in the guest-house with some very original features. The young men who run for the kava have a right to misconduct themselves *ad libitum* on the way back; and though they were told to restrain themselves on the occasion of our visit, there was a strange hurly-burly at their return, when they came beating the trees and the posts of the houses, leaping, shouting, and yelling like Bacchants. 1894 ÆT. 44

I tasted on that occasion what it is to be great. My name was called next after the captain's, and several chiefs (a thing quite new to me, and not at all Samoan practice) drank to me by name.

1894 ÆT. 44 And now, if you are not sick of the *Curaçoa* and Manu'a, I am at least on paper. And I decline any longer to give you examples of how not to write.

By the by, you sent me long ago a work by Anatole France, which I confess I did not *taste*. Since then I have made the acquaintance of the *Abbé Coignard*, and have become a faithful adorer. I don't think a better book was ever written.

And I have no idea what I have said, and I have no idea what I ought to have said, and I am a total ass, but my heart is in the right place, and I am, my dear Henry James, yours, R. L. S.

To Marcel Schwob

Vailima, Upolu, Samoa, *July 7, 1894*.

DEAR MR. MARCEL SCHWOB,—Thank you for having remembered me in my exile. I have read *Mimes* twice as a whole; and now, as I write, I am reading it again as it were by accident and a piece at a time, my eye catching a word and travelling obediently on through the whole number. It is a graceful book, essentially graceful, with its haunting, agreeable melancholy, its pleasing savour of antiquity. At the same time, by its merits, it shows itself rather as the promise of something else to come, than a thing final in itself. You have yet to give us—and I am expecting it with impatience—something of a larger gait; something daylit, not twilit; something with the colours of life, not the flat tints of a temple illumination; something that shall be *said* with all the clearnesses and the trivialities of speech, not *sung* like a semi-articulate lullaby. It will not please yourself as well, when you come to give it us, but it will please others better. It will be more of a whole, more worldly, more nourished, more commonplace — and not so pretty, perhaps not even so beautiful. No man knows better than I, that, as we go on in life, we must part from prettiness and the graces. We but attain qualities to lose them; life is a series of farewells, even in art; even our proficiencies are deciduous and evanescent. So here with these exquisite pieces, the XVIIth, XVIIIth, and IVth, of the present collection. You will perhaps never excel them; I should think the "Hermes" never. Well, you will do something else, and of that I am in expectation.—Yours cordially, 1893 ÆT. 43

ROBERT LOUIS STEVENSON.

To Augustus St. Gaudens

VAILIMA, SAMOA, *July 8, 1894.*

MY DEAR ST. GAUDENS,—This is to tell you that the medallion has been at last triumphantly transported up the hill and placed over my smoking-room mantelpiece. It is considered by everybody a first-rate but flattering portrait. We have it in a very good light, which brings out the artistic merits of the god-like sculptor to great advantage. As for my own opinion, I believe it to be a speaking likeness, and not flattered at all; possibly a little the reverse. The verses (curse the rhyme) look remarkably well.

Please do not longer delay, but send me an account for the expense of the gilt letters. I was sorry indeed that they proved beyond the means of a small farmer.—Yours very sincerely, ROBERT LOUIS STEVENSON.

1894
ÆT. 44

To Miss Adelaide Boodle

VAILIMA, *July 14, 1894.*

MY DEAR ADELAIDE,—. . . So, at last, you are going into mission work? where I think your heart always was. You will like it in a way, but remember it is dreary long. Do you know the story of the American tramp who was offered meals and a day's wage to chop with the back of an axe on a fallen trunk. "Damned if I can go on chopping when I can't see the chips fly!" You will never see the chips fly in mission work, never; and be sure you know it beforehand. The work is one long dull disappointment, varied by acute revulsions; and those who are by nature courageous and cheerful, and have grown old in experience, learn to rub their hands over infinitesimal successes. However, as I really believe there is some good done in the long run—*gutta cavat lapidem non vi* in this business—it is a useful and honourable career in which no one should be ashamed to embark. Always remember the fable of the sun, the storm, and the traveller's cloak. Forget wholly and for ever all small pruderies, and remember that *you cannot change ancestral feelings of right and wrong without what is practically soul-murder.* Barbarous as the customs may seem, always hear them with patience, always judge them with gentleness, always find in them some seed of good; see that you always develop them; remember that all you can do is to civilise the man in the line of his own civilisation, such as it is. And never expect, never believe in, thaumaturgic conversions. They may do very well

for St. Paul; in the case of an Andaman islander they 1894
mean less than nothing. In fact, what you have to do ÆT. 44
is to teach the parents in the interests of their great-grandchildren.

Now, my dear Adelaide, dismiss from your mind the least idea of fault upon your side; nothing is further from the fact. I cannot forgive you, for I do not know your fault. My own is plain enough, and the name of it is cold-hearted neglect; and you may busy yourself more usefully in trying to forgive me. But ugly as my fault is, you must not suppose it to mean more than it does; it does not mean that we have at all forgotten you, that we have become at all indifferent to the thought of you. See, in my life of Jenkin, a remark of his, very well expressed, on the friendships of men who do not write to each other. I can honestly say that I have not changed to you in any way; though I have behaved thus ill, thus cruelly. Evil is done by want of — well, principally by want of industry. You can imagine what I would say (in a novel) of any one who had behaved as I have done. *Deteriora sequor.* And you must somehow manage to forgive your old friend; and if you will be so very good, continue to give us news of you, and let us share the knowledge of your adventures, sure that it will be always followed with interest — even if it is answered with the silence of ingratitude. For I am not a fool; I know my faults, I know they are ineluctable, I know they are growing on me. I know I may offend again, and I warn you of it. But the next time I offend, tell me so plainly and frankly like a lady, and don't lacerate my heart and bludgeon my vanity with imaginary faults of your own

1894 ÆT. 44 and purely gratuitous penitence. I might suspect you of irony!

We are all fairly well, though I have been off work and off—as you know very well—letter-writing. Yet I have sometimes more than twenty letters, and sometimes more than thirty, going out each mail. And Fanny has had a most distressing bronchitis for some time, which she is only now beginning to get over. I have just been to see her; she is lying—though she had breakfast an hour ago, about seven—in her big, cool, mosquito-proof room, ingloriously asleep. As for me, you see that a doom has come upon me: I cannot make marks with a pen—witness "ingloriously" above; and my amanuensis not appearing so early in the day, for she is then immersed in household affairs, and I can hear her "steering the boys" up and down the verandahs—you must decipher this unhappy letter for yourself and, I fully admit, with everything against you. A letter should be always well written; how much more a letter of apology! Legibility is the politeness of men of letters, as punctuality of kings and beggars. By the punctuality of my replies, and the beauty of my handwriting, judge what a fine conscience I must have!

Now, my dear gamekeeper, I must really draw to a close. For I have much else to write before the mail goes out three days hence. Fanny being asleep, it would not be conscientious to invent a message from her, so you must just imagine her sentiments. I find I have not the heart to speak of your recent loss. You remember, perhaps, when my father died, you told me those ugly images of sickness, decline, and impaired reason, which then haunted me day and night, would pass away and be succeeded by things more happily characteristic. I have found it so. He now haunts me, strangely enough, in two guises; as a man of fifty, lying on a hillside and carving mottoes on a stick, strong and well; and as a younger man, running down the sands into the sea near North Berwick, myself—*ætat.* 11—somewhat horrified at finding him so beautiful when stripped! I hand on your own advice to you in case you have forgotten it, as I know one is apt to do in seasons of bereavement.—Ever yours, with much love and sympathy, 1894 ÆT. 44

ROBERT LOUIS STEVENSON.

TO MRS. BAKER

This refers again to the printing of some of his books in Braille type for the blind.

VAILIMA, SAMOA, *July 16, 1894.*

DEAR MRS. BAKER,—I am very much obliged to you for your letter and the enclosure from Mr. Skinner. Mr. Skinner says he "thinks Mr. Stevenson must be a very kind man"; he little knows me. But I am very sure of one thing, that you are a very kind woman. I envy you—my amanuensis being called away, I continue in my own hand, or what is left of it—unusually legible, I am thankful to see—I envy you your beautiful choice of an employment. There must be no regrets at least for a day so spent; and when the night falls you need ask no blessing on your work.

"Inasmuch as ye have done it unto one of these."—Yours truly, ROBERT LOUIS STEVENSON.

1894
ÆT. 44

To J. M. Barrie

This journal-letter to Mr. Barrie covers a period of a month. In the interval between two of its parts (August 6th and August 12th) the news of Mr. Barrie's engagement and marriage, which took place soon after his recovery from a dangerous illness, had reached Samoa.

VAILIMA, *July 13, 1894.*

MY DEAR BARRIE,—This is the last effort of an ulcerated conscience. I have been so long owing you a letter, I have heard so much of you, fresh from the press, from my mother and Graham Balfour, that I have to write a letter no later than to-day, or perish in my shame. But the deuce of it is, my dear fellow, that you write such a very good letter that I am ashamed to exhibit myself before my junior (which you are, after all) in the light of the dreary idiot I feel. Understand that there will be nothing funny in the following pages. If I can manage to be rationally coherent, I shall be more than satisfied.

In the first place, I have had the extreme satisfaction to be shown that photograph of your mother. It bears evident traces of the hand of an amateur. How is it that amateurs invariably take better photographs than professionals? I must qualify invariably. My own negatives have always represented a province of chaos and old night in which you might dimly perceive fleecy spots of twilight, representing nothing; so that, if I am right in supposing the portrait of your mother to be yours, I must salute you as my superior. Is that your mother's breakfast? Or is it only afternoon tea? If the first, do let me recommend to Mrs. Barrie to add an egg to her ordinary. Which, if you please, I will ask her to eat to the honour of her son, and I am sure she will live much longer for it, to enjoy his fresh successes. I never in my life saw anything more deliciously characteristic. I declare I can hear her speak. I wonder my mother could resist the temptation of your proposed visit to Kirriemuir, which it was like your kindness to propose. By the way, I was twice in Kirriemuir, I believe in the year '71, when I was going on a visit to Glenogil. It was Kirriemuir, was it not? I have a distinct recollection of an inn at the end—I think the upper end—of an irregular open place or square, in which I always see your characters evolve. But, indeed, I did not pay much attention; being all bent upon my visit to a shooting-box, where I should fish a real trout-stream, and I believe preserved. I did, too, and it was a charming stream, clear as crystal, without a trace of peat—a strange thing in Scotland—and alive with trout; the name of it I cannot remember, it was something like the Queen's River, and in some hazy way connected with memories of Mary Queen of Scots. It formed an epoch in my life, being the end of all my trout-fishing. I had always been accustomed to pause and very laboriously to kill every fish as I took it. But in the Queen's River I took so good a basket that I forgot these niceties; and when I sat down, in a hard rain shower, under a bank, to take my sandwiches and sherry, lo! and behold, there was the basketful of trouts still kicking in their agony. I had a very unpleasant conversation with my conscience. All that afternoon I persevered in fishing, brought home my basket in triumph, and sometime that night, "in

1894 ÆT. 44 the wee sma' hours ayont the twal," I finally forswore the gentle craft of fishing. I dare say your local knowledge may identify this historic river; I wish it could go farther and identify also that particular Free kirk in which I sat and groaned on Sunday. While my hand is in I must tell you a story. At that antique epoch you must not fall into the vulgar error that I was myself ancient. I was, on the contrary, very young, very green, and (what you will appreciate, Mr. Barrie) very shy. There came one day to lunch at the house two very formidable old ladies—or one very formidable, and the other what you please—answering to the honoured and historic name of the Miss C—— A——'s of Balnamoon. At table I was exceedingly funny, and entertained the company with tales of geese and bubbly-jocks. I was great in the expression of my terror for these bipeds, and suddenly this horrid, severe, and eminently matronly old lady put up a pair of gold eyeglasses, looked at me awhile in silence, and pronounced in a clangorous voice her verdict. "You give me very much the effect of a coward, Mr. Stevenson!" I had very nearly left two vices behind me at Glenogil—fishing and jesting at table. And of one thing you may be very sure, my lips were no more opened at that meal.

July 29th.

No, Barrie, 't is in vain they try to alarm me with their bulletins. No doubt, you 're ill, and unco ill, I believe; but I have been so often in the same case that I know pleurisy and pneumonia are in vain against Scotsmen who can write. (I once could.) You cannot imagine probably how near me this common ca-

lamity brings you. *Ce que j'ai toussé dans ma vie!* 1894 ÆT. 44
How often and how long have I been on the rack at night and learned to appreciate that noble passage in the Psalms when somebody or other is said to be more set on something than they "who dig for hid treasures—yea, than those who long for the morning"—for all the world, as you have been racked and you have longed. Keep your heart up, and you 'll do. Tell that to your mother, if you are still in any danger or suffering. And by the way, if you are at all like me—and I tell myself you are very like me—be sure there is only one thing good for you, and that is the sea in hot climates. Mount, sir, into "a little frigot" of 5000 tons or so, and steer peremptorily for the tropics; and what if the ancient mariner, who guides your frigot, should startle the silence of the ocean with the cry of land ho!—say, when the day is dawning—and you should see the turquoise mountain-tops of Upolu coming hand over fist above the horizon? Mr. Barrie, sir, 't is then there would be larks! And though I cannot be certain that our climate would suit you (for it does not suit some), I am sure as death the voyage would do you good—would do you *Best*—and if Samoa did n't do, you need n't stay beyond the month, and I should have had another pleasure in my life, which is a serious consideration for me. I take this as the hand of the Lord preparing your way to Vailima—in the desert, certainly—in the desert of Cough and by the ghoul-haunted woodland of Fever—but whither that way points there can be no question—and there will be a meeting of the twa Hoasting Scots Makers in spite of fate, fortune, and the Devil. *Absit omen.*

1894
ÆT. 44

My dear Barrie, I am a little in the dark about this new work of yours:[1] what is to become of me afterwards? You say carefully—methought anxiously—that I was no longer me when I grew up? I cannot bear this suspense: what is it? It 's no forgery? And AM I HANGIT? These are the elements of a very pretty lawsuit which you had better come to Samoa to compromise. I am enjoying a great pleasure that I had long looked forward to, reading Orme's *History of Indostan;* I had been looking out for it everywhere; but at last, in four volumes, large quarto, beautiful type and page, and with a delectable set of maps and plans, and all the names of the places wrongly spelled—it came to Samoa, little Barrie. I tell you frankly, you had better come soon. I am sair failed a'ready; and what I may be if you continue to dally, I dread to conceive. I may be speechless; already, or at least for a month or so, I 'm little better than a teetoller—I beg pardon, a teetotaller. It is not exactly physical, for I am in good health, working four or five hours a day in my plantation, and intending to ride a paper chase next Sunday—ay, man, that 's a fact, and I havena had the hert to breathe it to my mother yet—the obligation 's poleetical, for I am trying every means to live well with my German neighbours — and, O Barrie, but it 's no easy! To be sure, there are many exceptions. And the whole of the above must be regarded as private — strictly private. Breathe it not in Kirriemuir: tell it not to the daughters of Dundee! What a nice extract this would make for the daily papers! and how it would facilitate my position here! . . .

[1] *Sentimental Tommy:* whose chief likeness to R. L. S. was meant to be in the literary temperament and passion for the *mot propre.*

August 5th. 1894 ÆT. 44

This is Sunday, the Lord's Day. "The hour of attack approaches." And it is a singular consideration what I risk; I may yet be the subject of a tract, and a good tract too—such as one which I remember reading with recreant awe and rising hair in my youth, of a boy who was a very good boy, and went to Sunday Schule, and one day kipped from it, and went and actually bathed, and was dashed over a waterfall, and he was the only son of his mother, and she was a widow. A dangerous trade, that, and one that I have to practise. I 'll put in a word when I get home again, to tell you whether I 'm killed or not. "Accident in the (Paper) Hunting Field: death of a notorious author. We deeply regret to announce the death of the most unpopular man in Samoa, who broke his neck at the descent of Magagi, from the misconduct of his little raving lunatic of an old beast of a pony. It is proposed to commemorate the incident by the erection of a suitable pile. The design (by our local architect, Mr. Walker) is highly artificial, with a rich and voluminous Crockett at each corner, a small but impervious Barrièer at the entrance, an arch at the top, an Archer of a pleasing but solid character at the bottom; the colour will be genuine William-Black; and Lang, lang may the ladies sit wi' their fans in their hands." Well, well, they may sit as they sat for me, and little they 'll reck, the ungrateful jauds! Muckle they cared about Tusitala when they had him! But now ye can see the difference; now, leddies, ye can repent, when ower late, o' your former cauldness and what ye 'll perhaps allow me to ca' your *tepeedity!* He was beautiful as the day, but his day is done! And perhaps, as he was

1894 ÆT. 44 maybe gettin' a wee thing fly-blawn, it 's nane too shüne.

Monday, August 6th.

Well, sir, I have escaped the dangerous conjunction of the widow's only son and the Sabbath Day. We had a most enjoyable time, and Lloyd and I were 3 and 4 to arrive; I will not tell here what interval had elapsed between our arrival and the arrival of 1 and 2; the question, sir, is otiose and malign; it deserves, it shall have no answer. And now without further delay to the main purpose of this hasty note. We received and we have already in fact distributed the gorgeous fabrics of Kirriemuir. Whether from the splendour of the robes themselves, or from the direct nature of the compliments with which you had directed us to accompany the presentations, one young lady blushed as she received the proofs of your munificence. . . . Bad ink, and the dregs of it at that, but the heart in the right place. Still very cordially interested in my Barrie and wishing him well through his sickness, which is of the body, and long defended from mine, which is of the head, and by the impolite might be described as idiocy. The whole head is useless, and the whole sitting part painful: reason, the recent Paper Chase.

There was racing and chasing in Vailile plantation,
  And vastly we enjoyed it,
But, alas! for the state of my foundation,
  For it wholly has destroyed it.

Come, my mind is looking up. The above is wholly impromptu.—On oath, TUSITALA.

August 12, 1894. 1894 ÆT. 44

And here, Mr. Barrie, is news with a vengeance. Mother Hubbard's dog is well again—what did I tell you? Pleurisy, pneumonia, and all that kind of truck is quite unavailing against a Scotchman who can write —and not only that, but it appears the perfidious dog is married. This incident, so far as I remember, is omitted from the original epic—

She went to the graveyard
To see him get him buried,
And when she came back
The Deil had got merried.

It now remains to inform you that I have taken what we call here "German offence" at not receiving cards, and that the only reparation I will accept is that Mrs. Barrie shall incontinently upon the receipt of this Take and Bring you to Vailima in order to apologise and be pardoned for this offence. The commentary of Tamaitai upon the event was brief but pregnant: "Well, it 's a comfort our guest-room is furnished for two."

This letter, about nothing, has already endured too long. I shall just present the family to Mrs. Barrie—Tamaitai, Tamaitai Matua, Teuila, Palema, Loia, and with an extra low bow, Yours, TUSITALA.

TO DR. BAKEWELL

The following is to a physician in Australia.

VAILIMA, *August 7, 1894.*

DEAR DR. BAKEWELL,—I am not more than human. I am more human than is wholly convenient, and your

1894 ÆT. 44 anecdote was welcome. What you say about *unwilling work*, my dear sir, is a consideration always present with me, and yet not easy to give its due weight to. You grow gradually into a certain income; without spending a penny more, with the same sense of restriction as before when you painfully scraped two hundred a year together, you find you have spent, and you cannot well stop spending, a far larger sum; and this expense can only be supported by a certain production. However, I am off work this month, and occupy myself instead in weeding my cacao, paper chases, and the like. I may tell you, my average of work in favourable circumstances is far greater than you suppose: from six o'clock till eleven at latest,[1] and often till twelve, and again in the afternoon from two to four. My hand is quite destroyed, as you may perceive to-day, to a really unusual extent. I can sometimes write a decent fist still; but I have just returned with my arms all stung from three hours' work in the cacao.—Yours, etc.,

R. L. S.

To James Payn

Vailima, Upolu, Samoa [*August, 1894*].

MY DEAR JAMES PAYN,—I hear from Lang that you are unwell, and it reminds me of two circumstances: First, that it is a very long time since you had the exquisite pleasure of hearing from me; and second, that I have been very often unwell myself, and sometimes had to thank you for a grateful anodyne.

[1] *Sic:* query "least"?

They are not good, the circumstances, to write an anodyne letter. The hills and my house at less than (boom) a minute's interval quake with thunder; and though I cannot hear that part of it, shells are falling thick into the fort of Lotoanuu (boom). It is my friends of the *Curaçoa*, the *Adler*, and the *Bussard* bombarding (after all these — boom — months) the rebels of Atua. (Boom-boom.) It is most distracting in itself; and the thought of the poor devils in their fort (boom) with their bits of rifles far from pleasant. (Boom-boom.) You can see how quick it goes, and I 'll say no more about Mr. Bow-wow, only you must understand the perpetual accompaniment of this discomfortable sound, and make allowances for the value of my copy. It is odd, though, I can well remember when the Franco-Prussian war began, and I was in Eilean Earraid, far enough from the sound of the loudest cannonade, I could *hear* the shots fired, and I felt the pang in my breast of a man struck. It was sometimes so distressing, so instant, that I lay in the heather on the top of the island, with my face hid, kicking my heels for agony. And now, when I can hear the actual concussion of the air and hills, when I *know* personally the people who stand exposed to it, I am able to go on *tant bien que mal* with a letter to James Payn! The blessings of age, though mighty small, are tangible. I have heard a great deal of them since I came into the world, and now that I begin to taste of them — Well! But this is one, that people do get cured of the excess of sensibility; and I had as lief these people were shot at as myself — or almost, for then I should have some of the fun, such as it is.

1894
ÆT. 44
You are to conceive me, then, sitting in my little gallery room, shaken by these continual spasms of cannon, and with my eye more or less singly fixed on the imaginary figure of my dear James Payn. I try to see him in bed; no go. I see him instead jumping up in his room in Waterloo Place (where *ex hypothesi* he is not), sitting on the table, drawing out a very black briar-root pipe, and beginning to talk to a slim and ill-dressed visitor in a voice that is good to hear and with a smile that is pleasant to see. (After a little more than half an hour, the voice that was ill to hear has ceased, the cannonade is over.) And I am thinking how I can get an answering smile wafted over so many leagues of land and water, and can find no way.

I have always been a great visitor of the sick; and one of the sick I visited was W. E. Henley, which did not make very tedious visits, so I 'll not get off much purgatory for them. That was in the Edinburgh Infirmary, the old one, the true one, with Georgius Secundus standing and pointing his toe in a niche of the façade; and a mighty fine building it was! And I remember one winter's afternoon, in that place of misery, that Henley and I chanced to fall in talk about James Payn himself. I am wishing you could have heard that talk! I think that would make you smile. We had mixed you up with John Payne, for one thing, and stood amazed at your extraordinary, even painful, versatility; and for another, we found ourselves each students so well prepared for examinations on the novels of the real Mackay. Perhaps, after all, this is worth something in life — to have given so much pleasure to a pair so different in every way as were Henley and I, and to be talked of with so much interest by two such (beg pardon) clever lads! 1894 ÆT. 44

The cheerful Lang has neglected to tell me what is the matter with you; so, I 'm sorry to say, I am cut off from all the customary consolations. I can't say, "Think how much worse it would be if you had a broken leg!" when you may have the crushing repartee up your sleeve, "But it is my leg that is broken." This is a pity. But there are consolations. You are an Englishman (I believe); you are a man of letters; you have never been made C. B.; your hair was not red; you have played cribbage and whist; you did not play either the fiddle or the banjo; you were never an æsthete; you never contributed to —— *Journal;* your name is not Jabez Balfour; you are totally unconnected with the Army and Navy departments; I understand you to have lived within your income—why, cheer up! here are many legitimate causes of congratulation. I seem to be writing an obituary notice. *Absit omen!* But I feel very sure that these considerations will have done you more good than medicine.

By the by, did you ever play piquet? I have fallen a victim to this debilitating game. It is supposed to be scientific; God save the mark, what self-deceivers men are! It is distinctly less so than cribbage. But how fascinating! There is such material opulence about it, such vast ambitions may be realised—and are not; it may be called the Monte Cristo of games. And the thrill with which you take five cards partakes of the nature of lust—and you draw four sevens and a nine, and the seven and nine of a suit that you discarded, and O! but the world is a desert! You may see traces of

1894 ÆT. 44 discouragement in my letter: all due to piquet! There has been a disastrous turn of the luck against me; a month or two ago I was two thousand ahead; now, and for a week back, I have been anything from four thousand eight hundred to five thousand two hundred astern. If I have a sixième, my beast of a partner has a septième; and if I have three aces, three kings, three queens, and three knaves (excuse the slight exaggeration), the devil holds quatorze of tens!—I remain, my dear James Payn, your sincere and obliged friend—old friend let me say, ROBERT LOUIS STEVENSON.

TO MISS MIDDLETON

A letter from the lady to whom this is addressed, and who had been a friend of the Stevenson family in Edinburgh, had called up some memories of the Skye terrier Jura, of whom readers have heard something already.

VAILIMA, SAMOA, *September 9, 1894.*

DEAR MISS MIDDLETON,—Your letter has been like the drawing up of a curtain. Of course I remember you very well, and the Skye terrier to which you refer—a heavy, dull, fatted, graceless creature he grew up to be—was my own particular pet. It may amuse you, perhaps, as much as "The Inn" amused me, if I tell you what made this dog particularly mine. My father was the natural god of all the dogs in our house, and poor Jura took to him of course. Jura was stolen, and kept in prison somewhere for more than a week, as I remember. When he came back Smeoroch had come and taken my father's heart from him. He took his stand like a man, and positively never spoke to my father again from that day until the day of his death. It was the only sign of character he ever showed. I took him up to my room and to be my dog in consequence, partly because I was sorry for him, and partly because I admired his dignity in misfortune. 1894 ÆT. 44

With best regards and thanks for having reminded me of so many pleasant days, old acquaintances, dead friends, and—what is perhaps as pathetic as any of them—dead dogs, I remain, yours truly,

ROBERT LOUIS STEVENSON.

TO A. CONAN DOYLE

The following refers to the papers originally contributed by various writers to Mr. Jerome's periodical, the *Idler*, under the title "My First Book," and afterwards republished in a volume. The references towards the end are to the illustrations in the pages of the *Idler*.

VAILIMA, SAMOA, *September 9, 1894*.

MY DEAR CONAN DOYLE,—If you found anything to entertain you in my *Treasure Island* article, it may amuse you to know that you owe it entirely to yourself. *Your* "First Book" was by some accident read aloud one night in my Baronial 'All. I was consumedly amused by it, so was the whole family, and we proceeded to hunt up back *Idlers* and read the whole series. It is a rattling good series; even people whom you would not expect came in quite the

1894 proper tone — Miss Braddon, for instance, who was
ÆT. 44 really one of the best where all are good — or all but one! . . . In short, I fell in love with the "First Book" series, and determined that it should be all our first books, and that I could not hold back where the white plume of Conan Doyle waved gallantly in the front. I hope they will republish them, though it 's a grievous thought to me that that effigy in the German cap — likewise the other effigy of the noisome old man with the long hair, telling indelicate stories to a couple of deformed negresses in a rancid shanty full of wreckage — should be perpetuated. I may seem to speak in pleasantry — it is only a seeming — that German cap, sir, would be found, when I come to die, imprinted on my heart. Enough — my heart is too full. Adieu.— Yours very truly,

ROBERT LOUIS STEVENSON
(in a German cap, damn 'em!).

To Charles Baxter

The following was written on hearing of the death of his friend's father.

[*Received 15th September, '94.*]

MY DEAR CHARLES, — . . . Well, there is no more Edmund Baxter now; and I think I may say I know how you feel. He was one of the best, the kindest, and the most genial men I ever knew. I shall always remember his brisk, cordial ways and the essential goodness which he showed me whenever we met with gratitude. And the always is such a little while now! He is another of the landmarks gone; when it comes to my own turn to lay my weapons down, I shall do so with thankfulness and fatigue; and whatever be my destiny afterward, I shall be glad to lie down with my fathers in honour. It is human at least, if not divine. And these deaths make me think of it with an ever greater readiness. Strange that you should be beginning a new life, when I, who am a little your junior, am thinking of the end of mine. But I have had hard lines; I have been so long waiting for death; I have unwrapped my thoughts from about life so long, that I have not a filament left to hold by; I have done my fiddling so long under Vesuvius, that I have almost forgotten to play, and can only wait for the eruption, and think it long of coming. Literally, no man has more wholly outlived life than I. And still it 's good fun. R. L. S.

To R. A. M. Stevenson

Stevenson had received from his cousin a letter announcing, among other things, the birth of a son to the writer, and rambling suggestively, as may be guessed from the following reply, over many disconnected themes : the ethnology of Scotland, paternity and heredity, civilisation *versus* primitive customs and instincts, the story of their own descent, the method of writing in collaboration, education, sex and Christianity, anarchism, etc.; all which matters are here discursively touched on. "Old Skene" is, of course, the great Scottish antiquarian and historian, William Forbes Skene, in whose firm (Edwards & Skene, W. S.) Stevenson had for a time served, irregularly enough, as an unpaid clerk.

1894 ÆT. 44

[VAILIMA, *September, 1894.*]

DEAR BOB,—You are in error about the Picts. They were a Gaelic race, spoke a Celtic tongue, and we have no evidence that I know of that they were blacker than other Celts. The Balfours, I take it, were plainly Celts; their name shows it—the "cold croft," it means; so does their country. Where the *black* Scotch come from nobody knows; but I recognise with you the fact that the whole of Britain is rapidly and progressively becoming more pigmented; already in one man's life I can decidedly trace a difference in the children about a school door. But colour is not an essential part of a man or a race. Take my Polynesians, an Asiatic people probably from the neighbourhood of the Persian Gulf. They range through any amount of shades, from the burnt hue of the Low Archipelago islander, which seems half negro, to the "bleached" pretty women of the Marquesas (close by on the map), who come out for a festival no darker than an Italian; their colour seems to vary directly with the degree of exposure to the sun. And, as with negroes, the babes are born white; only it should seem a *little sack* of pigment at the lower part of the spine, which presently spreads over the whole field. Very puzzling. But to return. The Picts furnish to-day perhaps a third of the population of Scotland, say another third for Scots and Britons, and the third for Norse and Angles is a bad third. Edinburgh was a Pictish place. But the fact is, we don't know their frontiers. Tell some of your journalist friends with a good style to popularise old Skene; or say your prayers, and read him for yourself; he was a Great Historian, and I was his blessed clerk, and did not know it; and you will not be in a state of grace about the Picts till you have studied him. J. Horne Stevenson (do you know him ?) is working this up with me, and the fact is — it 's not interesting to the public — but it 's interesting, and very interesting, in itself, and just now very embarrassing — this rural parish supplied Glasgow with such a quantity of Stevensons in the beginning of last century! There is just a link wanting; and we might be able to go back to the eleventh century, always undistinguished, but clearly traceable. When I say just a link, I guess I may be taken to mean a dozen. What a singular thing is this undistinguished perpetuation of a family throughout the centuries, and the sudden bursting forth of character and capacity that began with our grandfather! But as I go on in life, day by day, I become more of a bewildered child; I cannot get used to this world, to procreation, to heredity, to sight, to hearing; the commonest things are a burthen. The prim obliterated polite face of life, and the broad, bawdy, and orgiastic — or mœnadic — foundations, form a spectacle to which no habit reconciles me; and "I could wish my days to be bound each to each" by the same open-mouthed wonder. They *are* anyway, and whether I wish it or not.

I remember very well your attitude to life, this conventional surface of it. You had none of that curiosity for the social stage directions, the trivial *ficelles* of the business; it is simian, but that is how the wild youth of man is captured; you would n't imitate, hence you kept free — a wild dog, outside the kennel — and came dam near starving for your pains. The key to the business is

1894 ÆT. 44 of course the belly; difficult as it is to keep that in view in the zone of three miraculous meals a day in which we were brought up. Civilisation has become reflex with us; you might think that hunger was the name of the best sauce; but hunger to the cold solitary under a bush of a rainy night is the name of something quite different. I defend civilisation for the thing it is, for the thing it has *come* to be, the standpoint of a real old Tory. My ideal would be the Female Clan. But how can you turn these crowding dumb multitudes *back?* They don't do anything *because;* they do things, write able articles, stitch shoes, dig, from the purely simian impulse. Go and reason with monkeys!

No, I am right about Jean Lillie. Jean Lillie, our double great-grandmother, the daughter of David Lillie, sometime Deacon of the Wrights, married, first, Alan Stevenson, who died May 26, 1774, "at Santt Kittes of a fiver," by whom she had Robert Stevenson, born 8th June, 1772; and, second, in May or June, 1787, Thomas Smith, a widower, and already the father of our grandmother. This improbable double connection always tends to confuse a student of the family, Thomas Smith being doubly our great-grandfather.

I looked on the perpetuation of our honoured name with veneration. My mother collared one of the photos, of course; the other is stuck up on my wall as the chief of our sept. Do you know any of the Gaelic-Celtic sharps? you might ask what the name means. It puzzles me. I find a *M'Stein* and a *MacStephane;* and our own great-grandfather always called himself Steenson, though he wrote it Stevenson. There are at least three *places* called Stevenson—*Stevenson* in Cunningham,

Stevenson in Peebles, and *Stevenson* in Haddington. And it was not the Celtic trick, I understand, to call places after people. I am going to write to Sir Herbert Maxwell about the name, but you might find some one. 1894 ÆT. 44

Get the Anglo-Saxon heresy out of your head; they superimposed their language, they scarce modified the race; only in Berwickshire and Roxburgh have they very largely affected the place names. The Scandinavians did much more to Scotland than the Angles. The Saxons did n't come.

Enough of this sham antiquarianism. Yes, it is in the matter of the book, of course, that collaboration shows; as for the manner, it is superficially all mine, in the sense that the last copy is all in my hand. Lloyd did not even put pen to paper in the Paris scenes or the Barbizon scene; it was no good; he wrote and often rewrote all the rest; I had the best service from him on the character of Nares. You see, we had been just meeting the man, and his memory was full of the man's words and ways. And Lloyd is an impressionist, pure and simple. The great difficulty of collaboration is that you can't explain what you mean. I know what kind of effect I mean a character to give — what kind of *tache* he is to make; but how am I to tell my collaborator in words? Hence it was necessary to say, "Make him So-and-so"; and this was all right for Nares and Pinkerton and Loudon Dodd, whom we both knew, but for Bellairs, for instance — a man with whom I passed ten minutes fifteen years ago — what was I to say? and what could Lloyd do? I, as a personal artist, can begin a character with only a haze in my head, but how if I have

1894 ÆT. 44 to translate the haze into words before I begin? In our manner of collaboration (which I think the only possible — I mean that of one person being responsible, and giving the *coup de pouce* to every part of the work) I was spared the obviously hopeless business of trying to explain to my collaborator what *style* I wished a passage to be treated in. These are the times that illustrate to a man the inadequacy of spoken language. Now — to be just to written language — I can (or could) find a language for my every mood, but how could I *tell* any one beforehand what this effect was to be, which it would take every art that I possessed, and hours and hours of deliberate labour and selection and rejection, to produce? These are the impossibilities of collaboration. Its immediate advantage is to focus two minds together on the stuff, and to produce in consequence an extraordinary greater richness of purview, consideration, and invention. The hardest chapter of all was "Cross Questions and Crooked Answers." You would not believe what that cost us before it assumed the least unity and colour. Lloyd wrote it at least thrice, and I at least five times — this is from memory. And was that last chapter worth the trouble it cost? Alas, that I should ask the question! Two classes of men — the artist and the educationalist — are sworn, on soul and conscience, not to ask it. You get an ordinary, grinning, red-headed boy, and you have to educate him. Faith supports you; you give your valuable hours, the boy does not seem to profit, but that way your duty lies, for which you are paid, and you must persevere. Education has always seemed to me one of the few possible and dignified ways of life. A sailor, a shepherd, a schoolmaster — to

your *Gleams of Memory*, No. 1; it then went to my wife, to Osbourne, to the cousin that is within my gates, and to my respected amanuensis, Mrs. Strong. Sunday approached. In the course of the afternoon I was attracted to the great 'all—the winders is by Vanderputty—which upon entering I beheld a memorable scene. The floor was bestrewn with the forms of midshipmen from the *Curaçoa*—"boldly say a wilderness of gun-room"—and in the midst of this sat Mrs. Strong throned on the sofa and reading aloud *Gleams of Memory*. They had just come the length of your immortal definition of boyhood in the concrete, and I had the pleasure to see the whole party dissolve under its influence with inextinguishable laughter. I thought this was not half bad for arthritic gout! Depend upon it, sir, when I go into the arthritic gout business, I shall be done with literature, or at least with the funny business. It is quite true I have my battlefields behind me. I have done perhaps as much work as anybody else under the most deplorable conditions. But two things fall to be noticed: In the first place, I never was in actual pain; and in the second, I was never funny. I 'll tell you the worst day that I remember. I had a hæmorrhage, and was not allowed to speak; then, induced by the devil, or an errant doctor, I was led to partake of that bowl which neither cheers nor inebriates—the castor-oil bowl. Now, when castor-oil goes right, it is one thing; but when it goes wrong, it is another. And it went wrong with me that day. The waves of faintness and nausea succeeded each other for twelve hours, and I do feel a legitimate pride in thinking that I stuck to my work all

1894
ÆT. 44

1894 ÆT. 44 through and wrote a good deal of *Admiral Guinea* (which I might just as well not have written for all the reward it ever brought me) in spite of the barbarous bad conditions. I think that is my great boast; and it seems a little thing alongside of your *Gleams of Memory* illustrated by spasms of arthritic gout. We really should have an order of merit in the trade of letters. For valour, Scott would have had it; Pope too; myself on the strength of that castor-oil; and James Payn would be a Knight Commander. The worst of it is, though Lang tells me you exhibit the courage of Huish, that not even an order can alleviate the wretched annoyance of the business. I have always said that there is nothing like pain; toothache, dumb-ague, arthritic gout, it does not matter what you call it, if the screw is put upon the nerves sufficiently strong, there is nothing left in heaven or in earth that can interest the sufferer. Still, even to this there is the consolation that it cannot last for ever. Either you will be relieved and have a good hour again before the sun goes down, or else you will be liberated. It is something after all (although not much) to think that you are leaving a brave example; that other literary men love to remember, as I am sure they will love to remember, everything about you — your sweetness, your brightness, your helpfulness to all of us, and in particular those one or two really adequate and noble papers which you have been privileged to write during these last years. — With the heartiest and kindest goodwill, I remain, yours ever, R. L. S.

1894
ÆT. 44

To Lieutenant Eeles

Vailima, Samoa, *November 24, 1894.*

MY DEAR EELES,—The hand, as you will perceive (and also the spelling!), is Teuila's, but the scrannel voice is what remains of Tusitala's. First of all, for business. When you go to London you are to charter a hansom cab and proceed to the Museum. It is particular fun to do this on Sundays when the Monument is shut up. Your cabman expostulates with you, you persist. The cabman drives up in front of the closed gates and says, "I told you so, sir." You breathe in the porter's ears the mystic name of *Colvin*, and he immediately unfolds the iron barrier. You drive in, and does n't your cabman think you 're a swell. A lord mayor is nothing to it. Colvin's door is the only one in the eastern gable of the building. Send in your card to him with "From R. L. S." in the corner, and the machinery will do the rest. Henry James's address is 34 De Vere Mansions, West. I cannot remember where the place is; I cannot even remember on which side of the park. But it 's one of those big Cromwell Road-looking deserted thoroughfares out west in Kensington or Bayswater, or between the two; and anyway, Colvin will be able to put you on the direct track for Henry James. I do not send formal introductions, as I have taken the liberty to prepare both of them for seeing you already.

Hoskyn is staying with us.

It is raining dismally. The Curaçoa track is hardly passable, but it must be trod to-morrow by the degenerate feet of their successor the Walleroos. I think it a

1894 very good account of these last that we don't think them
ÆT. 44 either deformed or habitual criminals—they seem to be a kindly lot.

The doctor will give you all the gossip. I have preferred in this letter to stick to the strictly solid and necessary. With kind messages from all in the house to all in the ward-room, all in the gun-room, and (may we dare to breathe it) to him who walks abaft.—Believe me, my dear Eeles, yours ever,

R. L. STEVENSON.

TO SIR HERBERT MAXWELL

VAILIMA, SAMOA, *December 1st, 1894.*

DEAR SIR HERBERT,—Thank you very much for your long and kind letter. I shall certainly take your advice and call my cousin, the Lyon King, into council. It is certainly a very interesting subject, though I don't suppose it can possibly lead to anything, this connection between the Stevensons and M'Gregors. Alas, your invitation is to me a mere derision. My chances of visiting Heaven are about as valid as my chances of visiting Monreith. Though I should like well to see you, shrunken into a cottage, a literary Lord of Ravenscraig. I suppose it is the inevitable doom of all those who dabble in Scotch soil; but really your fate is the more blessed. I cannot conceive anything more grateful to me, or more amusing or more picturesque, than to live in a cottage outside your own park-walls.—With renewed thanks, believe me, dear Sir Herbert, yours very truly,

ROBERT LOUIS STEVENSON.

THE HOUSE AT VAILIMA AFTER THE ADDITIONS.

1894
ÆT. 44

To Andrew Lang

The following refers, of course, to *Weir of Hermiston*, the chief character of which was studied from the traditions of Lord Braxfield, and on which Stevenson was working at the full height of his powers when death overtook him two days later.

Vailima, Samoa, *December 1, 1894.*

MY DEAR LANG,—For the portrait of Braxfield, much thanks! It is engraved from the same Raeburn portrait that I saw in '76 or '77 with so extreme a gusto that I have ever since been Braxfield's humble servant, and am now trying, as you know, to stick him into a novel. Alas, one might as well try to stick in Napoleon. The picture shall be framed and hung up in my study. Not only as a memento of you, but as a perpetual encouragement to do better with his Lordship. I have not yet received the transcripts. They must be very interesting. Do you know, I picked up the other day an old *Longman's*, where I found an article of yours that I had missed, about Christie's? I read it with great delight. The year ends with us pretty much as it began, among wars and rumours of wars, and a vast and splendid exhibition of official incompetence.—Yours ever,

R. L. Stevenson.

To Edmund Gosse

The next, and last, letter is to Mr. Gosse, dated also only two days before the writer's death. It acknowledged the dedication "To Tusitala" of that gentleman's volume of poems, *In Russet and Silver*, just received.

1894 VAILIMA, SAMOA, *December 1, 1894.*

ÆT. 44 I AM afraid, MY DEAR WEG, that this must be the result of bribery and corruption! The volume to which the dedication stands as preface seems to me to stand alone in your work; it is so natural, so personal, so sincere, so articulate in substance, and what you always were sure of—so rich in adornment.

Let me speak first of the dedication. I thank you for it from the heart. It is beautifully said, beautifully and kindly felt; and I should be a churl indeed if I were not grateful, and an ass if I were not proud. I remember when Symonds dedicated a book to me; I wrote and told him of "the pang of gratified vanity" with which I had read it. The pang was present again, but how much more sober and autumnal—like your volume. Let me tell you a story, or remind you of a story. In the year of grace something or other, anything between '76 and '78, I mentioned to you in my usual autobiographical and inconsiderate manner that I was hard up. You said promptly that you had a balance at your banker's, and could make it convenient to let me have a cheque, and I accepted and got the money—how much was it?—twenty, or perhaps thirty pounds? I know not—but it was a great convenience. The same evening, or the next day, I fell in conversation (in my usual autobiographical and . . . see above) with a denizen of the Savile Club, name now gone from me, only his figure and a dim three-quarter view of his face remaining. To him I mentioned that you had given me a loan, remarking easily that of course it did n't matter to you. Whereupon he read me a lecture, and told me how it really stood with you financially. He was pretty serious, fearing, as I could not help perceiving, that I should take too light a view of the responsibility and the service (I was always thought too light — the irresponsible jester — you remember. O, *quantum mutatus ab illo!*) If I remember rightly, the money was repaid before the end of the week — or, to be more exact and a trifle pedantic, the sennight — but the service has never been forgotten; and I send you back this piece of ancient history, *consule Planco,* as a salute for your dedication, and propose that we should drink the health of the nameless one who opened my eyes as to the true nature of what you did for me on that occasion. 1894 ÆT. 44

But here comes my Amanuensis, so we 'll get on more swimmingly now. You will understand perhaps that what so particularly pleased me in the new volume, what seems to me to have so personal and original a note, are the middle-aged pieces in the beginning. The whole of them, I may say, though I must own an especial liking to —

> I yearn not for the fighting fate,
> That holds and hath achieved;
> I live to watch and meditate
> And dream — and be deceived.

You take the change gallantly. Not I, I must confess. It is all very well to talk of renunciation, and of course it has to be done. But, for my part, give me a roaring toothache! I do like to be deceived and to dream, but I have very little use for either watching or meditation. I was not born for age. And, curiously enough, I seem

1894 ÆT. 44 to see a contrary drift in my work from that which is so remarkable in yours. You are going on sedately travelling through your ages, decently changing with the years to the proper tune. And here am I, quite out of my true course, and with nothing in my foolish elderly head but love-stories. This must repose upon some curious distinction of temperaments. I gather from a phrase, boldly autobiographical, that you are—well, not precisely growing thin. Can that be the difference?

It is rather funny that this matter should come up just now, as I am at present engaged in treating a severe case of middle age in one of my stories—*The Justice-Clerk.* The case is that of a woman, and I think that I am doing her justice. You will be interested, I believe, to see the difference in our treatments. *Secreta Vitæ* comes nearer to the case of my poor Kirstie. Come to think of it, Gosse, I believe the main distinction is that you have a family growing up around you, and I am a childless, rather bitter, very clear-eyed, blighted youth. I have, in fact, lost the path that makes it easy and natural for you to descend the hill. I am going at it straight. And where I have to go down it is a precipice.

I must not forget to give you a word of thanks for *An English Village.* It reminds me strongly of Keats, which is enough to say; and I was particularly pleased with the petulant sincerity of the concluding sentiment.

Well, my dear Gosse, here 's wishing you all health and prosperity, as well as to the mistress and the bairns. May you live long, since it seems as if you would continue to enjoy life. May you write many more books as good as this one — only there 's one thing impossible, you can never write another dedication that can give the same pleasure to the vanished TUSITALA. 1894 ÆT. 44

THE last words were prophetic; and the end came quite unexpectedly two days later. The reader may be glad to remember, what does not appear in the *Letters*, that in these last days, nay, on the last day of all, Stevenson had been once more enjoying keenly the highest pleasure of the artist — a consciousness of perfect command over his subject and his means. This came to him in dictating *Weir of Hermiston* more strongly than it had ever come to him before. On the afternoon of the 3rd of December he had brought his morning's work to his wife, the most exacting of his critics; had asked her whether it was not well done; and in her glow of admiring assent had found, within an hour of his seizure, his confirmation and his reward. The rest cannot be more fittingly told than in the words of the printed letter which was addressed to Stevenson's private friends by his stepson, Mr. Lloyd Osbourne, while his mind was full of the scenes and emotions of the time:

"He wrote hard all that morning of the last day; his half-finished book, *Hermiston*, he judged the best he had ever written, and the sense of successful effort made him buoyant and happy as nothing else could. In the afternoon the mail fell to be answered; not business correspondence — for this was left till later — but replies to the long, kindly letters of distant friends, received but two days since, and still bright in memory.

"At sunset he came down-stairs; rallied his wife

about the forebodings she could not shake off; talked of a lecturing tour to America that he was eager to make, 'as he was now so well,' and played a game at cards with her to drive away her melancholy. He said he was hungry; begged her assistance to help him make a salad for the evening meal; and to enhance the little feast he brought up a bottle of old Burgundy from the cellar. He was helping his wife on the verandah, and gaily talking, when suddenly he put both hands to his head, and cried out, 'What 's that?' Then he asked quickly, 'Do I look strange?' Even as he did so he fell on his knees beside her. He was helped into the great hall, between his wife and his body-servant, Sosimo, losing consciousness instantly, as he lay back in the arm-chair that had once been his grandfather's. Little time was lost in bringing the doctors—Anderson, of the man-of-war, and his friend Dr. Funk. They looked at him and shook their heads; they laboured strenuously and left nothing undone; but he had passed the bounds of human skill.

"The dying man lay back in the chair, breathing heavily, his family about him frenzied with grief as they realised all hope was past. The dozen and more Samoans that formed part of the little clan of which he was chief sat in a wide semicircle on the floor, their reverent, troubled, sorrow-stricken faces all fixed upon their dying master. Some knelt on one knee to be instantly ready for any command that might be laid upon them. A narrow bed was brought into the centre of the room; the Master was gently laid upon it, his head supported by a rest, the gift of Shelley's

THE LARGE HALL AT VAILIMA.

son. Slower and slower grew his respiration, wider the interval between the long, deep breaths. The Rev. Mr. Clarke was now come, an old and valued friend; he knelt and prayed as the life ebbed away.

"He died at ten minutes past eight on Monday evening the 3rd of December, in the forty-fifth year of his age.

"The great Union Jack that flew over the house was hauled down and laid over the body, fit shroud for a loyal Scotsman. He lay in the hall which was ever his pride, where he had passed the gayest and most delightful hours of his life, a noble room with open stairway and mullioned windows. In it were the treasures of his far-off Scottish home: the old carved furniture, the paintings and busts that had been in his father's house before him. The Samoans passed in procession beside his bed, kneeling and kissing his hand, each in turn, before taking their places for the long night watch beside him. No entreaty could induce them to retire, to rest themselves for the painful and arduous duties of the morrow. It would show little love for Tusitala, they said, if they did not spend their last night beside him. Mournful and silent, they sat in deep dejection, poor, simple, loyal folk, fulfilling the duty they owed their chief.

"A messenger was despatched to a few chiefs connected with the family, to announce the tidings and bid them assemble their men on the morrow for the work there was to do.

"Sosimo asked on behalf of the Roman Catholics that they might be allowed to recite the prayers for the dead. Till midnight the solemn chants continued, the prolonged, sonorous prayers of the Church of Rome, in commingled Latin and Samoan. Later still, a chief arrived with his retainers, bringing a precious mat to wrap about the dead.

"He, too, knelt and kissed the hand of Tusitala, and took his place amid the sleepless watchers. Another arrived with a fine mat, a man of higher rank, whose incipient consumption had often troubled the Master.

"'Talofa, Tusitala!' he said, as he drew nigh and took a long, mournful look at the face he knew so well. When, later on, he was momentarily required on some business of the morrow, he bowed reverently before retiring. 'Tofa, Tusitala!' he said, 'Sleep, Tusitala!'

"The morning of the 4th of December broke cool and sunny, a beautiful day, rare at this season of the year. More fine mats were brought, until the Union Jack lay nigh concealed beneath them. Among the new-comers was an old Mataafa chief, one of the builders of the 'Road of the Loving Hearts,' a man who had spent many days in prison for participation in the rebellion. 'I am only a poor Samoan, and ignorant,' said he as he crouched beside the body. 'Others are rich and can give Tusitala the parting presents of rich fine mats; I am poor and can give nothing this last day he receives his friends. Yet I am not afraid to come and look the last time in my friend's face, never to see him more till we meet with God. Behold! Tusitala is dead; Mataafa is also dead to us. These two great friends have been taken by God. When Mataafa was taken, who was our support but Tusitala? We were in prison, and he cared for us. We were sick, and he made us well. We were hungry, and he fed us. The day was no longer than his kindness. You are great people and full of love. Yet who among you is so great as Tusitala? What is your love to his love? Our clan was Mataafa's clan, for whom I speak this day; therein was Tusitala also. We mourn them both.'

"A meeting of chiefs was held to apportion the work and divide the men into parties. Forty were sent with knives and axes to cut a path up the steep face of the mountain, and the writer himself led another party to the summit — men chosen from the immediate family — to dig the grave on a spot where it was Mr. Stevenson's wish that he should lie. Nothing more picturesque can be imagined than the narrow ledge that forms the summit of Vaea, a place no wider than a room and flat as a table. On either side the land descends precipitously; in front lie the vast ocean and the surf-swept reefs; to the right and left, green mountains rise, densely covered with the primeval forest. Two hundred years ago the eyes of another man turned towards that same peak of Vaea, as the spot that should ultimately receive his war-worn body: Soalu, a famous chief.

"All the morning Samoans were arriving with flowers; few of these were white, for they have not learned our foreign custom, and the room glowed with the many colours. There were no strangers on that day, no acquaintances; those only were called who would deeply feel the loss. At one o'clock a body of powerful Samoans bore away the coffin, hid beneath a tattered red ensign that had flown above his vessel in many a remote corner of the South Seas. A path so steep and rugged taxed their strength to the utmost, for not only was the journey difficult in itself, but extreme care was requisite to carry the coffin shoulder-high.

"Half an hour later the rest of his friends followed. It was a formidable ascent, and tried them hard. Nineteen Europeans and some sixty Samoans reached the summit. After a short rest the Rev. W. E. Clarke read the burial service of the Church of England, interposing a prayer that Mr. Stevenson had written and had read aloud to his family only the evening before his death:

"'We beseech Thee, Lord, to behold us with favour, folk of many families and nations gathered together in the peace of this roof, weak men and women subsisting under the covert of Thy patience. Be patient still; suffer us yet awhile longer;—with our broken purposes of good, with our idle endeavours against evil, suffer us awhile longer to endure, and (if it may be) help us to do better. Bless to us our extraordinary mercies; if the day come when these must be taken, brace us to play the man under affliction. Be with our friends, be with ourselves. Go with each of us to rest; if any awake, temper to them the dark hours of watching; and when the day returns, return to us, our sun and comforter, and call us up with morning faces and with morning hearts—eager to labour—eager to be happy, if happiness shall be our portion—and if the day be marked for sorrow, strong to endure it.

"'We thank Thee and praise Thee; and in the words of him to whom this day is sacred, close our oblation.'"

INDEX

INDEX